William Leonard Courtney

Constructive Ethics

A Review of Modern Moral Philosophy in its Three Stages of Interpretation,

Criticism, and Reconstruction

William Leonard Courtney

Constructive Ethics
A Review of Modern Moral Philosophy in its Three Stages of Interpretation, Criticism, and Reconstruction

ISBN/EAN: 9783337079482

Printed in Europe, USA, Canada, Australia, Japan

Cover: Foto ©Thomas Meinert / pixelio.de

More available books at **www.hansebooks.com**

CONSTRUCTIVE ETHICS

A REVIEW OF MODERN MORAL PHILOSOPHY

IN ITS THREE STAGES OF

INTERPRETATION, CRITICISM, AND RECONSTRUCTION

BY

W. L. COURTNEY, M.A., LL.D.

FELLOW OF NEW COLLEGE, OXFORD

0558

New Edition

LONDON: CHAPMAN AND HALL, Ld.

1895

[*All rights reserved*]

By the same Author.

THE METAPHYSICS OF JOHN STUART MILL.
STUDIES IN PHILOSOPHY.
STUDIES NEW AND OLD.
THE LIFE OF J. S. MILL.
STUDIES AT LEISURE.

PREFACE.

As I tried to explain in the preface to the first edition of this book, my object in writing these pages is to give my readers an Introduction to what I conceive to be the proper and final form of Moral Philosophy—a system of Constructive Ethics. It was necessary to my purpose to show that the history of Moral Philosophy itself invites a reconstruction on the lines of that particular theory of ethical data which I have called indifferently Rationalism or Idealism. To this system, so far as I can read the phenomena, the early interpretative systems, as well as the critical systems of a crude and disappointing Utilitarianism, appear to be preliminary. If I am right in supposing that the progress of thought is a gradual transition from an ambitious and premature attempt to decipher ethical facts through a period of criticism, to a reconstruction of morals on a metaphysical and indeed an ontological basis, then it would seem clear that the ethics of the future, whatever other features they may contain, need not be merely interpretative, and must not be exclusively critical. It was further necessary to choose amidst the various schemes of reconstruction for that which answered best the conditions of the problem. Was the reconstruction to be made from the side of science, and from the recognized characters of an objective material order? Or was it to proceed from a particular world-theory which assumed a force or agency in things, to be called 'Will' with Schopenhauer, or 'the Unconscious' with von Hartmann? Reasons are advanced in the following pages for disbelieving in either alternative. The only system which remained was that which was inaugurated by Kant, developed by Fichte, illustrated and perhaps temporarily arrested by the brilliant vagaries of Schelling, and completed, at all events in characteristic features, by Hegel. Whether the details of the Hegelian system be or be not accepted, the contention of the present work is that a properly constructed system of morals can only be reared on the foundation of Absolute Idealism.

A further apology is perhaps needed for what some critics might term the slightness, but what the author prefers to call the terseness, of some of the criticisms made on rival theories. In some cases the fault is no doubt the author's own; in other cases, where points have been abundantly treated by other well-known writers, a repetition, which could but go over the main features of a tolerably familiar story, has appeared wholly unnecessary. Nor have these pages been in any way overburdened with references to other works, an omission for which the author can crave no indulgence, as it has been purposely designed.

Nevertheless, the obvious remark which this work suggests is that it either goes too far or not far enough. Such a criticism is more easily made than answered; for probably no author has ever completed a book without a profound scepticism of its value and the necessity of its publication. My object has been twofold. In the first place, I have desired to exhibit in a fairly popular form the chief characteristics of the different stages through which modern moral philosophy has passed. In the second place, it has been my intention to suggest the proper basis on which alone a satisfactory ethical system can be reared. For I believe that Ethics must be Rationalistic, and that they must repose on a metaphysical system designed to elucidate the full contents of an Absolute or Universal. To this Absolute or Universal I have not hesitated to ascribe the name of God, believing that thus alone can the character of the moral law be discovered, and the force of the moral ideal acknowledged as the life-aim of rational creatures.

October 1895.

ERRATA.

p. 30, *for* Frankinstein *read* Frankenstein
p. 58, *for* ethics presuppose *read* ethics presupposes
p. 68, *for* becomes plain *read* become plain
p. 73, *for* Pythagoranism *read* Pythagoreanism
p. 130, l. 13, *for* doctrine of stationariness *read* defect of stationariness
p. 147, l. 28, with the motive, *dele* with
p. 171, *for* ethics depend *read* ethics depends
p. 252, *for* ὑποκειμένον *read* ὑποκείμενον
p. 254, *note*, *for* p. 139 *read* p. 359

CONTENTS.

PART I. THEORETICAL.

CHAPTER I.

The discords in philosophy resolved in the progressive march of the human spirit—Interpretation, Criticism, and Reconstruction, the three necessary stages in all intellectual advance—Illustrations in the history of Philosophy, and in our personal experience—Necessity of the third stage: Reconstruction—The same law of progress exemplified in the history of modern Ethics—Reconstruction in Ethics ... ... p. 1

CHAPTER II. SUBJECTIVE IDEALISM.

The origin of the moral order, whence is it? First answer: It is the creation of the personal consciousness—What we know of the personal consciousness—Successive states and the personal Ego—Difficulties in supposing the world of thought and practice to be the creation of the Ego—The nature of the activity which the Ego, taken by itself, possesses ... p. 14

CHAPTER III. MATTER AND WILL.

Theory of Materialism and Theory of German Pessimists—The hysteron proteron of Materialism—The Will of Schopenhauer—The Unconscious of von Hartmann—Difficulty of founding an ethical system on such theories ... ... p. 26

CHAPTER IV. ABSOLUTE IDEALISM.

Superiority from an ethical standpoint of the principle of Absolute Idealism—Difficulties of calling this ultimate principle 'the Idea' with Hegel, or 'God' with the Spiritualists—Danger of overrating these difficulties—The real advantage of the Absolutist position, as rendering possible metaphysical cognition—The real advantage of the principle of 'God' as rendering a moral system possible—Attitude towards the logical and metaphysical difficulties connected with the conception of God ... ... p. 37

PART II. HISTORICAL.

BOOK I. INTERPRETATION.

CHAPTER I.

§ 1. Definition.

Right and Wrong—Difference between Right and Good, illustrated by contrast between Ancient and Modern Ethics—Sketch of the development of Man as a moral being—Value of the sketch, logical rather than historical ... ... p. 55

§ 2. Classification.

Modes of classification—The superficial descriptive method—The teleological method—Method depending on antithesis between *à priori* and *à posteriori*—The central idea in Ethics is Moral Obligation—Systems which give no proper explanation of moral obligation, *e. g.* Materialism and Mysticism—Systems which attempt to explain moral obligation, *e. g.* Egoism, Sentimental Altruism, Utilitarianism, Rationalism, and Evolutionistic Ethics ... ... p. 65

CHAPTER II.

§ 1. Egoism.

Hobbes as an Egoistic Hedonist—Criticism on Hobbes' system—Right, Duty, Contract, how explained—General criticism on Egoistic Hedonism—The paradox of Hedonism—The difficulties of the Hedonistic Calculus—The psychological fallacies   p. 80

§ 2. Sentimental Altruism.

Theory of Adam Smith—Deficiencies of Sympathy as a Moral Principle—Moral Sense, as explained by Hutcheson—Criticism of Sentimental Altruism—Its attack on Reason—Answer to such attacks ... ... p. 92

§ 3. Conscience.

Butler's Ethical Theory—Five principles in his scheme—Ambiguity of words, nature and natural—Benevolence, Self-Love, and Conscience, their relations—Conscience, as employed by Butler—Love of God ... ... p. 105

§ 4. Early Rationalism.

Distinction between early and late Rationalism—Explanation of good as 'fitness' by Clarke—Allusion to Wollaston, Malebranche, and Wolff—Good as a simple, irreducible idea—Theory of Price, the English Kant—General criticism on early Rationalism ... ... p. 118

BOOK II. CRITICISM.

§ 1. Early Utilitarianism.

Character of a critical period—Differences between Utilitarianism and Egoistic Hedonism—Importance of Hartley's principle of the Association of Ideas—Systems of Paley and Bentham   p. 135

§ 2. Later Utilitarianism.

James Mill—Austin—J. S. Mill's Utilitarianism—Sanctions of Utility as Ethical principle—Why Happiness is desirable—Use made of Association principle ... ... p. 146

§ 3. Considerations on Utilitarianism.

Happiness and Right—Philosophical objections to Utilitarianism—Popular objections ... ... p. 154

BOOK III. RECONSTRUCTION.

CHAPTER I. KANT.

§ 1. Kant as a Rationalist—The difference between the spheres of Ethics and Logic—Ethics depends on three ideas, Freedom, Immortality, God—Duty as a categorical imperative—The formulæ of right action—Philosophical justification of Immortality and the existence of God ... ... p. 167

§ 2. Criticism of the Kantian system—The distinction between the Phenomenal and the Noumenal sphere—The doctrine of Freedom—The value of the formulæ of Right Action—Absolute Duty and conflict of Duties—General value of the Kantian system   p. 182

CONTENTS.

CHAPTER II. THE SUCCESSORS OF KANT.

§ 1. JACOBI AND FICHTE.

Criticism of the Kantian Thing-in-itself—The subjective individualism of Kant, as evidenced in the treatment of the conceptions of Immortality and God—The elucidation of the Universal—The relation of Jacobi to Kant—Fichte—The Absolute as moral order—God as the necessary foundation of all knowledge and existence ... ... p. 200

§ 2. SCHELLING AND HEGEL.

Character of Schelling's Philosophy—Nature-Philosophy—The Philosophy of Identity—Character of Hegel's system—The Supremacy of Spirit—The Dialectical method—The fuller connotation of the Absolute ... ... p. 219

CHAPTER III. SCIENTIFIC THEORIES.

The progressiveness of Moral Philosophy—Mr. Herbert Spencer and the doctrine of Evolution—The application of Evolution to Ethics—Analysis of Conscience—Physical aspect of Ethics—Biological aspect—Psychological aspect—Sociological aspect—Professor Henry Sidgwick—Mr. Leslie Stephen's Science of Ethics—The social tissue—Criticisms on Utilitarianism—Prof. F. Pollock—General criticism on Scientific Theories—The sanction of Ethics—Assumption of a moral order—Absolute right and relative right—Successive transformations of the Self—Duty—Consciousness and Development ... ... p. 228

CHAPTER IV. PESSIMISM.

§ 1. Unreasoned Pessimism—The Greeks—The Indian Philosophy—Leopardi ... ... p. 278

§ 2. Schopenhauer—Analysis of the World as Will and Idea—Release from the burden of Unhappiness ... ... p. 290

§ 3. Von Hartmann and the Philosophy of the Unconscious—Relation to Schopenhauer—Character of the World-process—End of life—The Unconscious, as metaphysical principle—The birth of Consciousness—Final end of the World-process—Impossibility of finding a basis for Ethics in such a system—Deficiency of the Ethics of Pessimism ... ... p. 298

CONSTRUCTIVE ETHICS.

PART I.—Theoretical.

CHAPTER I.
INTERPRETATION, CRITICISM, RECONSTRUCTION.

THE alternatives of speculative thought vary with the ages. To one, it is a crude opposition between realism and nominalism; to another, it is a conflict between empiricism and idealism; to a third, it is a life and death struggle between science and metaphysics. Or, if we transfer ourselves to an ethical sphere, we shall see one of the earliest battles waged between pleasure and knowledge as competing ends of life, or between a doctrine of selfish egoism and a doctrine of disinterested emotion, or else between utilitarian morals and the ethics of rationalism. Everywhere the choice is offered between two sets of doctrines, animated by a different spirit; in each age of controversy the assumption is made by the respective disciples of the antagonistic schools that he who is not with us is against us. We are so accustomed to this radical difference of opinion that it never occurs to us as extraordinary that, in the intellectual progress of mind, points not only of such supreme but also of such universal importance should admit of contradictory views ; only here and there is the timid suggestion offered that possibly the doctrines may be complementary rather than antagonistic. Yet surely an ordinary acquaintance with psychological peculiarities might be sufficient to remind us that, though we oppose to each other the practical man and the idealist, the politician and the philosopher, the reformer and the mystic, the Platonist and the Aristotelian, we at the same time tacitly acknowledge that the human mind in its total contents can include within itself these differences, as broken lights and shadows of one comprehensive intelligence. In the same way, the history of philosophy can teach us that such internecine quarrels of thought with itself can be and are resolved into the total progressive march of the human spirit in its triple task of interpretation, criticism, and reconstruction.

Interpretation, criticism, reconstruction—these form the three invariable elements of all intellectual advance. The history of philosophy affirms them again and again. In its earliest era, the so-called systems of Thales and Heraclitus, Pythagoreanism and Eleaticism, Anaxagoras and the school of Atomists, were so many modes of interpreting the facts that met the gaze of the ancient inquirer. Here was the world in which we live, putting endless questions to the reflective mind—what was its nature? what its principles of activity? what its fundamental essence? The answers once given—given in that hardihood of ignorance which is at once the promise of future enlightenment and the dogmatism of unsatisfied inquiry—there follows a second stage, which is one of criticism and scepticism, the stage of the Sophists, Protagoras and Gorgias, and Socrates. Only when Sophistry has done its perfect work comes reconstruction by the hands of Plato and Aristotle. The drama repeats itself in much later ages. From Bacon and Descartes, through Locke down to Leibnitz and Wolff, is the age of interpretation. Criticism is concentrated in the critiques of Kant: then comes reconstruction in Fichte, Schelling, and Hegel. So too, if we confine ourselves to moral philosophy. What were the systems called Egoism and Altruism, the systems of Hobbes and Cudworth, of Hutcheson and Price, but modes of interpreting the moral data? Utilitarianism is essentially the spirit of criticism, as is also in certain aspects the doctrine of scientific ethics. Nor can it be doubted that the rationalism of Kantian ethics here begins the function of reconstruction, however little such a *rôle* may accord with the destructive spirit of the corresponding *Critique of Pure Reason*.

It does not need the exercise of much analytic ingenuity to prove that this is also the course of our own intellectual history. The stage of interpretation is indeed in many cases not consciously gone through. We receive our opinions from authority, from the common intellectual fund of our age, from the inherited discoveries of the past. They form the stock-in-trade, so to speak, with which the business is commenced, which we find ready to our hand, and have not been at the pains to acquire for ourselves. But the capital rarely remains undisturbed. The natural experiences of life, though they affect one man in one way and another in another, have always the same result of changing, transforming, and confusing the common notions with which life is commenced. Criticism can not be avoided, simply because the daily path of existence forms one continuous criticism. We may, it is true, refuse to acknowledge the change which has come over us. Nothing is commoner than the spectacle of a man who repeats to himself and to others the stereotyped formulæ which the public opinion of his age and his country has given him, while at the same time the unconscious testimony of his acts is all the other way. But this is because the habits of self-analysis are wanting, and the duty of a perfect fidelity to convictions is wrongly interpreted. The stage of criticism is inevitable, even to those who hardly lead an intellectual life. Dogmatism, for instance, we call the privilege of youth: what is this but to say that the criticism of life begets toleration? Rarely—so runs the maxim—do the ideals of earlier years escape the tarnish of a later experience: what else is this but to acknowledge that advancing years bring not only the deadening effects of sorrow, disappointment, and gloom, but also the testing, sifting spirit of analysis? It is the third stage which perhaps appears avoidable, rather than the second; for criticism does not seem necessarily to entail a further process of reconstruction. And certainly it is the characteristic of the contemporary age to rest in a state of intellectual suspense as if it were not so much transitional as final. Suspense —the critical weighing of divergent opinions—is on all hands acknowledged as a duty; but the consequent duty of reconstruction seems unreal and visionary, probably owing to the fatal facility with which such reconstructions are dissolved by a later criticism. Yet no man can really bring his mental history into any sort of accord with his life who does not in some fashion or other perform the reconstructive task. To fail to do so is the real scepticism, the scepticism of timidity and half-heartedness. The present condition of religious thought affords an easy illustration of this. Surely at no stage in the world's history was there so much of vacillation, inconsequence, and inconsistency as is exhibited in the religious attitude of most thinking men at the present day. Sometimes one is tempted to believe that there is an absolute divorce between profession and reality,—between the Christian doctrines that are on men's lips and the intellectual opinions, be they those of science or philosophy, which are in their minds. Here is a man who, living with full consciousness of the destructive criticism of his age, yet repeats the religious formulæ of mediæval Christianity. Here is another who has long since banished himself from the Christian communion, owing to the effects of a study of scientific methods, and who has learnt the lessons of Darwin and Haeckel; and yet if you ask him whether he believes in an impersonal Nature as the ultimate reality, he shelters his inability to answer under the convenient protest that scientific thought does not need to go back to first principles. Here is a third in a yet more piteous case, who feels all the attractive force of a spiritualistic creed, who acknowledges a sort of heart-hunger for a religion with some Absolute Spirit of Goodness as its object and its justification, and yet cannot shake himself free from the corroding idea that the criticism which has destroyed the universals of the past, has destroyed also the possibility of any future universal. But if the law of intellectual advance be rightly stated as a triple movement of interpretation, criticism, and reconstruction, we can not arbitrarily arrest progress at its second stage. Reconstruction of some sort there must be sooner or later. Indeed, it is a process which goes on whether we like it or no, independently of ourselves. To refuse to entertain its possibility, to acquiesce in the everlasting duration of this stage of criticism, is either indolence or cowardice.

It needs a certain disengagement from current controversy to see this law of progress in its best, and in some respects its highest, exemplification—moral philosophy. On the one hand, we are met by the oft-repeated assertion that moral philosophy is wholly unprogressive: on the other hand, all general statements of the law of progress afford an easy mark for the ridicule of those who are occupied with the bare detail of systems and particular opinions. The first objection may be sufficiently met by a counter-assertion of the reality of *the history* of ethical doctrine: the second requires a fuller consideration. It is maintained, for instance, that a general law of mental progress is nullified by particular systems which do not fall into the historical sequence demanded by the theory. For Hobbes' system, which is the earliest in the history of modern ethics, is nothing if not critical; while utilitarianism, which, according to our scheme, ought to belong to the critical age, is very largely constructive. Now, in the first place, it must be laid down dogmatically, that the value of laws of progress are only patent to him who can abstract from the particular divergences and apprehend the general tendency. When Comte affirmed his great law of the progress of intelligence, his 'loi des trois états,' that theology was succeeded by metaphysics, and metaphysics in turn by the positive spirit, he was met by a rejoinder which took particular notice of systems which were metaphysical before they were theological, or positive before they were metaphysical. To those who do not sympathize with the generalization, it is yet abundantly clear that Comte, from his own point of view, was justified in the abstract exposition of his law. For all generalizations are ideal rather than actual, or, as we should be inclined to affirm from a different standpoint, are reconstructive rather than critical. Reconstruction is nothing but the free handling of given materials, the redintegration of experimental data in accordance with an *à priori* synthesis. In this fashion, too, must be interpreted the general law of intellectual advance which we have laid down, so far as it affects the history of modern moral philosophy.

If we assume roughly that modern ethical theory commences with the two systems of Egoism and Altruism, that is to say with Hobbes, Mandeville, and La Rochefoucauld on the one hand, and with those other systems on the other, which, whether on rational grounds as Cudworth and Clarke, or on sentimental grounds as Shaftesbury and Hutcheson, oppose the doctrines of Egoism, and strive to establish a doctrine of benevolence and disinterestedness, we shall have a stage of interpretation of ethical data on the large scale; in other words, an exhibition of moral facts, so far as they can be explained either from the side of interest or sympathetic fellow-feeling. To this succeeds the school of utilitarianism, which is, in its essence, critical, which sifts the competing elements of selfishness and disinterestedness; and though it, at all events in its earlier division, decides for an explanation which is akin to selfishness, yet it is, in its own nature, negative, inquiring, and tentative. Of the same complexion are the modern systems of scientific ethics—the ethics of Darwin, of Herbert Spencer, and Leslie Stephen, though in certain points they undoubtedly begin the work of reconstruction. In the *Data of Ethics*, for instance, we have a critical examination of Egoism and Altruism, and a suggested conclusion that neither on the one side nor on the other do we find the absolute truth, but only in a combination of both aspects. Reconstruction, however, does not proceed on these lines. It assumes in large measure the truth or pertinency of the critical examination, but it is not satisfied with the result, which seems to flow from the premises. It would rather envisage these matters *à priori*, seeking to deduce from a higher law the concrete exhibition of moral principles. Such a reconstructive work was clearly begun by the Kantian *Critique of the Practical Reason*, which sought to deduce from the real validity of the Noumenal Ego the explanation of ethical laws and the authority of moral obligation. To the same category—if we abstract from particular divergences due to historical and psychological conditions—belongs the Subjective Idealism of Fichte and Schopenhauer. Of a different order, though equally reconstructive, are the so-called Subject-object of Schelling, the Idea of Hegel, and the Unconscious of von Hartmann; for here we attain, in the case of Hegel, to an absolute Idealism, and in the case, possibly, of Schelling and certainly of von Hartmann, to a Monism, which is not purely idealistic, but an alleged reconciliation of Idealism with Materialism. The one point which must be remembered in such large views of the development of ethical doctrine is the abstraction from temporal conditions. It is no objection to such theories that they confuse the exact historical sequence of philosophical systems. To some extent they do so; but from a freer standpoint, they affirm the real historic law of all progress in the study of ethical doctrine. The historical evolution is accepted in that comprehensive sense in which the salient tendencies are relieved of all disturbing and momentary accessories.

But is it true that criticism requires a subsequent era of reconstruction with regard to ethical theory? This is the point which yet remains to be made clear. Of course the real answer can only flow from a patient examination of the various systems, which is attempted in some measure in the ensuing book. Then only, after each representative system is tried at the bar, can it be properly affirmed that the reconstructive systems answer better to the tests which human consciousness demands from an adequate theory of its moral judgments. Meanwhile we can anticipate the conclusions from certain general considerations. The history of ethical systems makes it clear that there have all along existed two different modes of regarding the data of the science. The essential difference, for instance, between Plato and Aristotle as moral philosophers, is to be found not so much in their respective doctrines, (where as often as not they agree,) as in a radical contrast of standpoint. When Aristotle is criticising the Platonic idea of Good, it is quite clear that he can not understand Plato's conception. Perhaps Plato would be equally unable to understand Aristotle's use of logical method in the so-called Moral Syllogism. For in the interpretation of ethical data it makes all the difference whether we start from the notion that morality is an inquiry into the effects and tendencies of action, or whether it is only comprehensible on the pre-supposition of an *à priori* idea. To the ethical student of the first kind, it will be quite satisfactory to ask, what is the use of a knowledge of the idea of good, if a man does not know what is good for him? To a thinker of the second stamp, good is in itself inexplicable unless it be held to be innate in us in the form of an idea, given to experience, and therefore not to be abstracted from experience. Plato, at all events, seems to have held that the real seat and home of ethical determination is deep within the man's consciousness, and that only in the light of the illuminating *à priori* idea could moral judgments be passed on the contents of the sphere of experience. Aristotle, with his genuine scientific instincts, and his natural belief in the efficacy of a logical method which he had himself invented, desired to treat ethics as a system of laws, gained by induction from experience of the effects of action. And therefore Aristotle is always on the edge of the doctrine of 'the Relativity of Morals'—a doctrine which perhaps more than any other plays havoc with the utterances of our moral consciousness. If 'Good' and 'Right' be not in some sense the same for all men, we shall have ultimately to part company with the theory of moral obligation and duty. The same antithesis between what may be roughly called *à priori* and *à posteriori* ethics is exhibited over and over again in the later history of morals. It is found in the contrast between the Stoic and Epicurean systems, between the doctrine of Butler and the doctrine of Hobbes, between intuitionism and utilitarianism, between Kant and Spencer. There is all the difference in the world between Good as (in whatever sense) an *à priori* idea, and Good as a relation, a discovered result, an experimental discovery.

If we regard the question in another light, we shall see more clearly how this controversy stands with regard to those elements of intellectual progress which we have termed criticism and reconstruction. An analysis of ethical data, a resolution of complex facts into simple, an elucidation of a law which covers a multitude of single observations—all belong to a process, which, where it is not merely interpretative, is essentially critical. The title 'Data of Ethics' quite properly belongs to a work which thus critically establishes the dependence of ethical determinations on simple feelings of pleasure and pain, and shows the gradual evolution of conduct from reflex action on appropriate stimuli to conscious activities in view of purposed ends. When Kant proposed to analyse the conditions of knowledge as an indispensable preliminary to any future metaphysic, he with accurate consistency called his work a *Critique of True Reason*. But now come the inevitable questions of first principles. There is no question that morality is natural to man in the same way as language is: that is, if you give man time, he will undoubtedly develop an ethical creed. But on what does the ethical activity of man depend? From what ultimate principle or source is it all derived? What is it which thus evolves? Why does it evolve in one way and not in another? Why must it develop at all, unless there be an immanent idea which presides, so to speak, over the evolution? Such questions we call metaphysical, and sometimes seek to relegate them to the limbo of the empty and the void inane. But they have a fatal tendency to revive and undergo countless resurrections. Even Mr. Spencer has to fall back on an ultimate principle which he disparagingly calls the Unknowable, but has to hypostatise by giving it a capital letter. For these questions of their own nature belong to the reconstructive element of human knowledge. Reconstruction must have its rights. When we commence the reconstructive task, we then begin to base ethics on an elemental foundation in the consciousness: we talk of the Noumenal Ego with Kant, or of the Idea with Hegel, or the Unconscious with Hartmann, or of God with the Spiritualists. Ethics as a creation of man leads back to the essential character of man, and that in its turn leads to the absolute principle of things.

It is especially ethics which introduces these deeper inquiries. It is possible that a sincere student of nature might pass his life through without seeking to know more than the phenomenal world. It is possible, I say, though the prevalence of materialism, which is the creed of science, makes one doubt the possibility, for materialism is nothing if not ontological. It is also possible for the logician to be content with an analysis of knowledge, which adjourns the consideration either of the self or the not-self; to stop, for instance, where Kant stopped in the *Critique of Pure Reason*. But Kant wrote also the *Critique of Practical Reason*, as if to prove that the ontological instinct was undying. Here is a proof, if proof were needed, that ethics at all events will not be satisfied with a purely critical treatment. For ethics has the power to lead us out of the phenomenal into the real, and its problems end by transporting us straight into the arcana of metaphysics. Its problems are essentially problems of consciousness, to begin with: they deal with internal, subjective factors like will, conscience, motive, and responsibility. Then come the questions as to the personality, and its relation to the world at large, the torturing problem of the relation of the finite to the infinite, of the individual to the absolute. And finally the discovery that unless ethics is based on some form of ontology—whether matter or spirit, absolute self-consciousness or absolute unconsciousness, will or idea—the whole of our ethical science is floating in the air, a bubble with all the colours of the rainbow but still a bubble, a vast luxuriance of branches and leaves and flowers which have no trunk to support them or root to nourish.

CHAPTER II.

SUBJECTIVE IDEALISM.

ETHICS, as we have said, have a peculiar power of sending us back to the deeper bases of our being; as Plato would say, they are especially provocative of metaphysical thought. For not only are the main conceptions of ethics of a strictly subjective character, but the main problem with which ethics has to deal is of a nature which is remote from the commonplace traits of experience and understanding. If we regard man in his intellectual capacity, it is impossible to avoid the acknowledgment that he is in a state of subjection and passivity. For what is capacity but the possibility of being awakened by the touch of some external force? And what is growth in knowledge and culture but the gradual incoming of something outside the man, the communication of which to his spirit enlightens and enlarges it? His knowledge then is, in reality, dependence: as an intellectual being he is not free activity, but at most endowed with a certain reactive force on external stimulus. It may be, indeed, that to him large faculties are innate, vague, dreamlike outlines which will serve to mould the future material which is communicated to him.

But even so, the man's intelligence is waiting on the arrival of an alien somewhat; without which his innate capacities are as useless to him as digestive powers to a man in a desert. But, as a moral being, how different is the case! There is no passivity or subjection now; but rather the ceaseless activity of a free personal agent. It may turn out that man is not so free as he thinks. But his whole moral life is inexplicable except on the supposition of an autonomy of ethical function, by which he can set before himself an end towards which his life is to be devoted, and the fair outlines of an ideal such as was never yet on sea or land. Ethics is always aiming at that which neither is nor has been, but which ought to be; the ceaseless redintegration of ideal elements explains the hopefulness of a man after countless failures, and accounts for the possibility of reform, on which all our philanthropic endeavours are based. There is then no subjection to an alien external element; but only the active relation to an internal element—the will. For the moral life is only the prolonged effort to realize a certain moral order of the universe, which is so little due to the outside world, that it is rather the direct antithesis and masterful overthrow of that miserable external order which experience reveals.

Whence comes this moral order of the universe which men seek to fulfil? This is the crucial question which transplants us from criticism to reconstruction, and leads us at once into the region of metaphysics. Is it possible to escape this transference? Yes; by either of two alternatives: first, the supposition that men in their moral relations do *not* seek to realize a moral order; or secondly, that this moral order is not an ideal one. The first alternative is absurd, for then the assumption is that men are born perfectly moral, and that life can exhibit no advance. The second alternative is equally hard to sustain. Let us suppose that the moral order is adequately given by experience. Then, either we are born perfectly moral, which is the assumption already considered, or else the moral order is abstracted from the natural conditions of life, and the so-called ethical progress is in reality a progressively clearer view of the conditions under which we live. But then, how are we to explain that incessant reform which not only our best political and social science, but even nature herself, is for ever attempting? Is not the essence of reform an improvement, an amelioration of existing conditions? And if so, is it not the effort to realize an ideal rather than an actuality? And if all ethical progress be the attempt to give effect to an ideal moral order, the old question returns, whence came this ideal moral order? "The depth saith, it is not in me, and the sea saith, it is not with me." Where are we to find the inspiration which gave birth to the ideal moral order, which all conscious moral agents are seeking to realize?

The answers returned to this question form the different modes of reconstruction which are possible in ethics, the first principles of moral science. Thrown back as we are on the personality of man, a natural answer is, that the moral order is the creation of the personal consciousness. This is the answer furnished by Subjective Idealism, which we have first to examine.

What do we know of the internal consciousness—the

Ego? That is clearly the first point which we are bound to consider. But the unfortunate fact is that the logical or discursive understanding, which is the only organ of illumination which we possess as beings who do not so much feel as seek to understand, can tell us very little about such a matter. The internal consciousness, or Ego, either *is* the understanding, of whose critical and explanatory work we are conscious, or else is the parent or author or source of the understanding. No function or activity can tell us anything of its source; we may think ourselves lucky if it tells us anything of its own modes of working, other than the definite or concrete results of its activity, viz. its thoughts or ideas. Hence, if we trust to the logical understanding, we shall know very little of the Ego. What we do know can very shortly be resumed.

In the first place, we know the successive states of our consciousness. We know, for instance, that to-day we have passed through certain changing moods; we have entertained certain more or less evanescent sentiments; we have formulated, one after another, a few definite ideas. These are all, as Kant says, subject to the form of time, *i. e.* we apprehend them in succession, one coming and another going. Shall we say that we know them as a series? Not so, if we mean by series, not only a consecutive order, but a connected fabric. My impressions now in the year of grace 1886 do not in themselves contain any element or elements which my impressions bore in 1866. The experiment is perfectly easy. My consciousness at the present time bears a mass of different relations which it did not bear twenty years ago. It is true that I remember what I was in 1866, but my present thoughts contain no enduring elements which they also contained in 1866. Still there is my memory: that is, there exists a vague and indefinite bond of union which asserts that as I am in 1886, so also I was in 1866; that as the impressions *are* mine, so also they *were* mine. Moreover, I can project myself forwards, so to speak; I can with perfect legitimacy say that if I live to 1896 I shall then be conscious of certain impressions also. Memory and expectation—here are two powers of my consciousness which I am unable to forego, and in virtue of them I can speak of my personal identity. I was in the past, I am in the present, I shall be in the future: present sensation linked to memory and expectation form the decisive elements of my consciousness. So that it appears that when I speak of my internal consciousness, I mean only passing states, plus a certain link, necessarily vague and indeterminate, and only attested to by such powers as memory and expectation, which connects together past, present, and future states by the fact that these states are mine—that I think them. By what name we are to describe this personal identity is immaterial: Kant called it the synthetic unity of apperception. But the main point is to see to what narrow bounds is reduced this internal consciousness of ours, which we call personal identity, or Ego. For what does it become in itself when we abstract from it the passing states which we are inclined to call its functions or its manifestations? Apart from these it becomes a merely formal identity, $I = I$. This is all that the discursive understanding yields us as to our own most intimate self. And is this poor formal identity, this bare framework or skeleton, which holds together the bones of our thought, to prevent them from rattling and becoming mixed in confusion,—is this to furnish us with the moral ideal? the ethical order or law, which as conscious beings, we are in our practice to endeavour to fulfil? Who shall make these dry bones live? But let us, at whatever logical cost, throw overboard the discursive understanding, and let us assume that somehow or other—whether by Reason or Faith—we know that the Ego is a power conscious of itself; an efficient cause, an energetic force, able not only to contain, and be the subject of, its conscious states, but also to create and design in view of certain pre-determined ends. We will add to this the undeniable idealistic argument that all that we know is expressed in terms of consciousness; that nothing *is* except in relation to the conscious states of the Ego, which thinks it. And now we will review this idealistic position that the Ego is the complete master of its own world of thought and practice, which it both creates and comprehends. What are the difficulties of such a position?

One has to drive the philosophers into a corner in such matters, for they are apt to shirk the extreme consequences of their position, and cover themselves under a cloud of hollow-sounding and somewhat mystical utterance. The subjective idealist has to maintain that world in itself there is none; for the Ego creates it; and therefore that the world arises afresh, so to speak, in the birth of every single consciousness. Everything alike, whether sense-impression or idea, is the creation of consciousness, working according to laws which emanate from its own innermost activity. But now observe the difference between sense-impressions and ideas: the first are fortuitous, accidental, unexpected; the second are regular, orderly, and concatenated. It looks as if such a difference were due to difference of origin; it looks as if, while we created the second, and therefore everything is *en règle*, we did *not* create the first, and therefore have to wait on some alien force to suggest them to us. It looks, I say, as if sense-impressions were due to some world, or kosmos of things, independent of our own conscious activity : as if the Ego did not create such a world, but was subject to its impact and the in-rush of its energy.

The suspicion is confirmed when we regard the relation in which the conscious will stands to these two classes of mental phenomena—the impressions and the ideas respectively. For I can clearly recall a mental idea when and how I choose. Yesterday I formed an idea of comfort, composed of pleasant sensations of warmth and repose. To-day I can recall the idea; but I cannot recall the sense-impressions which accompanied it.' I can, it is true, remember that I was warm; but the sensation of warmth does not come at the bidding of the will. Yet surely if the Ego be cause of both ideas and impression, the latter ought not thus to elude the active, volitional capacity of the Ego. If it be due to something other than the Ego, the phenomenon is explained. But this is to admit that among the conscious states of the Ego, there are some towards which the Ego does not stand in a parental and active, but rather in a filial and passive, relation.

Think too, again, of the different order which obtains amongst mental states as compared with that which we usually believe to obtain in the so-called external sphere. I feel a sensation of warmth, and thence proceed to the inference that there was a fire which caused it. Now, if the subjective activity were all that had to be considered, the order of sequence ought clearly to be first warmth, then fire; from which it would naturally follow that the warmth was the antecedent, and fire the consequent. What is the fact, however? The scientific order of reality is exactly the reverse. The fire is the cause of the warmth, and therefore its antecedent. In other words, the real order is inverted in the subjective order, as though the latter were a reacting and reflecting medium, putting things backwards as in a photographic plate; yet surely, if the assumptions of subjective idealism were correct, we could have nothing but the subjective order to go by, and therefore the world would be interpreted according to the sequence of our mental states.

There are, besides, the difficulties connected with the existence of other conscious Egos. I, who am, according to our idealistic theory, the author of my own world, am, notwithstanding, always assuming that your world is the same as mine; and we both assume that our worlds are common to all other conscious Egos. Yet, strictly speaking, in the world which my consciousness creates, you are part of that creation. To me, your personality stands on precisely the same level as the tastes which I experience, and the phenomena which form for me a so-called objective world. By what right, then, can I transfer my impressions of a world to your consciousness? How can I call upon you to admire the beauty of a scenery which is only my creation, or appreciate the rare odour of a flower, which has only a right of appeal to my sensitive consciousness which called it forth? It is this isolation of the conscious Ego, this monomania of a self-begotten universe, which always forms the fatal weakness of subjective idealism. Does not the transference of thought from one Ego to other Egos itself presuppose the existence of a common objective reality to which they are all alike relative? We have not, however, yet exhausted the difficulties of this position. Berkeley saw long ago that the world of visual sensations must be one thing, the world of tactual sensations another. Yet we commonly assert that the different qualities revealed by the two sets of sensations cohere in the same object: we say that a given object, say a chair or a table, is both hard—a tactual sensation; and brown—a visual sensation. By what right do we thus make different sensations testify to the reality of one single object, unless, in some sense or other, there be a real single object, of which these are qualities? And what a strange inexplicable phantasy of our subjective notion it is, that only two of our senses, sight and touch, seem capable of revealing to us externality! From the side of our own consciousness we cannot make such a distinction between our senses. We stand in the same relation to all of them alike, and yet we construct our notion of externality almost exclusively out of only two of them. All these considerations seem to point to the conclusion that there must be something beside the conscious Ego to account for the world as we know it. At all events, if we may not speak of an objective something, we must at least assume an universal something, which shall stand to all the conscious Egos in the relation of a common cause of inspiration or enlightenment; some Universal Consciousness, or Absolute Spirit, or God, which can account for the fact that my world is identical with yours, and mine and yours shared with all other thinking intelligences.

We have been hitherto dealing with considerations which are more or less popular in their scope, and which perhaps offend the metaphysician, because they do not breathe that air of solemn mystery with which he loves to surround his speculations. From a strictly metaphysical standpoint, however, there is one difficulty which is always present to the subjective idealist, and which he is for ever making fitful attempts to surmount.

The Ego is to be considered as engaged in the work of evolving all those rich stores which we possess in our conscious life. It is spinning them, remember, out of itself, according to the modes of its own activity. Now, try as much as we can, we cannot conceive of consciousness arising in this process, so long as the Ego is merely affirming itself. Why? Because the essence of consciousness is comparison and distinction, and so long as the Ego is merely affirming itself, comparison and distinction are impossible. All that would flow from the active revolution of the Ego would be an eternal 'I,' 'I,' 'I.' No comparison or distinction, because no contrast; only everlasting identity, and therefore no consciousness. Activity there might be, unceasing, unwearying; but we could never be conscious of it, any more than we can say that the endless repetition of a single note constitutes a piece of music. The Ego then must meet with some obstacle, some check; it must throw out from itself something alien to itself, from the shock of which, as though by attrition, the spark of consciousness is to leap forth. Here we are at once face to face with the famous *Anstoss* of the theory of Fichte, who quite rightly sees that consciousness has three elements or movements: first, the activity of the Ego; then the impact on something alien; thirdly, the harmonization or rather the return to the Ego-activity, all the richer for the surmounted obstacle. But now, the important element here is clearly the alien element, the obstacle which causes the momentary shock from which consciousness results; and if we are to preserve our idealist theory, we must somehow explain this obstacle *as itself a creation of the Ego*. But how can this be? The brain reels under the effort to comprehend how the Ego can throw out from itself something which is not itself, and which is to cause it a shock—just as though a man were to create the lamp-post against which he then incontinently runs his head. It is clear that subjective idealism must be hard-driven to preserve its consistency, if it is to lend itself to such an assertion as this. And if this falls to the ground, we have no other alternative but to assert that our conscious states can only arise if there be something other than the Ego; or, to speak in less pretentious language, our world, as we know it, must be due to the influx of something from the outside on which our internal activities then re-act.

If, then, the assumption of subjective idealism be

untrustworthy, if it be not true to assert *totidem verbis* that the Ego creates its own world, we are relieved from all necessity of considering whether the Ego can of itself create a moral order to which it thereupon aspires to rise. The absolute principle which ethics presuppose, and on which it rests as presupposition, can not be the conscious personal Ego.

CHAPTER III.

MATTER AND WILL.

THERE appears, then, to be no doubt, that however much morality may be due to the co-operation of the subjective consciousness of mankind, it cannot be entirely created by that consciousness. It is perhaps unnecessary to say that this holds true not only of the empirically-ascertained consciousness of any single individual, but also of consciousness as the possession or spirit of humanity at large. No one probably in his senses would affirm that he, as one individual Ego, or that any other member of the human race, created morality. This excessive subjective relativity of morals could only be found to be the doctrine of one of those early Sophists whom Plato first travesties and then laughs at. Still it might be maintained, and it has been maintained, that morality was a creation of the impersonal and general consciousness of humanity. The doctrines have been laid down that humanity by means of the evolution of intelligence gradually formulates an ethical ideal, that it lays on itself the obstacles, the conquest of which constitutes its morality; that it puts on its own shoulders the burden which it calls Duty and Responsibility. It is an attractive theory, for it seems to explain many of our difficulties; it brings, for instance, man's moral activity into line with his activity in speculative knowledge. To Fichte and to Kant, the Self, which was at the bottom of all our synthetic activity in constructing for us the world as we know it, was also at the bottom of our practical energy in formulating the moral law. But if there be any truth in our previous discussion, it would appear in the first place that consciousness itself is impossible without the presupposition of something not itself, against which it has to react; and in the second place, that moral effort is equally incomprehensible without the notion of something to be surmounted, or at all events reacted against. If ethics requires the notion of a moral ideal, given in some fashion to the struggling, aspiring personal Ego, an ideal which he has by daily efforts and in spite of daily failures to attempt to make his own; then it is absurd to say morality is the creation of the consciousness. Human consciousness at large seems to require the supposition of some larger, comprehensive element, or agency, or object, common to all individual Egos, and to which they are all alike relative, which is to meet its activity, either check it, or rebuke it, or inspire it; at all events cause it to react, and so enable it to increase its theoretic capacity on the one hand, and give it an object for its practical activity on the other.

But now, what is the nature of this necessary complement to the subjective consciousness? In what language of metaphor and allegory shall we interpret it? For to speak of it in terms precise and definite, such as are applicable to the definite and concrete products of human thought, is *ex hypothesi* impossible, since we have agreed that it is *not* a product of conscious intelligence. We can only then construct it to ourselves, partly by using figurative and emblematic terms, partly by dealing in negative definitions, *i. e.* saying what it is not. But it does not follow that because we have to define it negatively, it is in its essence a purely negative and privative thing (as some English critics are fond of affirming with regard to such descriptions as infinite and immortal), any more than it must needs be a piece of poetical illusion, because our language with regard to it is from a strictly logical point of view, a metaphor, a hope, an allegory. Logic, at all events, on the one side, and the moral consciousness on the other seem to have driven us to see its necessity, and shall we then try to deny its reality, because we have not the terms to describe its essence? We may call it what we choose, provided that we are not the victims of our necessarily imperfect nomenclature.

This comprehensive element, then, this Noumenon, or *Ding-an-sich*, which is the complement to our thinking consciousness, may be figured in one of two ways. Either it is the antithesis to our consciousness, something alien, opposed, and contrasted in its essence; or else it is homogeneous with our consciousness, and only opposed in the sense that while our consciousness is limited and partial, it is unlimited and universal. Each of the two ways of regarding it may be still further broken up. If we take the latter alternative first; namely, that it is in essence homogeneous, we may describe it as either Universal Consciousness or Idea (in the Hegelian sense), or God in the language either of theology or of theistic philosophy, say of Jacobi. For whether we call it Universal Consciousness, or God, it is construed as of one kind with ourselves, figuring in a sense as *object* to our intelligence, because it is all comprehensive, because it illuminates, it inspires, it uplifts. If we take the other alternative, and suppose that it is in essence contrasted with ourselves, then we may call it Nature or Matter, with the Scientists and Materialists; or Will, with Schopenhauer, or the Unconscious, with von Hartmann. For in all these descriptions the idea is the same, that the ultimate groundwork of Reality, which calls out our intelligence and our consciousness, is alien to ourselves; is so far opposed that it confronts us with an essential difference of kind. It is with the second of these modes of regarding the Noumenon that we shall be in the present chapter concerned.

Although both alike agree that the ultimate reality of things is of a kind which is alien to and contrasted with our own conscious intelligence, yet there is a radical difference between the Nature of the Materialists and the Monistic principle, whether Will, or Unconsciousness, of the German Pessimists. There is a frank brutality about the Materialistic hypothesis, which is absent in the other theories. For this 'Nature' is either a congeries of atoms, or a combination of energies, or a world-force of some kind, whose essential nature it is to be blind, irrational, and unintelligent. It knows nothing of design, for all teleological interpretation is an abomination to the scientific materialist, and the notion of a final cause is one which can only dawn for a conscious intelligence. On the other hand it knows (if the word 'know' may be pardoned in such a reference) a good deal. It works by means of a struggle for existence, in which millions of creatures perish. Its evolution, though the term is in reality inappropriate to that which works on in blind and aimless energy, is accomplished by the survival of the fittest, who has made his way to the top, wading, as it were, knee-deep in blood. That such an alogical element as this is a necessary complement to our consciousness is truly, as Plato would say, an ἄγροικός σοφία. But further, it is actually incomprehensible. For its essence is, that it should be absolutely devoid of all that we include in elements of consciousness; and yet, if its impact on the Ego is to evoke consciousness, consciousness must somehow be able to envelop it, transmute it, and make it one with itself. Let us grant that this process is somehow accomplished; that the alogical has become logical; for unless that be granted, the very existence of a theory about the world-evolution is impossible. We know that the Materialists have formulated a theory about Matter and its laws of development, and therefore for them, at all events, the gigantic task has been accomplished, the unknowable has become knowable. But now, further, what are we to say when the Materialists tell us that this Matter is the ultimate cause, parent, and origin of consciousness? Shall we not say that Kronos is being overthrown by his own offspring? —that this matter which has been in a real sense constructed by consciousness is like the monster of Frankinstein, treating as its victim that to which it owes breath? Let us shake ourselves free from this ugly dream. The materialistic assumption is one enormous *hysteron proteron*. For us, conscious intelligent beings, to think that material atoms or dynamical forces are the sole origin of our conscious life, is an impossible conception. The theory is too brutal, λίαν ἄφιλον καὶ ἄμουσον. I think it the less necessary to say much here of this materialistic hypothesis, because we shall have the opportunity of seeing some of its difficulties when we consider the scientific or evolutionist ethics, as expounded, for instance, by Mr. Herbert Spencer.

The other variety of doctrine remains, which avoids in great measure the repulsive character of the materialistic theory, by choosing principles like Will, or Will and Idea, which have more affinity with our own conscious life. If it be granted that the monistic tendency is a legitimate, and even an unavoidable one, it is natural so to construe the ultimate principle, that we can at once claim some relationship with it. Now our own individual activity appears a sort of personified will. By a legitimate extension of meaning, we may call Will—though now an impersonal and absolute one—the ultimate principle of the universe. For the undeniable character of that which makes us and the universe at large is clearly activity; and it is by a perhaps pardonable analogy that we attempt to understand that grand primal activity by the only form of activity of which we as individuals are conscious, viz. energy and force of will. What, then, Kant designated by the term 'Practical Reason or Noumenal Ego,' and made the author of that Categorical Imperative under which we live as moral creatures, appears in Schopenhauer under the name of 'Will.' The conception, however, though fathered by Kant, is strikingly dissimilar. Schopenhauer's Will is a great blind, irrational force impetuously rushing into being, and constantly creating a disorder and an excess of suffering, such as is enough to justify the creed of Pessimism. At one stage in this headlong process the Will threw out from itself intelligence and consciousness, to which now is assigned the dreary task of surveying, without being able to arrest, the misery caused by the ceaseless activity of Will. But in what sense can there be any explanation of morality in such a system? Can such pessimism have an ethic? Clearly, in the first place, conscious intelligence as it exists in us, can have no duty, can not live under any law of obligation; it can at most recognize a certain task or tasks as the suggestion of expediency, in order to release itself so far as it can from the wild and whirling moods of Will. What is, then, the best course it can pursue? According to Schopenhauer it can, on a lower level, cultivate sympathy, and try to lose itself in Art-Ideas, because these are universal, and therefore raised out of the slough of particularity and despair; but the only high task that is assigned to it is the denial of the will to live, the effort by asceticism (though not by suicide) to wither up the volitional activity at its source. How it is possible for an individual consciousness, the late and ineffectual product of a gigantic will, to negate the universal force, which is the formal activity of the universe, Schopenhauer does not explain. But even granted that this is possible, the whole scheme fails to account for the content of our ethical consciousness. In the first place, it does not explain the law of obligation or authoritative duty under which we live; in the second place, its version of the moral ideal towards which we are to aspire is, if not revolting, at least too paradoxically inadequate. To tell us that the ideal, towards which our conscious efforts are to be directed, is in reality the denial of effort by means of asceticism, is at once to affirm and deny in the same breath, to invite us to strive in order that we may learn to give up striving.

It seems to be generally admitted that Schopenhauer's Pessimism, which is rather a splendid *bizarrerie* of genius than a serious system, has no ethic; but von Hartmann assures us that his so-called *Philosophy of the Unconscious*, albeit that it too is Pessimism, can provide us with a moral scheme. English critics are sometimes inclined to assume that von Hartmann is merely the disciple of Schopenhauer, and that whatever differences may exist between them are small as compared with the pessimistic conclusion in which they both agree. In reality, the differences are almost vital, and the pessimism of the so-called disciple might very well be considered as an almost accidental appendix to his main ideas. For the effort of von Hartmann is to reconcile Schelling and Hegel (together with the subjective idealism of the first book of *The World as Will and Representation*) with the creed of modern science, and to provide the world with a sort of modernized version of Spinozism. Here the absolute principle of the universe is formally indeed monistic, for it is called the Unconscious, but really it is dualistic—Will and Idea. It is impossible, so von Hartmann thinks, to conceive of Will's activity without some idea to guide it, for volition would be mere automatic mechanism without the illumination of some end and the perception of the proper means. So that the *Ding-an-sich* for von Hartmann is not merely blind, purposeless activity, but even at its earlier stages Idea was side by side with Will. For us, the puppets of this world-force, it is some comfort to know that the 'Unconscious' of von Hartmann is more like the will, of which we are conscious in our individual experience, than the tyrannical monstrous energy of Schopenhauer.

Yet still we are strangers and aliens to this world-force, in that it is called the 'Unconscious,' and it is argued that consciousness is a late, and so far as we can see, an accidental, product of its activity. How then can it supply us with a moral ideal? How can it furnish us with an explanation of the law of duty? Von Hartmann is ready with his reply. Our duty is to help on the world-process. Our ideal is to effect the emancipation of intellect from the will. For the world is full of pain, and we are mistaken if we put the happiness of which we are in search either in the present world or in a transcendent other world, or in the future ages of humanity. At most we can attain to painlessness, and this only by a corporate act on the part of humanity, not by an individual act, as Schopenhauer wrongly affirmed. Moreover, even this painlessness can only be gained by the emancipated consciousness setting up a counter will of restfulness to negate the will of restless activity. All this gives a strange air to our ethics; for even if we grant that our duty really is to help on the world-process, yet we are inclined to assume that co-operation in the world-process is the fulfilment of some large ideal of blessedness—the consecration of all our active energies rather than their complete cessation. It must be a paradox to make the ideal of morality, which is nothing if not a continuous striving, consist in a cessation of striving, and the ethics of von Hartmann become just as impossible as the ethics of Schopenhauer.

But further, von Hartmann is very explicit in telling us that morality is a predicate of the conscious will—of the will as illuminated by consciousness—not of the great Unconscious Will. The Unconscious is not either good or bad: it is, in fact, Nature, and nature is not either good or bad, but only natural, *i. e.* self-adequate. Now the individual will is good or bad, because it is related to some external object. But to what external object could the 'Unconscious' be related? The Universal Will has nothing outside itself. Hence no moral attribute can attach itself to its action.[1]

I lay stress on this passage, because it puts before us very succinctly the character which all ethics must assume, if once we grant that the absolute principle of nature and life is unconscious, blind, alogical. Ethics becomes a diverting pastime for us partial creatures, living in a partial world; not that which is the veritable heart and essence of all reality. The great Noumenon or Ding-an-Sich knows nothing of the way in which the whole creation groaneth and travaileth together; if not removed to a serene and cloudless sphere, like the Epicurean Gods, it is at all events non-moral. If, however, we strictly analyze the contents of the ethical consciousness, we find three elements involved. There is, first, the conscious activity of the Ego; secondly, a baffling opposition which we have to surmount; thirdly, an infinite ideal

[1] The passage will be found in Sect. (B) chap. iv. of von Hartmann's work (*The unconscious in Character and Morality*).

which we progressively try to realize by overcoming the baffling opposition. Now according to the hypothesis of 'the Unconscious' just as much as on the supposition of the materialist, the second and third elements are furnished by one and the same absolute principle. The 'Unconscious' or 'Matter' at once opposes our conscious effort, and supplies our moral ideal. But then the essence of morality, which is the effort to surmount a given opposition, can not be also the fulfilling of an ideal furnished by the same principle which gave us the opposition. The issue is that we must either assume that the Absolute Principle is non-moral, or that morality is not effort. It is surely more logical as well as simpler to accept the popular version of these elements, which assumes that God gives us the ideal, and Nature gives us the opposition: that it is Nature which is non-moral, and God whose essence is Goodness.

CHAPTER IV.

ABSOLUTE IDEALISM.

The systems which profess as their ultimate principle either 'Matter' or some unconscious element akin to our own nature, be it 'Will' or a combination of 'Will' and 'Idea,' fail equally to supply the foundation we need; but they fail for different reasons. Materialism fails for metaphysical reasons, because it can not explain and account for knowledge, as it grows within us, and the consciousness which is always present to us; the theories of Schopenhauer and von Hartmann fail, for ethical reasons, because on such presuppositions ethics become a futile and mutilated science. They can, in a measure, supply a metaphysical basis for an *Erkenntnisstheorie*, but when we seek to construct from the principles they give us an adequate theory of the contents of our ethical consciousness, their manifest deficiency becomes patent. For the 'moral ideal' and the 'law of moral obligation' as explained, say by von Hartmann, are very different things from what they appear to quite nine-tenths of humanity.

We must linger a little longer over these two salient points in the ethical consciousness, in order that we may see what demands they make upon any ultimate principle, which is to serve as their support. The law of moral obligation has been enunciated by Kant in a manner which leaves nothing for further criticism to add. Men live under a great 'I must,' a categorical imperative, which comes upon us with a sanction and a force to which all other authority seems to yield. All other imperatives addressed to our nature are hypothetical; the moral imperative alone admits of no hypothetical clause, it is simply assertorial and categorical. From a strictly ethical standpoint, *i. e.* viewed as a formal principle of our nature, the law of duty admits of no exception. On the other hand, the moral ideal has been and may be differently interpreted. For in one sense, it is concerned with the contents of the moral law, and the empty form of Duty can have its contents supplied from many quarters. In another and truer sense, however, it is strictly ideal; it holds up before us an infinity of perfection, which we are to aspire to through an infinite series of efforts. Now both these conceptions seem for us, as individuals, to be necessarily based on a dualism; the word 'obligation' is meaningless, unless there is both the obliger and the obliged; the term 'moral ideal' is only comprehensible on the supposition that there is besides the individual some ultimate and absolute reality of perfection which to him as individual is an ideal. If we say that the Ego lays command on itself, or that the Ego supplies the ideal to which it therefore has to aspire, we are conscious of a certain delusive sense in both 'obligation' and 'ideal.' On the other hand, neither the law under which we live, nor the order which we have to fulfil must be so far removed from our own conscious nature, as to be incapable of being taken up into the life of intelligence and practical activity. It is no good telling us that 'Nature' or some alien force of 'Will' lays commands upon us, for these smite us, so to speak, across the void: in order that they may even begin to lay command on us, they will have to be assimilated to consciousness, and then they cease to be anything but purely subjective principles. It is to meet this double requirement of the ethical consciousness, that we have now to seek for its ultimate principle in 'God' or 'The Idea.' For these are certainly not removed from our own conscious life. They are ours, and yet not ours: we know them, but we only know them in part: they are one in kind with ourselves, but yet different, because the Absolute Consciousness is a totality, and we are only partial. Such a principle is sufficiently removed from the personal Ego to give a real meaning to terms like 'Obligation' and 'Moral Ideal,' and yet not so far removed as to be an alien force. We can know it in the sense that it serves for us as the necessary presupposition alike of knowledge and morality. It is one with us, though infinitely higher, greater, more real.

Though, from the point of view just indicated, such principles as 'Absolute Consciousness,' 'Idea,' 'God,' seem adequate to the problem before us, none the less are they exposed to great difficulties of their own, which it would be mere affectation to ignore. The Hegelian principle, for instance, 'the Idea,' has one central difficulty to meet before it can serve as the foundation for a theory of Knowledge and Reality. According to the Hegelian view, the Idea alone is the

Being of the world: logic is consequently ontology: the dialectic self-movement of the concept is the world-process. Now what are the underlying assumptions in this position? In the first place, the Idea, which is a self-enclosed totality and omnipotent within its own sphere, must nevertheless find a reason or motive for coming out of its shell, so to speak—for expanding, that is to say, into a world-process: in the second place, logic, whose principle is self-consistency, and therefore from the formal point of view mere identity ($A = A$), must yet somehow include other elements so as to break up its formal identity into equivalence of differentiated parts ($2A = 3B$, for instance).* In the third place, from the standpoint of the individual consciousness, this complete totality, the Idea, must be capable of being communicated, as it were, piecemeal to our intelligence. Let x stand for the Idea; and a, b, c, d, &c. stand for our partial and progressive knowledge. Then $a + b + c + d +$ &c. indefinitely added to, must $= x$. These are really only three ways of stating what I have called the central difficulty, but it is well to regard it in its different expressions. Undoubtedly we have here a formidable problem; for it seems that the Idea requires some other and opposed element to give it a motive for expanding, and if such another element be supposed, the Idea cannot be the monistic principle which it is alleged to be. Clearly, too, in order to account for reality as we know it, *i.e.* the contingent as well as the necessary, the logical principle of self-consistency must be supplemented by a non-logical element—some such principle, for instance, as Leib-

* Cf., however, what is said on p. 225.

nitz called the principle of Sufficient Reason. It is no good laying it down axiomatically that the dialectical movement consists of three parts, 'position,' 'contradiction,' 'subsumption into a higher unity'; for it is the possibility of 'contradiction' which urgently requires to be explained. For contradiction to the Idea can only apparently come from that which is not Idea—an alogical element, like Not-Being, or Plato's ἐκμαγεῖον, or Aristotle's ὕλη. So again, it is a common criticism on sensationalist and empirical schemes which attempt to arrive at the notion of infinity by infinite addition of empirical parts, to say that infinite addibility is not and cannot be equal to an infinite unity. But the reverse process appears also impossible, for if infinite addibility does not equal infinite unity, then neither can infinite unity be capable of being broken up into an infinite addition of parts. And yet to account for the progressive increase of our knowledge, as well as to explain our progressive fulfilment of a moral ideal, the infinite unity, the omnipotent, self-enclosed, and total Idea must be capable of being communicated to us, as was said just now, piecemeal. Equal difficulties surround us if, instead of calling our ultimate principle 'Idea' or 'Absolute Consciousness,' we prefer to call it 'God.' For not only have we all the difficulties confronting us which gather round the 'Idea' as ultimate reality, but we have, superadded to these, the special difficulties caused by the inevitable suggestions of anthropomorphism in construing the nature of God. God, we naturally suppose, has a consciousness, and a consciousness like our own; but is not consciousness itself a limitation? Our own consciousness seems bound and tied in the chains of an inherent Dualism of Subject and Object. Can we suppose that God's consciousness is similarly bound? If so, there is either a radical contradiction in his nature, or else there is beside God something outside himself which effectually limits and restrains him. Then he ceases to be self-sufficient, he ceases to be the one Ultimate Reality. Or again, is God a person? So we love to assume: so all religions in the world agree in representing him. But if a person, then not possessed of a personality in any sense intelligible to us. Personality to us signifies either from an ethical point of view a certain capacity of self-judgment, a certain power of aspiring to a moral ideal, a certain sense of responsibility: or else from a metaphysical point of view it is the common subject of all acts of conscious activity—thought, emotion, will. The former sense is clearly inapplicable to God: the second is equally so, because the underlying assumption involved is the relation of the individual personality to something not himself, a relation to what we call Nature, or the World, or Humanity at large. Without such relation to a not-itself, the metaphysical idea of Personality is devoid of content and is meaningless. But it is the very essence of the nature of God as Ultimate Reality that there is nothing beside himself. Once more. If God be a conscious person in the anthropopathic sense, the old problem of Evil in the World appears in its most baffling and bewildering form. For if he created such a world as that in which we live, why are there such phenomena as pain and disease? Was there some dull, dead, and obstructive

Matter to limit his benevolent activity, and to serve as the principle of Evil? Then he is not omnipotent. If he is to retain his omnipotence, he must surrender his other attribute of Goodness. He cannot be Good, for he has caused Evil.

I do not desire to underrate these difficulties; but I think they can be very much exaggerated. If we dwell solely on these difficulties, and shut our eyes to the other and enormous theoretical advantages of such principles as 'Idea' and 'God' (which is the usual procedure of sceptical 'esprits forts'), then doubtless the difficulties so fill the whole intellectual sky that it becomes impossible for a man to accept these Absolute principles for himself as the illuminating principles of his metaphysic. Fichte was probably right when he said that it very much depended on the character of a man what metaphysic he accepted.

What is, then, the preponderating speculative advantage of the theories that we have just been considering? It is that while, if we envisage our primal unity as 'Absolute Idea,' we get an explanation of knowledge; if we envisage it as 'God' we get an explanation of morality. What, let us begin by asking, is the main condition of metaphysical knowledge? Since the Copernican revolution of Kant, there can be but one answer. It is undoubtedly the identity of Thought and Being, the essential homogeneity of Thought and its object. Without this condition, the possibility of metaphysical knowledge is absolutely inconceivable. For unless that which we progressively know is one with the knowing faculty as in us constituted,—the unity of which our knowledge is partial, the whole of which we are fractions, the Absolute in relation to which we are limited and conditioned individualities,—then nothing can be known whatsoever. For since all that we apprehend is for us related to and couched in terms of consciousness, an absolute invasion into our consciousness of something alien and heterogeneous is impossible. If that be so, then the thing we get to know is not something antithetical to our consciousness, but is as much *in* consciousness as the faculty which we say gets hold of it. This is the only doctrine which reconciles the fantastic theory of Plato, that knowledge is reminiscence, with the standpoint of modern metaphysics. I need not enlarge on the point, because any student who has fully realized the meaning of the Idealistic criticism, which for ever renders materialism impossible, must also end by accepting the identity of Being and Thought. Of course it may still be urged, that even with this condition granted, we have only hypothetically established metaphysical cognition: we have proved that, supposing knowledge to exist, it must conform to this condition. This is true, and therefore whatever value there is in the objection will always be a sort of excuse for scepticism to assert that knowledge *may* be a subjective dream. But one thing is clear, that to those who have made up their minds that knowledge is a real thing, it must depend on the condition we have postulated. But now if knowledge depends on a homogeneity between the Thinker and the Thought, observe how incomparably effective is the theory which makes the ultimate reality of things to be 'Idea' or 'Absolute Consciousness.' For here we have a principle which is at one with our own consciousness, which appeals to us, as it were, with the face of a friend, which is not so much a stranger as an all-powerful and ancestral relation. This we have some chance of gradually getting to know, for Primal Source and Final End are essentially one with the thinker who strives to interpret them to his consciousness.

The difficulties, before adverted to, still remain; but now we may perhaps face them with a lighter heart. In the first place, the seemingly necessary antithesis between subject and object is, it must be remembered, a fault of *our own* consciousness; how far these are essential elements of an Absolute Consciousness, we simply have no means of determining. In the second place, we are, at all events, better off than we were on the supposition of subjective idealism. While starting from the Ego, it is well nigh impossible to see how there can arise an 'Anstoss,' for there is, *ex hypothesi*, nothing but the Ego; if we start from the idea, we can get a relation between the Ego, on the one hand, and that which serves for it as object on the other, viz. that part of the absolute which reveals itself in Consciousness. In the third place, difficulties with regard to the possibility of the Idea gradually developing itself to us, and the general relation in which the Individual stands to the Absolute, are partly difficulties of language, because language has no term in which to express the relation: partly they arise from the notions of a limited individuality, which we try to stretch, so as to fit the measure of an Universal. Especially must we remember, in this connection, the invincible inclination to transfer notions of time, which are only true for us, to that which is wholly outside the temporal category. We ask, How is it possible for an Absolute Idea to evolve itself, forgetting that development belongs to the category of time, and is therefore inapplicable to the Absolute Totality and Unity. I do not say that the difficulties are removed by these considerations, but certainly their importance is lessened when contrasted with the overplus of substantial value which inalienably belongs to the theory.

If the statement of the Ultimate Principle as 'Idea' or 'Absolute Consciousness' thus serves as an adequate foundation for metaphysics, the conception involved in the term 'God' answers best the requirements of ethics. We must once more patiently interrogate the content of the moral consciousness, in order to appreciate all that it involves and presupposes. We start with an idea of Good. Let it be granted that Reason gives us the idea, and that, therefore, it is for us as individuals *à priori*, in the sense that our experience, at all events, did not formulate it or call it into being. But if Good be an *à priori* idea of Reason, it cannot help but be tautological. That is good which Reason constitutes as an end for active moral beings. But what is the end which Reason constitutes? That which is the Good. From the circle of this tautology we cannot advance a step, so long as we argue from the individual platform; that is, so long as we attempt to estimate the constituents of morality from the side of the personal consciousness. Yet still the conception of Good is not a vacant ideal. By it men have been inflamed to serve their generation according to the best of their ability; nay, even to lay down their lives in its service. Good, therefore, can not be a meaningless tautology, which can only be expressed in terms of itself: it must be a pregnant idea, with power to move and to inspire. So, too, when we say that the duty which is laid upon mankind is to fulfil a moral order, it is clear that this moral order must exist in some completed and realized form, if not here and now in our experience of the actual world, then somewhere and somehow, idealiter and in transcendental fashion. But how are we to give concrete shape to such notions, except on the supposition that the Absolute Reality of the Universe is God? Here we have a Divine Consciousness, which contains within itself the completed notion of that Good, which in imperfect fashion we seek to realize, and the full content of that moral order, the progressive aspiration towards which constitutes for us the moral life. God gives me the Good which I am under an obligation to fulfil: God is the moral order which my highest duty is to seek to make prevail. It is the peculiarity of the moral problem, that it causes that which in a theory of knowledge we apprehend as the Absolute, to wear for us, from an ethical standpoint, the lineaments of a Consciousness who wills Good. Obligation then becomes the law of God: Good the ordinance of His will: the moral ideal the completed notion or final end of the universe.

Of course such conceptions are vague, but they are not therefore unreal. For we know by experience that they have served as inspirations to the best and holiest men who have ever lived. It is curious how little use has been made by ethical science of a psychological analysis of men whom the world agrees to call 'holy.' Such men as Francis of Assisi, or the late General Gordon, or still more St. Paul should surely form the best exemplifications of the relations of the Divine to the human in the moral life. The essential characteristic of such men was that their individual consciousness was held by them to be interpenetrated by an Absolute Consciousness; that alike in their feelings and their conduct, their aspirations, and their ethical activity, the keynote is expressed in the assertion, 'not I, but God.' In the revelations of their own inner nature, a pendulum-like swing is observable between the ascription of what they did and felt to themselves in alternation with a greater than themselves. But what is this but the confession that the individual in his ethical activity is complemented, so to speak, by the Universal, the finite by the Infinite? Is this mysticism? It is no greater mysticism than the corresponding assertion in the theory of knowledge that the individual consciousness finds in the Absolute Idea at once the completion of its own slow and step-by-step advance, and the discovery that what it learns to know is after all not another but its own highest self. If there is mysticism in one department, there is at least equal mysticism in the other; only without such mysticism, neither metaphysics nor morality are possible.

But now crowd in upon us the difficulties which we have already signalized. This God, which is declared to be the only principle which can explain morality,—how can he communicate himself to the individual, if he be at the same time an Universal and a Totality? Is God an individual? Is he a conscious person, who talks to us in dreams, and to whom, as to a magnified and non-natural man, we can address our prayers?

How can he be the author of a confessedly imperfect and largely evil universe?

Some of these questions are only pertinent in a philosophy of religion, and with that we have nothing to do. For instance, when we are asked whether God can listen to prayers, that is a question to be answered by an analysis of the religious consciousness, and we are only concerned with an analysis of the moral consciousness. It may well be that if philosophy on other grounds decides that God can in no intelligible sense be a person, it may have to tell the religious consciousness that prayer, in the ordinary sense of the term, is an absurdity. But this is no more than some of the most devotional of men have already admitted. For, as Emerson says, not prayer, but rather 'a glad and conspiring reception' would appear to be the proper religious attitude of the finite to the Infinite. It is God in us, as he says elsewhere, which checks the language of petition by a grander thought. But whatever be the answer, the question is not one with which moral philosophy need be troubled, for in morality we do not need to know whether prayer can be addressed to God, but whether moral activity can fulfil the moral order of the Divine Absolute. So again, it may well be that the religious life is the glad and joyful doing of that which the moral life does painfully and with striving, as though the God which the moral life seeks to realize is present in the religious consciousness with a blithe sense of imposing actuality. But again, it is enough for us to know that the essence of morality is effort, progressive effort to a divine ideal. The most moral men have had an energizing faith that they are helping

E

God in the world. This is, of course, the language of a merely finite and limited consciousness, but it expresses well enough the notion that morality involves the struggle towards a final end.

If we think accurately the demand for a proof of God is illogical. The ordinary method of proof is by causality: we prove one thing from another by showing that the first depends by way of causation on the second. But God is the Absolute First Cause. How then, can we find the cause of that which is *ex hypothesi* uncaused? How can we deduce the existence of that which is the sole ground of existence? If we succeeded we should have to admit that there was something on which God depended, which was therefore more of an Ultimate Reality (if the expression be allowed) than God. All so-called proofs of God fall under the edge of this criticism. They become attempts at once to affirm and deny in the same breath that God is the First Principle of the universe. But if that be so, how can we be sure of this First Principle? Only indirectly, by seeing that without it the metaphysical structure of knowledge and the ethical structure of well-doing fall to the ground. Will it be yet asked, How can the individual, who is finite, know God who is Absolute? Well, but how does a man know of himself that he is a personal Consciousness? Certainly logic will not assure him of his personal reality. It will tell him, with Hume, that he is a bundle of perceptions and sensations, or with Kant's Critique that he is a bare formal identity of $1 = I$. Partly he knows himself to be a real, personal Consciousness by a sort of intellectual intuition; but much more he gets the necessary assurance by studying the problems of morality. Just so with his consciousness of God. Logic will not help him here: nor yet, perhaps, adequately, metaphysic; but, logic or no logic, he has an intellectual intuition, and, metaphysic or no metaphysic, he realizes the one grand presupposition of ethical science.

Many of the difficulties of the conception of God are purely ethical versions of the corresponding metaphysical difficulties in the case of the Absolute Idea; and, in many respects, a solution must be found in the recognized incapacity of the Individual Consciousness, which seeks to pass judgment. Notoriously is this the case with the problem of evil. Evil is always construed by metaphysicians as limitation, negation, partiality. The assumption is clear. Evil is only a relative conception, not an absolute idea. Nor must we shrink from the consequence that therefore with Evil, God as absolute Idea has nothing to do, for fear that it will make God cease also to be the author of Good. For Good is in our interpretation connected with the final end of the world, whereas Evil is not. We ascribe Consciousness to God, but we do not ascribe the limited consciousness of individuality. Now it is only in relation to the latter, that Evil becomes a positive thing: to an Universal Consciousness it is not positive, but a negation, that is to say unreal. In what sense, however, can God have a Consciousness other than the Individual Consciousness? In the sense that he is the sum of individual consciousnesses, to whom he serves as common subject. If God be the cause of consciousness, he must himself have consciousness, though not in the form in which it is in us constituted. He is a Consciousness in that he is at once primal Cause and final teleological principle of all individual consciousnesses. This is, it is true, not consciousness in our sense, but in one in which by analogy we can yet find a meaning, and, indeed, an explanation of what we mean by good.

After all our attempted explanations, the notion of God remains peculiarly baffling and obscure. But for this we have been prepared by the discovery that we can only construe to ourselves a notion by means of a higher notion; and if we in this way elucidated the notion of God, we should have also to admit that a higher notion than God existed, which then in its turn we should have to call God, and so on *ad infinitum*. The matter has been admirably put in that scripture which says that "verily our God is a God who hideth himself," and by that philosophical theologian in the book of Job, who asked, "Canst thou by searching find out God?" All the more need have we to be thankful for such elucidation as is granted by the moral consciousness. For by an ethical analysis it appears that the idea of God is necessary, not indeed for that base reason which Kant affirms in the *Critique of the Practical Reason*, in order to assure a perfected satisfaction for the individual, but to give a sanction for the Moral Law, an explanation of Moral Good, and a content for the Moral Ideal.

PART II.
HISTORICAL.

BOOK I.—INTERPRETATION.

CHAPTER I.

§ 1. Definition.

What is Moral Philosophy? The question is not unnecessary, nor is the answer obvious, since upon it depends the view we take of the progressiveness of ethical science—whether there is any progress, and if so, what kind of progress there may be. How, then, can we best define its subject matter so as to find a place for it, separate and distinct, among other sciences and investigations obviously connected with it, such as Biology, or Anthropology, or Psychology?

Moral Philosophy is a systematic study of the conditions which make right Right, and wrong Wrong. The history of Moral Philosophy is essentially an account of the different explanations given by students of human nature of the words 'Right' and 'Wrong,' as applied to human action. And it is because words apparently so simple are found to involve in reality so many complicated considerations that their explanations are so numerous and so conflicting.

Observe that the words employed are 'Right' and 'Wrong,' and not 'Good' and 'Evil.' I desire to make the distinction for a particular reason. When we use the terms good and evil, we employ expressions for the full connotation of which all sorts of considerations, historical and scientific, are necessary, and by making Moral Philosophy deal with the investigation of good and evil, we are making its province overlap and include the provinces of Anthropology, Biology, and History. The essence of the ethical problem is the *human attitude* to certain historical and scientific data. I may ask, for instance, whether a particular social state or a particular legal enactment is a good one or no, and the answer will depend on what I conceive to be the proper lines of progress in the human race—a question of science, or history, or politics. The answer is very important to the student of morals, but the ethical question is rather this—Is such a course of action right or wrong for the human agent? To determine the answer to such a question, I have to know under what *motives* the actions were performed, and with what *end* or goal of activity before them the agent embarked on the course of action. Both of these two elements, the motive and the end, are involved in the question whether an act is right or wrong, but I may decide whether the act is good or evil by general considerations of science which do not necessarily touch either of these elements.

There is another way in which the distinction between 'right' and 'good' may be illustrated. The Greek moralists, we are often told, asked, What is good?—while the modern moralists ask the question, What is right? If we inquire, then, what are the consequences of asking the Greek question, we shall be able to see the issues involved in the distinction. Now in determining the conditions of the good, the whole basis of the inquiry was laid by the Greek moralist in politics, very much as, in a modern day, the solution of the same question is by Darwin or Spencer expressed in terms of science. In the one case as in the other the foundation overpowers the superstructure. The chief good of the citizen—a political question,—or the chief good of the human animal—a scientific question,—serves to obscure the lineaments of Duty, to determine which is the essential problem of the moralist. When the Hellenic state-system was broken up, first by the Macedonian supremacy and then by the Roman conquest, the true question slowly struggled to the light in the systems of the Stoics and the Epicureans. When men begin to see that the evolution of the human animal is not the real ethical problem, but at most, a doctrine presupposed by the moralist; or, better still, when the true bearings of idealistic analysis reveal somewhat of the deeper principles which underlie both nature and man, then, perhaps, again will ethics flourish as an independent inquiry. But besides subordinating ethics to politics, the determination of the conditions of 'the good' had another result. The ancient moralist, asking the question what is the *summum bonum*, proceeded to detail the characteristics of this *summum bonum*, as though it was some rare work of artistic skill, like a picture or a statue. The 'good' was to consist of such and such elements, and include such and such beautiful qualities. But however splendid the ideal might be made, the human being in the face of it might be left perfectly cold and untouched, unless some reasons were adduced to prove that the struggle towards the ideal was obligatory on him. It is the last consideration which is peculiarly important in ethics, not the earlier inquiry as to the characteristics of the ideal perfection. Good, described in terms of art, fails to bring out the difference between artistic creation and moral effort, and the confusion between the two spheres was, as a matter of fact, never quite got over by Greek thinkers. That it is a confusion hardly needs any proof, for directly we begin to consider the paramount importance of the Will in moral action, and its unimportance in the sphere of art, we begin to realize in what sense the human attitude towards good and evil, to which we apply the terms right and wrong, is the truly ethical point, instead of the constitution of good and evil themselves. Perhaps this distinction will enable us in the sequel to discriminate between adequate and inadequate moral systems, and justify us in affirming that some plausible and extensively popular ethical inquiries are not really ethical at all, but leave the moral problem exactly where they found it.

It was said, however, that the elucidation of right and wrong involved many considerations, and that this explained the divergence of moral systems. What are these considerations? Roughly speaking, they are of two kinds. There are certain data which may be called properly ethical; *e.g.* the test or criterion of morality, the announcement of the moral faculty, and the end or aim of a moral life. These are inwrought into the very texture of ethics. There are other questions, the solution of which ethics presuppose; questions psychological in one sense, ethical in another, because ethics gives them their peculiar colour and importance. Of the latter sort are the following:—What is the part played by the will in human action? Is the will free or determined? What is the relative importance of feeling and reason in determining action? Is there a special faculty active in moral judgments? Though logic may in a measure keep these classes distinct, it is naturally impossible to sever them completely in the elucidation of the question—What is meant by the assertion that we are moral?

Why are we moral? Let us attempt to narrate in some fashion this development of moral activity, with, at all events, enough precision to serve our purpose, which is to throw light on the divergence of ethical systems. At the outset of the history of the human being, we find a series of acts which are purely instinctive. There are certain rudimentary impulses, certain desires towards objective ends, which appear to act on the human being, as we say, without rhyme or reason. There is hunger, which instinctively desires the objective end—food. There is curiosity, which is the rudimentary instinct to know. There is the combative instinct, which is the effort to assert one's own position in the world; and many other impulses, sufficiently observable in every nursery. Are any of the actions ensuing to be called moral? Assuredly not. They are purely instinctive, natural, animal. There gradually supervenes on these rudimentary activities the exercise of volition. The rudimentary instincts are naturally diffusive and arbitrary in their tendency. The human being likes to indulge them all in turn, and he makes no choice between them. The pressure of external circumstance, however, teaches him that in order to secure a definite result he must learn at once to limit and to concentrate. He is not living in a world where everything can be got for the asking, but in one in which much must be sacrificed in order that something may be secured. He selects, therefore, and narrows down, as it were, his efforts on one or two given ends, because otherwise power is lost and fruition delayed. This is the beginning of the exercise of the volition, and the stage of development—if stage it ought to be called—is the wilful one. But now there dawns upon the human being the power of his reason, the power of abstracting, of ideating, of comprehending, which has several notable effects upon his activity. The first result is, that the man gradually acquires the notion of his own personality or self, as something to which all the separate ends of his activity must be subordinated: he learns to develop his powers in one direction, curtail them in another, in order to secure for himself the maximum of benefit and the minimum of injury, hoping thereby to establish his own position in the scale of human beings. Is action directed to this end and guided by this view of self to be called moral? Many moralists (including the whole of the hedonistic body) assert that it is: in the development of my thesis I may perhaps be allowed to assert, for the present dogmatically, that it is not. It is only when a second result of the action of reason asserts itself that a man can properly be termed a moral being. For the second result is the comprehension that a man is but one unit among many, that he is part of a social order which is made up of many personalities and many selves. Now the question comes before him as to the relation in which he stands to the social order, not as a question of antagonistic self-assertion, but of profound theoretical and practical interest. The discovery that there is such a thing as a social order constituted by a number of individuals makes him attempt to determine not only his proper relations to this order, but how best he can secure its welfare. And so arises the notion of Duty, which in its full sense till that moment had not seen the light. It is the work of reason to lift purely personal questions into the sphere of the universal, and it is this difference of air and atmosphere, this contrast between universality and individuality, which makes the difference between duty and expediency. I ask, does an act benefit myself?—though reason enables me to give the reply by its idea of self as something to work for, I am asking a question of expediency, of interest. But if I ask, Is this act which I am meditating one which is equally incumbent on all human beings in my position?—then I ask a question of duty. With such an universal end in view, the motive under which I act is a moral one; with an individual or relative end in view, my motive, though not necessarily immoral, is non-moral. Nor must the implied consequence be shirked that, therefore, from this point of view there are, strictly speaking, no duties to oneself. To the hermit in his cell, or the man on a desert island, the matter of course assumes another form. Motives are interpenetrated with feelings, sentiments, emotions of all kinds. These are the mainsprings of activity. But it is only when reason definitely brings before a man universal ends of action, that is to say, the idea of humanity at large, and himself as one member of that humanity, a being whose nature cannot be defined except in relation to a social order, that we can speak of moral action, or moral motive, or duty. Why, then, am I a moral being? Because I am one member of a social order, one unit in a human series. Why *must* I be moral? Because reason has enlightened me as to my position, and when once the enlightenment has come, there is no going back to the purely instinctive, or wilful, or even selfish stage. By the ordinance of his reason, a man lives for ever under a law of obligation.

In this rough and hasty picture of the development of morality, it will be well to guard against misconception. It is in all probability impossible to discriminate between the modes of human activity with any final or decisive boundaries, as different stages of ethical advance. In one sense Reason is implicit in a human being from the outset; in another sense it is a late acquisition,—the first birth of, or perhaps identical with, self-consciousness. Nor is it possible for a man to act either wholly from emotion, or wholly from rational motive, every act being a complex of reason and sentiment where reason gives the end and the idea, and sentiment the local colouring. Still, even in the history of the development of races the lines of social advance are found to run in a manner very similar to the moral development of the individual. A broad survey of ethnological divisions would probably reveal the fact that just as the human embryo is said to represent in its various changes the rudimentary types of lower animals, so the moral development of the individual finds its special history illustrated by racial divisions. There is, for instance, the earliest stage of selfishness and wilfulness illustrated by the Australian aborigines, the lowest in the scale of humanity and the oldest of existing races, or by the North American Indians, who exhibit much of that instinctive cruelty which is found connected with the wilfulness of childhood. The African, with his paroxysms of passion, sensual indulgence and intoxication, is only an exaggerated parallel of the emotional phase in human life. The earlier stages of rational comprehension, the beginnings of the use of experience, and its adaptation to the needs of a thinking self, find their illustration in some of the mental characteristics of the Chinese and the Japanese; while the stage of positive morality is only reached in the social condition and ethical enactments of the Egyptians, the Hebrews, the Greeks and the Romans. Thus in the stages of growth from childhood to manhood the human being appears to reproduce the stages of the development of humanity at large.[1]

Let us grant, if need be, that this picture forms a logical discrimination of elements rather than a precise historical order; yet for us, in our attempt to get a logical definition of the scope of ethics, it is important to distinguish between three modes of human activity. First, the purely instinctive and emotional; second, that action which is rational and calculative in view of a self which needs satisfaction; third, the rational action which finds its motive power and its final aim in the idea of one self among many selves,—the idea, as we say, of a common humanity. For here we have hit on again, though in a different form, those three elements of interpretation, criticism, and reconstruction, which we found to enter as moments

[1] Cf. Wake's 'Evolution of Morality,' Vol. I. Hegel's 'Philosophy of History,' Introduction.

into all intellectual progress. The ethical systems which base themselves on instincts and emotions are mainly interpretative. Those which are absorbed by the notion of one all-engrossing self, are systems of criticism; they use the reason, but arrest the rational activity too soon. When Reason has done its perfect work, then only do we have systems of reconstruction.

§ 2. CLASSIFICATION.

To avoid the distraction of endless details, some classification of ethical systems is absolutely necessary. But on what principle or principles is such a classification to be made? Every writer on Morals has probably his own principle, but they fall generally into three well-marked species. There is the superficial descriptive method, when systems are looked on *ab extra*, and some obvious characteristic is selected to serve as a basis for a descriptive epithet; or there is the teleological method, when we start from a given view of what ethics should be, and then inquire how far the philosophical systems have either attained to or fallen short of this ideal conception. Or again, ethics being considered as a department of general philosophy, the fundamental antagonism in philosophical method, the different ways of approach, known respectively as the *à priori* or the *à posteriori* methods, have been employed to divide the various systems into two antithetical divisions. It may prove of some interest to take an instance of each in turn.

The first—the superficial descriptive method—can be illustrated by one of Mr. Spencer's classifications in the *Data of Ethics*. Ethical systems[1] are divided

[1] 'Data of Ethics,' p. 49.

into four—theological, political, intuitional, and utilitarian, a division in which the author is guided by the obvious external characteristics in each case. The theological system of ethics, for instance, is one which makes actions respectively good or bad simply by divine injunction. Political systems are those which make state enactments the sources of right and wrong, implying the belief that moral obligation originates with Acts of Parliament, and can be changed this way or that by majorities. Intuitional systems are those which hold that moral perceptions are innate in some original faculty or sense which belongs to all men alike. Utilitarian systems are those which estimate conduct by observation of results, by discovering, that is to say, whether conduct is useful or the reverse. Such a mode of classification clearly gives us only superficial aspects, and makes us lay stress rather on the differences between the systems than on their less obvious though perhaps more important resemblances. A far better classification, it must be admitted, is found in the same work[1] where Mr. Spencer divides ethical systems according as they take into consideration either the character of the agent, or the nature of the agent's motive, or the quality of his deeds, or the results of his deeds.

The second mode of classification is illustrated by Professor Sidgwick's remarks in the opening chapter of *The Methods of Ethics*. He begins by setting forth the scope of Moral Philosophy. In his judgment, morality is 'a doctrine of ends,' an account of the different objects and aims which men pursue. What are the different ends which ought to be pursued?

[1] 'Data of Ethics,' p. 32.

They are mainly two—*perfection* or *excellence*, and *happiness*. Each of these can be further subdivided according as the perfection on one hand, or the happiness on the other, is held to be universal or individual. But no sooner is the principle of classification expounded than an explanation has to be added which diminishes its value. For there are many moralists, as Mr. Sidgwick has to admit, who are careless of these ends, and who regard ethics as only a set of absolute rules. In the development of their systems, however, these moralists, we are told, can for all practical purposes be identified with those who make perfection or excellence the object of pursuit. We get accordingly a threefold division of moral systems, to which more technical names can now be given. A first system is called *Intuitionism*, including those who partly devote their attention to the elaboration of the absolute rules of morality, and partly profess to find in perfection, whether individual or universal, the end of human existence. A second system is *Egoistic Hedonism*, the system of those who make individual happiness the only object of moral endeavour. A third class is composed of those who substitute universal happiness for individual, and this system is called *Universalistic Hedonism*, or more shortly *Utilitarianism*.

Dr. Martineau's classification in his recent work, *Types of Ethical Theory*, affords another example. According to Dr. Martineau the true form of ethical theory is psychological; ethics should be based on psychology. On this principle we can at once divide systems into those which accept this legitimate basis, and those which do not,—a division which in the hands of its author, roughly accords with the ethics of Christianity and unchristian ethics. Unpsychological ethics may be of two kinds—metaphysical, like those of Plato, or Descartes, or Spinoza; or physical, like that of Comte and Positivism. Psychological ethics has also two varieties, *heteropsychological,* when the attempt is made to reduce moral phenomena to those exhibited by some mental faculty other than conscience, such as sense, or reason, or the artistic faculty; and *idiopsychological,* where we start with a definition of the inner facts of conscience itself, and deduce our system therefrom. It is an assumption of Dr. Martineau that Christianity introduced psychological ethics (a statement which is rendered somewhat doubtful by the essentially psychological character of the ethics of the post-Aristotelian schools), and that psychology in the narrower sense of mental analysis should be the sole foundation of ethics. The disadvantages of such a course becomes plain, when it is seen what the absence of metaphysical analysis entails. Conscience becomes almost a fetish; and reason, with all its ethical prerogatives curtailed, takes revenge on the moralist by landing him in the most uncompromising and unmetaphysical dualism.

Perhaps our third method of classification needs only a few words of explanation. It consists of a rigorous application of the antithesis between *à priori* method and *à posteriori.* How shall we approach the consideration of moral questions? Shall we begin by assuming good to be an *à priori* idea, which for this very reason cannot be defined otherwise than tautologically, like time or space? Then we are dealing with ethics in the spirit of all those moralists from

Plato to Kant, who find the seat of moral distinctions in the intimate essence of man's spiritual nature, and deduce moral rules from an intuitive conception. Or shall we approach ethics, like any other science, from the side of experience? Shall we look at actions from the point of view of their results rather than their motives, and classifying and tabulating them in this spirit, gradually rise by an inductive method to the general rules and laws of morality? Then we shall put ourselves on the side of the other great division of ethical writers who begin with Aristotle, and find their latest exponents in Darwin and Spencer.

There can be no question which of these three methods of classification is at once the most inviting and the most satisfactory. It is indubitably the second. For we must interpret the value of systems in accordance with some idea, and this idea must be capable of finding its proper place in a general metaphysical system. It does not appear to be of much use to say, generally, that Morality is a doctrine of ends, any more than to make the assertion that all true ethics are psychological. Such statements are wanting in precision, or rather the idea which is to serve as the basis for classification, is not sufficiently clear, simple, and far-reaching. For æsthetics are also psychological, and politics is a doctrine of ends, ἕνεκα τοῦ εὖ ζῆν. Remembering that all classifications have only a provisional value, let us begin by asking, Is there any central idea in ethics which may serve to distinguish it from other studies like Psychology, or Social Physics, or Natural Science? All these latter sciences, it appears, deal with the systematization of facts; ethics takes the form of the enunciation of a law. What is this law? It is what we call moral obligation, which may be differently stated as the sense of Duty, Responsibility, or the necessity of self-regulation. Ethics, having for its sphere of study the courses of human action, is confronted with this fact, which it is therefore bound to explain, that in man there are not only the various lines of activity which flow from desire, impulse, and volition, but also the ineradicable conviction that a necessity is laid upon him to do the conduct which is right, whatever interpretation of the word right may be ultimately given; that if he does not do it he will suffer in some way, if not externally then internally, by the feeling of remorse : and that thus man is what is termed responsible—responsible for the right direction of his powers and activities and impulses, and, so far as is implied in this description, possessed of the capacity of self-direction. It is the unique character of this conception of obligation which serves to preserve ethics as an independent science. Is the conception one which can find its proper basis and explanation in a metaphysical system? If it be the essence of the metaphysical problem to unroll the full contents and meaning of spirit as it explains alike the physical, moral, and intellectual worlds, it is also clear that spirit is nothing if not free. How freedom is to be reconciled with the consciousness of law, how in this sense both freedom and necessity are integral notions in the evolution of spirit, is precisely the problem on which above all other studies ethics appears to throw most light; for responsible action, which means freedom, and obligation, which means necessity, are so little inconsistent in their application to ethics that they appear not only different aspects, but at bottom one identical phase of the moral life. In this way the sense of obligation seems to take us back to the essential characteristics of the spiritual Ego, which in its turn requires to be supplemented by a metaphysical theory of the universe, which shall be idealistic of one kind or the other, either subjective idealism or absolute idealism.

If the law of obligation, then, answers to both our tests, if it is at once the central conception of ethics, and in itself an essentially metaphysical principle, it may be taken as the *fundamentum divisionis* in our classification. We may at once divide moral systems into (1.) Those which give no explanation of moral obligation. (2.) Those which give some explanation, satisfactory or unsatisfactory.

1. The first class requires some further specification. In giving no explanation of moral obligation, the systems may either categorically deny its existence, or preclude its existence by the general tenor of their speculations. Many systems may be found which in one way or the other take up this attitude towards the central conception of ethics, such as Scepticism, Materialism, Mysticism, Quietism, Pessimism, and perhaps Pantheism. For the sake of illustration let us look at two of these,—Materialism, which denies the fact of moral obligation, and Mysticism, which precludes it by the tenor of its speculations. With regard to all these systems it is probably true that they are not primarily concerned with ethical speculation. They start with other and different inquiries; they either speculate concerning the conditions of knowledge, or else they are wholly possessed by some metaphysical idea, or they are occupied with

physical studies, or the character of their thought is found to be merely the reflection of certain historic conditions of misery, unsettlement, or despair. Their conclusions, therefore, in the moral sphere are only deductions from other conclusions in which they are more interested. Materialism, so far as it is a system at all, is certainly in this case. A Materialist is primarily occupied with scientific studies of Physics and Biology. The study of Physics yields the result that certain changes of matter account for the opposite and changing effects of nature. As applied to man the same material basis is found for those affections, desires, loves, antipathies which he exhibits; even his intellectual life is said to have a physical basis. Now comes the deduction in the sphere of ethics. As all life is thus implicitly bound up with material organization and material form, the activity of man, as directed to what we term right and wrong, becomes also a mere question of organization and matter, in which we, as individuals, have no voice and interest. Let us listen to the utterances of Dr. Maudsley, who is in this respect the most uncompromising of speculative materialists. In a lecture on Conscience, published in his work *Body and Mind*, Dr. Maudsley says: "There is the strongest desire evinced, and the most strenuous efforts are made in many quarters, to exempt from physical researches the highest functions of mind, and particularly the so-called moral sense and the will. Are we, as physiologists, to allow an exemption from physical research to any function of mind, however exalted; or shall we maintain through good and through evil report that all its functions from the lowest to the highest are equally functions of organization?" He proceeds: "One thing is certain, that moral philosophy cannot penetrate the hidden springs of feeling and impulse; they lie deeper than it can reach, for they lie in the physical constitution of the individual, and going still farther back, perhaps in his organic antecedents. Because the fathers have eaten sour grapes, therefore it often is that the children's teeth are set on edge. Assuredly of some criminals, as of some insane persons, it may be truly said, that they are born, not made; they go criminal as the insane go mad—because they cannot help it. A stronger power than they can counteract has given the bias of their being." A clearer statement could scarcely be found of the ethical aspect of materialism, and no words are necessary to show that such a system as this denies what is to us the central conception of ethics—the law of obligation.

Mysticism, though it perhaps hardly denies, still by the tenor of its speculation precludes, the reality of moral obligation. The great age for mysticism was that which succeeded the disruption of the state system in Greece, when especially in Alexandria, neo-Platonism and neo-Pythagoranism combined with certain Eastern elements in a philosophy of Quietism. In a time of considerable external misery, when individual thinkers were thrown back upon their own narrow individualities, deprived as they were of all opportunity of political action, philosophy took three main lines: one, the Stoic, found within man a certain fortitude to resist and to be content under unhappy circumstances; the Epicurean turned more and more to a pursuit of pleasure—that last infirmity of disappointed minds; while the Mystics chose to renounce all effort, to resign themselves to their own weakness, and to find in certain ecstatic conditions, which they called 'swooning into the godhead,' the solace for all unhappiness. Mysticism rests on three principles. First, the fact that human life can at the best afford very imperfect good; second, that even this good, such as it is, cannot be obtained except by an effort which is against nature, and followed by extreme lassitude; third, that in consequence there is a large preponderance of evil in life. Hatred of the flesh, hatred of the world, contempt for action—such are some of the gloomy ascetic results which follow. The only intellectual activity the Mystics allowed themselves was contemplation rather than study, and their ideal state of existence was one of complete passivity, followed, as such a state invariably is, by unreal conditions of ecstacy and hallucination. The moral consequences are for us the more important. If all action is equally fruitless, there can be no moral distinction between actions, as Plotinus actually affirmed. Man has no end to pursue on earth, and therefore there can be for him no good or evil. Hence, too, no duties and no moral obligation. For the truth is that it is just the arduousness of human life and the pressure of a seemingly hostile world, which makes man an active, unconquered, individual unit, with duties to perform and an ideal to realize, defection from which is moral failure.

There were, indeed, Mystics before Alexandrian times, and it is the doctrine of these early sages in the Indian peninsula which Schopenhauer adapted to the uses of his Pessimism. Nor are the moral deductions in this case essentially dissimilar. Listen to the final page of Schopenhauer's *Die Welt als Wille und Vorstellung:* "Before us there is certainly only nothingness, but that which resists this passing into nothing, our nature, is indeed just the will to live, which constitutes ourselves and is our world. But if we turn our glance from our own needy and embarrassed condition to those who have overcome the world, in whom the will, having attained to perfect self-knowledge, freely denies itself, and who then merely wait to see the last trace of it vanish with the body which it animates; then instead of the restless striving and effort, instead of the constant transition from wish to fruition and from joy to sorrow; instead of the never-satisfied and never-dying hope which constitutes the life of the man who wills, we shall see the peace which is above all reason, the perfect calm of the spirit. . . . But we must banish the dark impression of that nothingness which we discern behind all virtue and holiness as their final goal, and which we fear as children fear the dark: we must not even evade it like the Indians through myths and meaningless words such as reabsorption in Brahma, or the Nirvana of the Buddhists. Rather do we freely acknowledge that what remains after the entire abolition of will is for all those who are still full of will certainly nothing; but conversely, to those in whom the will has turned and has denied itself, this our world which is so real, with all its suns and milky ways, is nothing." *Nichts* is the ominous word with which the whole system ends.

2. Let us turn to the other division of ethical systems. To these moral obligation is a fact which requires some explanation. Man is a creature who, in

the face of the circumstance of life, feels or thinks a certain course of conduct to be right, and feels or thinks himself obliged to pursue it. The points in which these philosophical systems differ is the different mode of interpreting the obligation which they all in a measure allow to exist. Five varieties may be distinguished.

(1.) The first of these is Egoism, or pure Hedonism, of which the best exponent in modern ethics is perhaps Hobbes. The obligation, in his view, that is laid upon human beings is the careful ministration to self, an obligation dependent upon a certain sensitive organization, and gaining its validity from its supreme naturalness and originality.

(2.) A second system may be called the disinterested school, or the school of sentimental moralists, or intuitionists. These philosophers believe in the disinterestedness of moral action, and explain obligation as due to a sentiment or intuitive feeling of some sort; either a sixth sense which morality adds to the other five, or else a combination or result of simple feelings. There are many forms of this system of ethics; thus, for instance, Shaftesbury and Hutcheson spoke of what they called a moral or reflex sense, a certain internal feeling or disposition towards actions, some of which it approves, while others it disapproves. Adam Smith made the feeling of sympathy the main principle of morality. Butler, who must be classed with these philosophers, shows that in conscience and the internal feeling which it inspires, resides the moral faculty of man.

(3.) A third system is the Utilitarian, which may perhaps be not unjustly described as the modern form of the selfish theory of Hobbes. It is in every way an improved form, for instead of explaining obligation as the necessity of ministering to self, it explains it as the necessity of ministering to society at large. The duty of man is to secure the greatest happiness of the greatest number; the end is still happiness, *i.e.* a feeling of gratification, but it is enlarged, or as some would say disguised, under a widely philanthropic form. The writers, who would be classed under this head are Locke, Hume, Hartley, Paley the utilitarian theologian, Bentham the utilitarian without the theology, Austin, the two Mills, and some later writers.

(4.) Rationalism and rationalist systems form a fourth variety. The general position is explained in the assertion that morality is determined not by feeling but by thought, reason, intellectual considerations. Rationalist philosophers interpret moral obligation as a purely rational mode of action, and refer the idea of good to an *à priori* concept of reason. They differ, however, in their views as to the character of this idea. Some, like Cudworth and Price (to whom also from this point of view Kant must be added), make good a simple and irreducible idea; others, like Clarke, Wollaston, Malebranche, and Wolff, treat the idea of good as complex, and attempt to resolve it into what they deem simpler ideas.

(5.) A fifth and last variety of ethical systems is the Naturalistic or Scientific Ethics—the Ethics of Evolution. In accordance with the idea of evolution the notion of duty is supposed to have been slowly evolved from other and alien elements, from the selfish greediness of animal instincts, from the fear of the departed chieftain, from reverence for a ruling chieftain, from superstitious alarm at invisible deities, and from calculations of social expediency. These are the ethics of Darwin and Spencer, and they form the latest development of ethical thought to be found in England.

The stages of moral advance which were referred to in the earlier portion of this chapter, afford curious and instructive parallels to these systems. The early wilful stage of human action is well represented by the simple instinctive selfishness of Hedonistic moral schemes. The second or emotional stage will then find its analogue in those systems which we have called sentimental, with their reliance on moral emotion and moral sensibility. To that will succeed Utilitarianism, which adequately represents that early Empiricism which is the first result of intellectual comprehension. Partly to this stage, partly to a later one, will also belong that which in modern times has taken the place of Utilitarianism, Naturalistic Ethics, or the Ethics of Science. In the final and concluding stage of the development of reason will be placed Rationalistic Ethics—the implication being that here we are touching on the full and completed development of Morality. A similar guiding clue is furnished by that principle, already more than once adverted to, that interpretation is followed by criticism, and criticism by reconstruction. It will then appear that while early forms of Hedonism, Intuitionism, and Rationalism form an interpretative stage, Utilitarianism is, above all, the stage of criticism, and reconstruction commences partly with the Ethics of

Evolution, but much more with the Kantian Rationalism, together with its historical sequel in philosophy. If such an arrangement of systems as is adopted in the following pages appears to savour too much of a *parti pris* in the disputed questions of ethical science, it must be remembered, on the other hand, that dogmatism, despite certain obvious drawbacks, should possess at least two advantages, clearness and consistency.

CHAPTER II.

§ 1. Egoism.

[Thomas Hobbes, 1588—1679.—'Translation of Thucydides,' 1628.—'Elementa Philos. de Cive,' 1642.—'Leviathan, or the Matter, Form, and Authority of Government,' 1651.—'Human Nature, or the Fundamental Elements of Policy,' 1650.—'De Corpore Politico, or the Elements of Law, Moral and Political,' 1650.]

MORAL PHILOSOPHY begins, in accordance with the development of mankind, and also in accordance with the development of a human individual, with the purely selfish stage. Just as in the history of the peoples of the world, the lowest and earliest stage is found in the Australian aborigines; just as in the history of a man, the earliest scene is the simple, self-regarding vitality of the child, so in the history of modern ethics, the selfish or hedonistic system of Hobbes and Mandeville must be considered as the first step in the development of moral notions. The history of ancient ethics is framed on exactly similar lines. When first Moral Philosophy began to be articulate in the paradoxes of the Sophists, it espoused a purely selfish form; only afterwards, in the systems of Plato and Aristotle, does it present those larger and fairer lineaments which indicate the change from selfish isolation to a self-sacrificing social activity. Nor does the analogy stop here. For philosophy began as it were anew, after the break up of the Hellenic state system, and one of the earliest moral systems after Aristotle was that founded by Epicurus, which made pleasure and pain the tests of moral activity—the system which suited so well the pleasure-loving Romans at Baiæ and Herculaneum, and lasted probably longer than any ancient school of thought.

Hobbes is in many senses a typical philosopher of selfishness: he is not such "a buffoon and ale-house sophist as Mandeville, nor is he such a vain, shallow, sensual jester as Helvetius."[1] If you grant him his premises, he will be found to be an acute and consistent logician. His style of writing is a model of clear, simple, and unaffected English, and he is animated by a sincere political idea that an absolute monarchy is the one remedy for the evils of England. Hobbes begins his philosophical theory by picturing the conditions of humanity before society began. In this early pre-historic age every man's hand was against his neighbour's. Each was, as Hobbes picturesquely says, "a wolf to his brother" (homo homini lupus). An internecine war raged without stint or stay, and men were fairly equal, for where they were inferior in brute strength they regained their equality by means of cunning and fraud. Such a state of things was naturally full of inconvenience; possession was uncertain, and enjoyment precarious; and possibly through sheer weariness or through the gradual increase of reasonableness men at last agreed to frame certain conditions of peace. These articles of peace

[1] Mackintosh's 'Ethical Philosophy,' p. 87.

consisted of simple requirements, bidding men to give up that right to everything which nature seemed to allow to each; ordering them so far as possible to seek peace and ensue it, to cease from injuring on condition of not being injured, and to abide by and perform their contracts. But how were such articles of peace or 'laws of nature' (in contradistinction from 'rights of nature') to be stringently enforced? Only one way seemed practicable: an absolute despot must be elected whose duty it should be to see that men adhered to the compacts they made with their fellows. "This is the generation of that Leviathan or mortal god," whose absolute authority is thus referred to the natural history of man's development; the ancient prototype of the monarch possessed of a divine right and an inviolable person, who figured so disastrously in the imagination of the Stuart dynasty. Such is Hobbes' position as a political writer and student of society, and in both capacities the course of modern speculation has left his views high and dry on the shores of time. Republican England, since the Revolution, is justly intolerant of the pretensions of an absolute monarchy; and the idea of an original social contract between men, though popularized by the names of Locke and Hobbes and Rousseau, has long ago passed into the limbo of exploded fallacies.

We are, however, more concerned with Hobbes as a moralist. His principles are so simple that they can be stated in a very few words. The aim of all action among human beings, as indeed we might well gather from the conduct of Hobbes' pre-historic wolves, is personal well-being—a persistent course of grubbing and grasping to secure the maximum of individual pleasure. The only motive of action is the love of well-being, combined with a fear of the dreary alternative of personal misery. The conclusions involved in this principle are easily formulated. In the first place, the only moral quality of actions is their pleasurableness or painfulness: all acts are indifferent except on this ground. ("Whatever is the object of any man's longing that he calls good; whatever is the object of aversion or hatred in him, that he calls evil or vile.") In the second place, there is only a single passion in our nature—the love of personal well-being. In the third place, the individual is the only judge of his own good, for good and evil are relative terms, to be understood always in reference to the person who uses them, the only standard of judgment being the individual pleasure or pain involved. From such a standpoint some commonplace mental states wear strange forms. Fear is aversion, with the thought of mischief to follow: anger is sudden fortitude: laughter is sudden self-glorification: magnanimity is the contempt of little helps and hindrances: pity or compassion is the pain arising from the consideration that what has happened to another man may happen to ourselves: benevolence is inspired by the fear that we also may suffer. There is no such analyst of motives as Hobbes, for he starts from a single principle which makes all analysis easy. Human nature is not complex or multiform. It is absolutely simple. It surrenders all the secrets of its activities to the single key of self-love.

Such in outline is the ethical system of Hobbes—

one of the most consistent and logical systems of pure hedonism that has ever been presented to a selfish age. Inasmuch as I have taken it as characteristic of a particular stage of thought, it will be better to mention a few points of criticism which are applicable to Hobbes' system alone, before proceeding to those general considerations which affect it in common with all other attempts to make morality and the pursuit of pleasure convertible terms. For there are one or two technical terms employed by Hobbes which naturally invite examination. Three meet us at the outset—the words *right, duty, contract.*

1. What does Hobbes mean by *right?* Every man has naturally a right to everything. Nature has given each man a right to seize and hold everything for his own personal advantage; and this natural right (*jus naturale*) is by each man surrendered in the formation of society, not on any grounds which we should call moral, but solely because by such a surrender he thinks that he can better secure his own advantage. Now ordinarily *right* involves two conceptions:

(*a.*) There can be no *rights* without corresponding duties.

(*b.*) A *right* is of a sacred character, which every one is bound to acknowledge.

Comparing these two conceptions with Hobbes' version of the term *right*, it is, in the first place, tolerably clear, that if every one has a right to everything, no single person can have any particular duties answering to rights. My right to secure what conduces to my well-being naturally leads me to disregard other people. I can have no duties therefore towards them, for they simply stand in the way of my wellbeing. Further, they can have no duties towards me for a precisely similar reason. My right, then, is of such a nature that it involves no consideration whatever on my part of those around me, nor any consideration on their part with regard to me. A second consequence then follows. This right which belongs to every one by nature is clearly one which no other person need acknowledge. It lays no obligation whatever on other people; on the contrary, it is controverted at every moment, whether successfully or not depends on the individual strength. Or we may put it even more strongly. My natural right to secure my own well-being is one which every one else has a natural right to disregard. The fact is that the word *right* itself has no meaning as applied to the so-called natural condition of man. Right is a term correlative to a complex set of duties, and this complex set of duties can only arise after society has been formed, and not prior to its formation; while, as legal right, it is the result of positive enactment, defining the relation of men to one another; as moral right, it is interpreted as having reference to a certain moral order of the world, not to anarchic disorder.

2. What does the word *duty*, or *moral obligation*, in Hobbes' system mean?

The duty of man is to follow out his own interest, to secure his own well-being. Self-interest considered from a sufficiently wide point of view declares that it is better for a man to give up some of his own rights and to live in society, because his self-interest is better secured by peace than war. The duty therefore of man becomes obedience to the ordinances of the autocratic government which he has set up. Now, supposing that a man does not see that it is his interest to give up some of his personal rights, what can Hobbes say to him? He has told us that the only motive of action is self-interest, he has begun by expressly referring us to an individual criterion. What can be done to this recalcitrant? He can be punished by the State, is Hobbes' answer. But observe what is involved in this reply. It is implied that the only sanction of duty is the coercive and punitive power of the State. We ordinarily mean by a moral sanction an internal feeling of some sort, to which such words as 'conscience,' 'responsibility,' and 'remorse' are correlative. So even Mill tells us when in his 'Utilitarianism'* he asserts that the only sanction of morality is an internal sentiment of some kind, which is the essence of what we mean by conscience. Such an internal feeling is simply non-existent in the system of Hobbes. Duty is not personal, it is civic; it does not mean obedience to an internal standard, but a subservience, willing or unwilling, to an external and arbitrarily constituted authority.

3. Lastly, if Hobbes gives a new version to the words *duty* and *right*, what shall we say to the word *contract* itself? Our wolfish forefathers made a contract, says Hobbes, but those who make a contract are already in society and not before it. For how should a contract be comprehensible to the 'wolves' of Hobbes? The obligation to keep a promise, to fulfil one's word, to maintain a contract, is correlative to certain moral ideas and duties; apart from such conception it has no meaning. Here, once again, Hobbes

* *Utilitarianism*, c. iii.

is transferring words, the connotation of which has only been gradually evolved by the courses of human progress, to a state of nature in which they have no meaning, in which they are vacant forms devoid of all content whatsoever.

Let us now turn to considerations which have a wider reference than to the isolated system of Hobbes, and which are applicable to the general system which is called egoistic hedonism. The end of life, we remember, is held to be individual pleasure, the only motive is self-interest, the only paramount feeling in human nature is desire for personal gratification. Let us begin with the single motive of "self-interest." In attempting to trace the gradual development of man in the last chapter, I tried to distinguish between three stages: first, a purely instinctive stage of action; second, a stage where reason has begun to formulate the notion of a self as something for which we ought to work; thirdly, a stage where reason carrying out its reflective functions discovers that the world is composed of many selves, and that in point of fact an individual self can only be defined by its relations to other selves. These three clearly-marked stages of advance are confused and contracted by Hobbes into one absorbingly selfish stage. In the first place there is a confusion of the selfish motive of action with the instinctive motives of action. Yet unless mankind had at first instinctively pursued certain objective ends, like food and knowledge and the like, had instinctively felt hunger and curiosity and the combative impulse, the very notion of self could never have been formulated. Therefore the selfish motive could not possibly have been the earliest motive of human action. In the second place Hobbes has arbitrarily arrested the work of reason at its most primitive stage. For no man who has once formed the notion of self can avoid the discovery that his self is limited and controlled in a thousand ways by other selves, and that his life problem is not that of a Crusoe on a desert island. And the discovery—and it is one which every practised voluptuary has made—involves a serious curtailment of the one motive of self-interest. On grounds of mere expediency, man becomes bound to consider others.

Observe, too, what a mutilated picture of human feeling a characteristic hedonist like Hobbes gives us. Pleasure is mere personal gratification, says Hobbes; the only paramount feeling is love of personal gratification. But other elements are involved even in pleasure. Sympathy is a pleasure, pity is a pleasure, generosity and benevolence are pleasures. For in reality the fact that sympathy is innate and instinctive is that which enables us to traverse Hobbes' assertion that society is against nature, by the opposite assertion that man is by nature a social being. Sympathy, in the form of the social instincts, is the great proof that man's natural state is not a state of war. When Aristotle said, "Man is a political animal," he expressed a truer as well as a more humanitarian maxim than Hobbes' dictum, "Every man's hand is against his brother's."

There are three other general considerations which may be referred to as affecting this selfish system of ethics known as hedonism.

The first is called the paradox of hedonism. The

paradox is this. Pleasure is asserted to be the only end of activity; pleasure, therefore, is clearly that which we ought to set before our eyes in any and every form of action. We make the experiment, and we find that experience gives the lie to our dogma. If there is one thing more certain than another, it is that to do an action because of the pleasure it brings is precisely the way to lose the pleasure. Pleasure, therefore, which is that we are told to aim at, is exactly that which we must not aim at if we desire to secure it. A paradox indeed, when the end of human activity is found to be secured only on the express condition of not making it the end of activity

A second consideration is suggested by the scheme of life which this system inevitably suggests. We have to secure the maximum of pleasures; therefore we must compare pleasures one with another to see which is greater, which less. Therefore pleasure must admit of comparison. Do pleasures as a matter of fact admit of being compared? Can I set my pleasure in comparison with yours? Is there any meaning in the sensualist telling the philosopher that he underestimates the pleasure of sensual gratification, or the philosopher telling the sensualist that he ignores the pleasures of philosophic meditation? Nor can a man form a comparative estimate even of his own pleasures. When he is recovering from sickness, nothing is so pleasant as repose; when he is in health, nothing is so distasteful as repose. He estimates the pleasures of eating in a different spirit before and after dinner. The pleasures of youth are not comparable with the pleasures of maturity, nor can the pleasures of manhood be set in the same balance with the pleasures of old age. If pleasure is to be the end of life, the standard must vary with every year of life, and almost with every phase of conscious feeling. Nor, further, is the attitude of self-seeking calculation one which is likely to secure the largest amount of self-gratification. Happiness is the gift of expansive emotional natures, and not of calculative machines. These are some of the difficulties of what we may call the hedonistic calculus.

The third is a question of deeper import, and touches on questions of metaphysics. What a notion of the self does this moral system present! Can the self be exhausted by an enumeration of its conscious states? Can a series of isolated feelings be summed up at all, or can we say that each man's self is nothing but a bundle of sequent feelings? The experience of human kind, so far as our present subject is concerned, points to a different conclusion. What is a more trite and commonplace discovery than that pleasure is a phantom, a will of the wisp, a fleeting and treacherous thing? Here one moment, it is gone the next, and the man who attempts to pursue it is breaking up his life into isolated and disconnected moments, is planting his feet every instant in the quagmire of disappointment and despair. The pleasure is sought for, possibly it is secured, and it turns, like Dead Sea apples, into ashes in the mouth. The man whose self is something above any or every conscious feeling which he entertains, vindicates his own higher nature by a divine dissatisfaction, which is the best disproof of that narrow psychological basis on which all systems of hedonism rest. And this consideration let us add to those we have already referred to under the name of the psychological fallacy of hedonism. All three considerations point to the same result. Whether we regard the absurdity of the hedonistic paradox, or the difficulties of the hedonistic calculus, or the fallacy of the hedonistic psychology, we are led to the conclusion that moral aims, moral ideals, can never rest on the foundation of sense or feeling. The only ends of the rational human life must be fixed by the reason.

§ 2. SENTIMENTAL ALTRUISM.

[Adam Smith, 1723—1790: 'Theory of the Moral Sentiments.'— Shaftesbury, 1671—1713: 'Characteristics of Men, Manners, and Times.'—Francis Hutcheson, 1694—1747: 'Enquiry into the Ideas of Beauty and Virtue,' 'Treatise on the Passions,' 'A System of Moral Philosophy' (1755).—[Joseph Butler (1692--1752): 'Fifteen Sermons on Human Nature.']—Thomas Reid, 1710—1796: 'Essays on the Active Powers of the Mind.'—Dugald Stewart, 1753—1828: 'Philosophy of the Active and Moral Powers.'—Thomas Brown, 1778—1820: 'Lectures.']

A GREAT part of the ethical speculation of the earlier period of the eighteenth century may be described as a reaction on different lines to the selfish doctrines of Hobbes. The earliest opposition to that philosopher took the form of a vindication of morality on grounds of Reason, in the writings of Cudworth and Clarke, to whom I shall have to refer under the head of Rationalistic systems. The commoner form however of protest, which it is convenient in many ways to take first, was the assertion, accompanied with abundance of indignant rhetoric, that men were spontaneously and instinctively unselfish, because they possessed original feelings and impulses, enlisted in the service of generosity, sociability, and morality. I class such systems together as forming a school of sentimental altruism, meaning thereby, that in them morality is based on a feeling or sentiment of some kind (by whatever name called, Moral Sense, Taste,

Tact, Instinct, Conscience, or Sympathy), such feeling or sentiment being an original element of human nature, and also essentially disinterested and unselfish.

There are indeed many varieties in this school of sentimental moralists, but it would be tedious and useless to go through each variety in turn. In general terms its position is defined by its contrast to Hobbes and Egoism on the one hand, and to the Rationalist writers, Cudworth and Clarke, on the other. In antagonism to Hobbes, it asserts that the essence of morality is unselfishness: in antagonism to Cudworth and Clarke it maintains the familiar dictum that morality is a matter of the heart and not of the head, being based on feeling rather than intellectual discrimination. The general problem of the school is to discover and illustrate the generic difference between moral feelings and other feelings in men's nature. Their method is to trace the history of human feeling through its various phases, and when the discovery is made that moral feelings are incapable of resolution into other and simpler feelings, the conclusion naturally is that they must be assigned to a special faculty. As a matter of fact, then, the different sections of these ethical writers may be said to have been merely illustrating some one characteristic of moral judgment. Having asked themselves to what train of mental phenomena our moral conceptions bore the closest resemblance, they gave them and their faculty a name derived from this resemblance. Thus it was that Adam Smith, struck with the sympathetic character of moral feelings, described his moral faculty as Sympathy. Shaftesbury and Hutcheson, from motives of a parallel kind, called their faculty Moral Sense, or Moral Taste. Butler (whose importance, however, demands a separate treatment), engrossed with the authoritative nature of moral perceptions, gave to his ethical faculty the name of Conscience, which, though he sometimes called a power of judging, he yet as often treated as emotional. I propose to illustrate the system of sentimental altruism by taking these three characteristic answers to the moral problem. What is the source of our moral perceptions? One answer is sympathy; another is moral sensibility; a third is conscience. Adam Smith will fitly illustrate the first answer, Hutcheson the second, Butler the third.

1. Adam Smith's theory need not detain us long. He was not essentially a psychologist; still less was he a metaphysician. His aim was to give the world a popular treatise on the system of morality, which should be sustained by several practical considerations, and adorned with eloquent exhortations to rectitude. He was, as we have seen, peculiarly struck by the sympathetic character of moral sentiments. In the first chapter of his book he draws out, with some elaboration, the workings of sympathy in human nature. We are naturally attracted by humanity and repelled by cruelty: we feel for another person what that person does not feel for himself. We feel, for instance, for the insane what they clearly do not feel for themselves. Our sympathy extends even to the dead. It is this instinctive unreasoning sentiment which in Adam Smith's judgment constitutes the difference between right and wrong. To see in what sense it can have such power we must pass to a second point in Adam Smith's

system. Sympathy operates through a peculiar medium. It draws us out of ourselves and the circle of our narrow selfish interests, and puts us in the situation of the other party. Allied with the imagination, it transports us from our present feeling to what we should feel, as we say, "in another man's shoes." Consequently, the best definition of the ethical judgment is, that it is the "judgment of the impartial spectator or critic." It is in this fashion that sympathy can give rise to a discrimination between right and wrong, for our judgment as to what is right or wrong is gained by reference to what an impartial spectator would approve or disapprove. It is sympathy which makes us impartial, and an impartial view of the situation *is* the right and wrong of the situation.

It is quite clear that to lay stress on sympathy is to do a substantial service to the cause of morality. A man is in many senses a moral being according as he can enter into and realize the feelings, sentiments, and opinions of others. The very existence of society depends on the innateness of certain feelings which are mainly sympathetic feelings. Society means mutual co-operation and protection by acts of reciprocal self-sacrifice, and self-sacrifice is at all events facilitated by, if it is not largely due to, sympathy. When we have said as much as this, however, we have given Adam Smith all that is his due. For it is impossible not to see that if we base morality on sympathy, we are in large measure depriving it of its restrictive power and authority. Sympathy might attract men to one another, it could hardly keep them together in perpetuity. But the chief difficulty of Adam Smith's system is to understand the working of his objective standard,—the judgment of the impartial spectator. For according to the application of that standard, the virtue of an act does not reside in the act itself, but in the perception of the beholder. What, then, was the original motive of the act? Clearly, a sort of sympathetic pleasure in being in harmony with the general tone of society as expressed in the impartial critic's judgment. Then it must be the pleasantness of an act which is the quality causing a moral feeling, and the consequence follows, that the act called virtuous is never done for the sake of its virtue (for that is a quality relative to the contemplator, not to the doer), but to obtain a pleasure, the pleasure of sympathy, and to avert a pain, the pain of discord with the general tone of society. The idea of moral obligation too vanishes; for the phrase 'ought' or 'ought not,' in the case of action, does not express the relation of the act to the doer, but only its relation to beholders; it is the beholder who says, in looking at an action, it ought or ought not to be done. It is therefore not essential to a virtuous or to a vicious act, that it should be done either in conscious obedience to, or in conscious violation of, a law within the doer's self.[1]

As soon, then, as we attempt to analyse an ethical system which bases morality on sympathy, we find it crumbling away beneath our hands. It is difficult on the one hand to make any clear distinction between that sympathetic pleasure on which Adam Smith relies, and that selfish pleasure which Hobbes makes

[1] Cf. 'Popular Philosophy in its Relation to Life,' 'North British Review,' No. 95, pp. 148, 149.

the motive of morality. On the other hand, the
idea of moral obligation which we accept as the test
of the validity of a moral system, is left totally
unaccounted for. Adam Smith is hardly perhaps
concerned with the scientific basis of morality. He
describes the ideal condition of man as one in which
he is in health, out of debt, and with a clear conscience—an admirable popular compendium of ethics,
but hardly a scientific account of the matter.

2. I pass to a second variety of this disinterested
school, which asserts the existence of a moral sense
or faculty. The first intimation of a distinct moral
faculty, seems to have been given by Dr. Henry
More, in his book entitled *Enchiridion Ethicum*.
He spoke of a faculty which he called 'the boniform faculty,'[1] meaning by this uncouth term to
describe that innate principle in humanity, which
seized and apprehended the good and evil of actions,
and visited them with approbation, or the reverse.
In somewhat similar fashion, Shaftesbury invents a
convenient addition to our five senses, which he
terms reflex sense, or moral taste. There are certain
dispositions or actions, which after being contemplated
by this reflex sense, become the objects of love, or
the reverse. Virtue or merit only arises after the
working of reflective sense on actions, which thereupon invests them with moral approbation, or the
contrary. But what the origin of this moral sense
might be, Shaftesbury never inquired. The most
characteristic advocate, however, of the moral sense is

---

[1] 'Enchiridion Ethicum,' præcipua moralis philosophiæ rudimenta complectens, per Henricum Morum, Cantabrigiensem, p. 135. Londini. 1668.

Hutcheson, a contemporary of Butler. It is his system which both Reid and Stewart repeat with variations, and Brown, though he never uses the exact term, equally accepts the doctrine of the innate moral sense.

A human being, Hutcheson tells us, has his actions influenced by his desires. These desires may be of two kinds, calm or turbulent. Turbulent desires are those appetites and passions whose end is simply and solely their gratification, and which cease when gratification is gained. Calm desires, on the other hand, are invariable constant impulses towards some large end of human activity and ambition, where the emotion is probably deeper just because it is less violent, and the final accomplishment more difficult to attain. Either of these two varieties of desire may be either interested or disinterested, selfish or benevolent. Hunger, for instance, is a selfish, turbulent desire; pity is a turbulent, benevolent one. Or again there may be a calm desire of our highest happiness, the attitude of the experienced Epicurean; as well as a calm constant impulse towards the general happiness of others, the attitude of the systematic philanthropist. But the selfish and the benevolent systems are diametrically opposed, and the question becomes of paramount importance—which is to yield to the other? And here it is that Hutcheson introduces his characteristic doctrine of the moral sense, to solve the discord of which he has made human nature the arena. The conflict between benevolent and selfish desires is settled by the moral sense, which decides in favour of the former. What is this moral sense? The definition of Hutcheson is to be found in the fourth chapter of the First Book of 'the System of Moral Philosophy.'

Why, he asks, do we approve conduct which is moral and benevolent? It is not owing to sympathy, as Adam Smith thought; it is not due to considerations of personal pleasure, as was the opinion of Hobbes; nor is it explained by rationalist views of conformity to truth, fitness, or law. We approve moral conduct simply in virtue of a moral sense, a natural immediate feeling of the excellence of some actions and of the ignominy of others. This quality of excellence, though perceived by a sense, is not perceived by any of the five senses with which we are familiar; nor yet is the moral sense, which does perceive it, in any way dependent on the bodily organs, like the five senses. Yet a sense it is and remains, just like hearing and seeing, only superior, because moral action is superior to sounds or sights. It can be trained like the other senses, educated to discern finer excellences, and give closer or more exact decisions of approbation or the reverse. It can be trained, for instance, to approve the general happiness, rather than the chance relief of beggary; or, in other words, it can be trained to prefer the exercise of calm benevolent desires in preference to that of the turbulent benevolent ones. But for unselfishness as such it always decides; and if we ask why it should be held to be superior, why it should control all other mental powers, Hutcheson's answer is that this is a matter of immediate consciousness. We always do, as a matter of ordinary experience—such is his bold and somewhat hazardous assertion—prefer the moral good to the objects of our other powers of apprehension.

But we naturally object that there are all kinds of variation in the moral code of different nations. How are these to be explained on the hypothesis of a natural moral sense congenital in all men? On this Hutcheson has one or two remarks which are worth attention.

(*a.*) The sense is not uniform possibly, but still it exists, just as the human palate is not uniform, but still the faculty of taste exists in all men.

(*b.*) There are in different nations very different views as to the elements and constituents of happiness. These explain to a large extent the variety in the moral code, without impugning the existence of a moral sense.

(*c.*) Besides, men approach the considerations of action from such very different sides, and animated by such different forms of bias—sect, party, country, for example. One of the principal disturbing agents is, according to Hutcheson, men's view of the supernatural. Men have very different views as to what the Deity is supposed to command or forbid, and their view of the Divine will is often permitted to overpower their moral sense. In pursuance of such principles, apparent exceptions are not found to interfere in any vital manner with the doctrine of the moral sense.

The general position of the school of sentimental altruism, so far as is necessary for our present purpose, has now been indicated. The standpoint may, from a popular point of view, be summed up in the phrase which has been before referred to, that "morality is a matter of the heart, and not of the head." A popular phrase need only be answered in a popular fashion. It will be enough to assert in contravention of such a dictum that there is no such victim of delusions as the heart, which makes it a dangerous foundation on which to rest the structure of morality. A conviction that reposes on the basis of feeling is the most isolating, the most disintegrating principle in the world, for it is exactly in the sphere of feeling that men have differed and will differ for ever; whereas morality should be a common fund of principles for humanity at large. It is the heart which has justified most of the unnatural cruelties which have retarded the progress and civilization of mankind. In politics, it distorts the judgment of truth and tends to elevate party above purity; in morality it is the source of mystical rhapsodies or else of ascetic follies. It is the heart which mistakes mystery for mastery, emotional feverishness for a dominant conviction; and there are few who begin by professing to guide their lives by feeling, who do not end by being the most narrow-minded and dangerous of sentimentalists.

Apart, however, from popular prejudices, towards which this school, it must be remarked, has certain definite leanings, there are two philosophical antagonisms which explain the ethical position. These moralists are animated by two antipathies—an antipathy to selfishness, and an antipathy to the office of reason in morality. They dislike the selfish school because they mutilate human nature, their picture of humanity being wanting in that large section of disinterested feeling to which experience seems to testify. Let it be granted that in this criticism they took up a defensible ground: it is more to our present purpose to discover the motives of their antagonism to reason. The arguments appear to be twofold.

1. The reasoning process can tell us what a thing is, can discriminate one act or feeling from another, but cannot tell us which is *good*. To Reason, in its pure exercise, because it is a mere power of intellectual discrimination, all acts are ethically indifferent. To Reason, then, there can be no such thing as good and evil: for good and evil imply some relation to our sensitive nature, and it is conformity or want of conformity to the constitution of that sensitive nature which serves to define good and evil—a conformity which we cannot reason about, but *feel*.

2. Reason cannot give the motive to action: as Aristotle said, pure intelligence moves nothing, has no kinetic power. The power by which man is impelled to one course and deterred from another, can never reside in the cold and somewhat colourless functions of Reason, but in the fervid sphere of emotion and feeling.

The position is undoubtedly a strong one, but it is not unassailable. Let us take each argument in turn. "Reason cannot discern what is good." Granted, if it be meant that the particulars of moral action must be intuitively estimated. But the very divergencies of the school prove that they are not sure of this proposition. What is it that the moral sense suggests? The rightness of particular acts, or the rightness of general rules? Hutcheson says the first; Brown, Reid, and Stewart say the second. Hutcheson's position is almost indefensible, for it would seem to preclude the possibility of any moral progress, and would place all mankind on exactly the same moral platform, which is historically false. But now if it be the general rules rather than the particular acts on which the moral sense passes verdict, is it so certain that the reason cannot discern moral rules? For it is only reason which can discern an absolute end of action for man, which thereupon illuminates all the necessary means. Having discerned the end of activity by means of his reason, a man naturally turns to the instinctive impulses to discover how they must each and all contribute to the securing of this end. "Reason does not influence the will." But in morality the paramount motive is Obligation, which is incomprehensible without rational activity. Instinct, it is true, primarily influences the will in the early non-moral stages of human activity. As soon as Reason has delineated the absolute good for man, it can and does influence the will by the transcendent motive of obligation.

There are, however, other elements of weakness in the position of this school. There is, first, the want of a scientific unity of principle. So it comes that we have the introduction of this sixth sense of Moral Taste to be added to our other senses as a sort of *Deus ex machinâ*, to cut the problem without solving it. So, too, we have the deficiency of analytic power which could rest in these principles as ultimate, merely because consciousness seemed to affirm them to be so, without any attempt to discover whether they might not themselves be resolved into simpler ones. A more special difficulty follows. The moral faculty being on the level of an instinct, the good at which it aims must rest on the level of the several goods at which our other instincts aim. Then there must be as many goods as there are instinctive feelings. When, therefore, we have to ask, What is the highest good at which men can aim ? the question must be answered arbitrarily, or by falling back on the deceptive verdict of consciousness. Thus Adam Smith arbitrarily selected Sympathetic Pleasure; and Hutcheson contented himself with affirming that the object of the Moral Sense is highest of all the objects of the senses, because consciousness testifies to the fact. This leads us to another point; that in these moralists there is always a dangerous proximity to a circular form of argument. What is good? That which the Moral Sense approves. What sort of action does the Moral Sense approve? That which is good. Or, once again. The character of *authority* can never be explained on the assumption of a moral sense. For, if it be a sense, we ask, *why* should one sense be in authority over other senses? The old test returns, by which this school must be tried and found wanting. How do you explain Moral Obligation?

In point of fact, both selfish and unselfish schools of English Moral Philosophy base themselves on the Empiricism of Locke and Hume. They all proceed on the supposition that reason follows in the wake of sense, merely working up the intimations which sense gives. The selfish school, however, openly admits, while the instinctive school seeks to avoid, the consequences of its metaphysics.

§ 3. CONSCIENCE.

[Joseph Butler, 1692—1752: 'Fifteen Sermons, delivered in Rolls Chapel.'—'Dissertation on Virtue,' appended to the 'Analogy.']

IN the earlier portion of this chapter Butler has been included in that school of moralists who make the motive and disposition to morality, as well as its sanction, depend on a feeling or sentiment of some kind. But in truth it is more for the convenience of classification than for any exact similarity of doctrine that Butler has been classed with such men as Shaftesbury and Hutcheson. 'Conscience,'[1] the leading principle in man's nature, according to Butler is not quite on the same level as Hutcheson's 'Moral Sense,' or Adam Smith's 'Sympathy.' It is

[1] 'Conscience' is by Dr. Martineau, in his new and important book, *Types of Ethical Theory* (ii. 56), defined as "the inner sense of difference along the scale of impulses, without regard to the absolute force of any." There are two noticeable points in the definition. In the first place, Dr. Martineau's moral faculty is clearly on the level of Hutcheson's 'moral sense.' It is defined as a sense, and is naturally instinctive. In the second place, it appears to be not the author of illumination or growth. For illumination and growth affect both the qualitative and quantitative differences of the various impulses, giving force to one and taking it away from another. Conscience, therefore, it would seem, is no originating or constitutive faculty, neither is it, strictly speaking, a faculty of judgment; it is simply reflex and passive, an inner register, which belongs to all men alike, and to all men always.

partly intellectual and partly emotional. For the first reason Butler might, from one point of view, be placed in the Rationalistic ranks. It is because the emotional elements appear to be of paramount importance, and because Butler in Sermons XIII. and XIV. seems to insist on the love of God as his moral principle, which is nothing more nor less than an emotional aspiration, that Butler has been classed with the school of sentimental altruism. Nor yet is Butler purely an apostle of unselfishness, for he elevates self-love into the rank of a principle of human nature, side by side with benevolence. For the truth is, that Butler in his moral scheme had two pervading influences acting upon him. On the one hand, he, together with the better spirits of his time, was repelled by the undisguised selfishness of the system of Hobbes. On the other hand, preaching to the court worldings at the Rolls Chapel, he had to make the best of a bad case, and argue that 'a cool self-love' led to much the same ethical results as a disinterested benevolence.

Butler begins by stating the proper method of studying ethics. There are two ways, he says in his preface, in which the subject of morals may be treated. "One begins with inquiring into the abstract relation of things, the other from a matter-of-fact, viz. what the particular nature of man is, its several parts, their economy or constitution, from whence it proceeds to determine what course of life it is which is correspondent to this whole nature." In the former method the conclusion is expressed thus—"That vice is contrary to the nature and reason of things"; in the latter thus—"That it is a violation or breaking in upon our own nature." "The following discourses," he goes on to say, "proceed chiefly in this latter method."

We observe then, at the outset, that Butler abjures an *à priori* view of ethics in favour of one founded on the constitution and nature of the human mind. He will not begin from some transcendental standpoint, nor will his method be deductive, but the appeal shall be to experience, and the method shall proceed from a consideration of facts to the establishment of such general principles as those facts may warrant. The important point is to consider what we mean by the nature of a thing; what we understand by calling human nature a system, an economy, a constitution; for such words clearly imply the notion of a plurality of parts, of the proper relations of those parts to one another, and of their subordination to a ruling principle or principles. If we understand what the nature of man is, we shall understand what the morality of man is,—for it is that course of action which is strictly in accordance with his nature. "To follow nature" is, in point of fact, as the Stoics discovered (ὁμολογουμένως τῇ φύσει ζῆν), a very good principle of ethics. But we must be careful as to what we mean by nature. It is used in three senses, and in only the third of these does it become suitable as an ethical maxim.[1]

1. By nature is often meant no more than some principle in man, without regard either to the kind or degree of it. Thus the passion of anger, and the affection of parents to their children would be called equally natural. In this sense of the term a

[1] Sermon II.

man may by the same act both follow and contradict his nature. He may by the natural passion of anger contradict the natural affection to his parents.

2. Nature is frequently spoken of as consisting in those passions which are strongest and which have most influence on actions. In this sense a man is, as we say, born a tyrant; in this sense, too, St. Paul says, that "the Gentiles are by nature the children of wrath."

3. In neither of these two senses, however, does Butler propose to use the word 'Nature.' By the nature of man he means, the system or economy of man, that is to say, the proper relations which subsist between the various feelings and impulses of his character taken as a whole. If we can enumerate these various parts and show their proper subordination to a ruling principle, we can safely say that morality means to follow nature.

How, then, shall we describe the component elements of human nature? Butler's scheme consists of three divisions. On the lowest plane there are a number of 'propensions' and 'appetites' concerned with merely objective ends, instinctive, unreflective, and irrational. Some of these seem to tend to public good, as, for instance, the desire of esteem, which is called a public passion; others tend to private good, like the appetite of hunger, the end of which is the preservation of the individual. Above these, on a higher level, are two principles, the antagonism between which is more apparent than real—benevolence and self-love. What benevolence is to society, that self-love is to the individual, the former tending to public good, the latter to private. These are not instinctive but reflective: they arise after the particular appetites have secured their particular ends; they are calm reflective desires for public and private good. That they are not antagonistic in reality is proved according to Butler by the fact that the greatest satisfactions to ourselves depend on our having benevolence in a due degree, and that self-love is the one chief security for our behaviour towards society. We ascend, however, to a higher level than these. There is a third principle, a principle of reflection, by means of which men distinguish between, approve and disapprove, their own actions. "We are plainly constituted such sort of creatures as to reflect upon our own nature. The mind can take a view of what passes within itself. In this survey it approves of one thing, it disapproves of another, and towards a third it is indifferent. This principle in man, by which he approves or disapproves his heart, temper, and action, is Conscience." This is the supreme principle which nature has designed to be the authoritative or ruling element in man. It has all the symbols of authority, and if it had might as it has right, it would govern the world.[1]

Such is briefly the ethical system of Butler, and from Sermons I. to XIV. he is concerned in various ways with its elaboration. There emerge then as many as five different ways of stating the principles of ethics. The first answer to the ethical problem, How shall I be moral? is, "Follow nature" (Preface). A second answer is, "Be guided by benevolence" (Sermons III. and XI.). A third answer is, "Be guided by cool self-love," for, as Butler is at some

[1] Sermons I. and III.

pains to prove, reasonable self-love leads to results identical with benevolence (Sermons III. and XI.). A fourth and better answer is, "Obey conscience" (Sermons I. II. III.). Last of all, in Sermons XIII. and XIV. we are introduced to a fifth principle of ethics— "the love of God" becomes the whole of morality, because to love goodness is to be good. Or, to put Butler's principles in another way, they might be stated thus:—(1.) "Be true to your own nature," will furnish men with a good general description of a moral life. (2.) The really moral man is the truly benevolent man. (3.) The best principle of practical life is cool reasonable self-love. (4.) The supreme principle of the moral nature of man is conscience. (5.) Or, if you view the matter from the spiritual standpoint, the supreme principle of man's nature is the love of God.

At the very outset, the number of these principles is embarrassing. It is a characteristic of philosophy, which moves merely on the popular level, that it gives us different principles in accordance with the different phases of mental activity, just as if there were in truth no unity of self-consciousness, and as if the single human being, transferred to these different scenes of action, himself underwent change—was one person in practical life, and another in speculative study, and yet a third in religious feeling. From a deeper standpoint, it has to be acknowledged that he is throughout one being, dominated by a few ruling principles which constitute his personality, and that he interpenetrates with his own essential power every sphere and province of action, ethical, spiritual, political, or practical. It is an ungracious task to find points of criticism in so thoroughly earnest and profound a student as Bishop Butler, but the newer studies, and the more recent lights of modern times have given, as I think, an almost old-world air to Butler's position; because the problems of ethics, though fundamentally ever the same, vary from age to age in their setting forth and elucidation, and the arguments of a man who lived in the age when Hobbes was the prophet of radicalism in ethics, while the conservative teacher was, let us say, Shaftesbury, with his 'Characteristics,' do not prove convincing to a generation that has been nurtured on Teutonic metaphysics or English positive science.

Let us begin by noticing Butler's earliest exhibition of his moral principle as conveyed in his axiom, "Follow nature." 'Nature' and 'natural' are indeed ambiguous terms, and any one who has studied the struggles of the Stoics to explain the maxim which they were the first to profess, will hardly fail to acknowledge the fact. What do we mean by the word 'natural' in our ordinary parlance? If we analyze the common usage of the term, we shall find that three meanings, at least, are indicated. The natural, means either 'the normal,' 'the original,' or 'the ideal.' When we say that a man is naturally inclined to use his right hand rather than his left, we mean that such is the normal habit of humanity; or, when we say that man is naturally predatory, or naturally migratory, we mean that that was the original characteristic of humanity, which would have existed till now had it not been altered by circumstances and institutions. Or lastly, if we say that man is naturally free, we mean that such is the ideal state of mankind, to which we should endeavour, as far as possible, to approximate. Now when man erects an idol to nature, and asserts that the natural is the moral, he is in reality guilty of an equivoque or *double entendre*. Every aphorism must savour of the paradoxical, and the paradox in this instance, is the supposed simplification of the moral problem, by a reference to the less involved and less complicated cases of natural agency and life. But what our aphoristic moralist, if he is in earnest, means by nature, is not the simpler, less artificial modes of life, but the more evolved and ideal processes which culminate in Divine and fully perfected existence. And in this latter sense, the maxim "Follow nature," does not help a man one whit, for he still desires to know wherein the ideal life differs from the normal or original one, and how his life is from the two last to develop into the former. "To follow nature" is in reality the hollowest of phrases, for if Nature means the primitive, the physical, the biological, it is an inhuman doctrine; while, if Nature means God, it would be far simpler language to say at once that the essence of morality is the imitation of the Divine.

From the general and vague assertion of the moral principle, we pass to a more particular examination of the elements, which, in Butler's opinion, meet to form the nature of man. There is much that might be said of the absolute opposition which Butler draws between particular propensions and appetites, unreasoning and instinctive, and those higher principles, which are reflective, and can only arise after the appetites have reached their particular ends. But this point depends on that crude severance between feeling and thought, as two absolutely self-contained processes of man's nature, which Butler inherited from the psychology of Locke. Much, too, might be said of the absence in Butler's system of any theory of the Will; whereas, on the recognition of the importance of the Will in moral action, depends the satisfactoriness of any ethical system. "There is nothing so good in the world as a good will," said Kant, at the very outset of his consideration of Moral Philosophy.

But I pass to the three 'Principles' of human nature, on which Butler alternately laid such stress— Benevolence, Self-love, Conscience. For it is very difficult, if not impossible, to understand the relations which they are supposed to hold to each other. Speaking generally, benevolence and self-love are held to be co-ordinate principles of human nature, apparently antagonistic, but in many respects, coincident in their results. Benevolence is treated sometimes as a 'natural affection,' sometimes as 'a principle of virtue;' but in each case, seemingly, co-ordinate with self-love—for the balance between Self-love and Benevolence constitutes virtue. Now, if Benevolence is a merely natural affection, it must rest on the same basis as those natural passions and appetites, which have their own particular ends, like hunger or resentment, and which Butler calls 'propensions.' In that case it cannot be in any sense a supreme principle in man's nature, unless each of such natural 'propensions' be in turn supreme. Therefore, too, if Benevolence be not a principle, Butler cannot insist on the disinterested character of the main principle of action. If, on the other hand, Benevolence is a principle of virtue, it must be reflected on, it must be a sort of reflective desire for good in the world. As merely a simple propension it might be disinterested, but as reflected on, it must become interested: for directly a desire is lifted from the natural propension-stage by being reflected on, it becomes viewed in connection with self as a whole—it becomes related to that self, or in other words, it becomes 'interested.'

Thus, then, we see that Butler's co-ordination of Self-love and Benevolence leads to this awkward dilemma. If Benevolence be a reflective principle of action it must be interested: if it is disinterested it is only a natural propension, and therefore not a principle of virtue. And so while in Sermons XI. and XII. Butler is apparently aiming at giving benevolence the prerogative of being the spring of all virtue, his main idea in his first three sermons tends rather to the recognition of self-love—cool self-love—as a moral principle: for if the moral nature is reached when the man becomes conscious of himself, then all moral action being related to this self, to live for self must be in some sense morality. What is the way to extricate oneself from this dilemma? To remember that self is not merely individual but also universal. Each of us is a complex, a focus of relations towards those around us, and so to live for self is, it is true, to live for morality; but in that morality there are other constituents besides personal aims,—ends of action which are universal, not individual,—the gratification of others, the performance of duty, the doing of the will of God.

What shall we say of Conscience in Butler's scheme? Is it an immediate sense or feeling, a moral sense, as Shaftesbury and Hutcheson would regard it? Then, of course, it must yield in supremacy to that reflective principle of human action which we have found Butler calling 'Cool self-love.' But Butler's language does not make it merely feeling or sense. It is with him an authoritative faculty of judgment; it is a faculty of reflex approbation or disapprobation. Is it then Reason, Thought? If it were, then we could understand its supremacy, for it would in truth constitute the unity of the self-conscious man. But Butler does not identify it with this constitutive reason. Conscience is not supposed to constitute the man. It is not the whole nature, it is only part of our nature, alongside of another part which is called appetite or affection. Why, then, we ask, should it claim supremacy over this part? For clearly it is from the appetites and affections that it derives the objects of man's action with reference to which it judges. There being certain desires and affections in man's nature issuing in certain activities, Conscience says that some of them are right, some wrong. Why are they wrong? The only reason appears to be that the indulgence of some of them is harmful to the self or to others. In other words the rationale of that reflex approbation or disapprobation performed by Conscience is simply utility. It appears then that the real rightness of actions depends on utilitarian considerations. Conscience exists as a mere name: a symbol for that process of ratiocination which discovers what is, or is not, beneficial. It has the insignia of power without its reality, it has to decide on right or wrong, not simply by itself, but in reference to a standard given by self-love, in which case Conscience is the servant of an enlightened selfishness.[1]

If this is the pass to which Butler's co-ordination of Benevolence, Self-love, and Conscience as competing principles of our nature has brought us, what are we to say of the final principle, which Butler introduces in Sermons XIII. and XIV. as the 'Love of God?' It has sometimes been thought that Butler intended the 'Love of God' as the final principle which should harmonize and unite with itself all the other principles of human nature. He appears to escape with something like a sigh of relief from those philosophical distinctions which were all that the narrow psychology of his time could give him, to the language of religious fervour and emotional aspiration. But if we ask how the love of God is to be the harmony of the warring principles of our nature, it is very difficult to say except by an answer which frankly deserts logical procedure for mysticism. Of course it might be said that the love of God, though as much a part of ourselves as any appetite, transports us from the narrow self to the universal self, so that "our will is lost and resolved up into God's." Or it might be said, that it is only another form of Conscience; but Conscience is a faculty of *judgment*, the love of God must be a feeling. If the identification is in any way to be made, if the love of God is to be in any sense the harmonization of the principles of our nature, it must be made an intellectual love, having before it an intellectual idea

[1] Cf. 'North British Review,' No. xcv. 139—143.

or standard—the idea of completeness or perfection. As it stands it is a sort of beatific vision. It is Spinoza's 'Amor Intellectualis,' or Plato's 'Idea of the Good,' the contemplation of which not only makes all men in its own likeness, but is itself the highest goal of human love and philosophic endeavour.

§ 4. EARLY RATIONALISM.

[Richard Cumberland, 1632—1718: 'De Legibus Naturæ Disquisitio Philosophica' (1672).—Ralph Cudworth, 1617—1688: 'Treatise concerning Eternal and Immutable Morality' (1731).—Samuel Clarke, 1675—1729: 'A Discourse concerning the Being and Attributes of God, the Obligation of Natural Religion,' &c. (1705).—William Wollaston, 1659—1724: 'Religion of Nature Delineated.'—Richard Price, 1723—1791: 'A Review of the Principal Questions in Morals' (1758).—(Malebranche, 1638—1715.—Wolff, 1679—1754.)]

THE distinction between earlier Rationalism and later Rationalism is one which, proceeding to some extent in defiance of historical order, yet serves to mark the difference between a merely ethical system and one which carries its rationalistic deductions into ethics as a consequence of its general metaphysical position. As matter of history, Cumberland, Cudworth, and Clarke, belonging to the seventeenth century, proposed their Rationalist systems as an answer to Hobbes. Price, on the other hand, who belongs to the eighteenth century, has as his antagonists men like Shaftesbury and Hutcheson. Price is in fact the contemporary of Kant, and may well figure as Kant in English dress. But there is all the difference imaginable, in point of elaboration and systematic procedure, between the English moral philosopher and the German professor. Price, too, would have to be described as an Ethical Realist; Kant is a Critical Idealist. It is this essential difference in content and signification which makes it necessary to draw a boundary line between the earlier and the later forms of Rationalism. Kant's 'Critique of the Practical Reason' belongs, not indeed historically, but in logical order, to the Reconstructive stage of ethics; or rather, it inaugurates a period of Reconstruction in which man's inner self, which is proved to have such authoritative influence in morality, is the same self, without which the theory of knowledge would be meaningless and inexplicable. But the cruder forms of rationalism belong to an interpretative stage. They are isolated ethical disquisitions, in the first place; and in the second, they represent that period in which various phases of the moral life are being set forward in turn, between which the future choice has to be made. That choice must not be unduly accelerated. There must first be a negative period of criticism and suspense, and it is only the thinker who bases ethics on psychology first and metaphysics afterwards, who has any right authoritatively to determine what that choice shall be.

The general outlines of the Rationalist position can be clearly seen if a brief contrast is instituted between it and other positions. The question turns on the origin and nature of the Good. The Selfish school asserts that Good designates the greatest satisfaction of our nature according to a standard of pure hedonism; in which case the motive to morality, ordinarily termed moral obligation, is that aggregate or consequence of primitive desires called self-love. The school of Altruistic Sentimentalists who based themselves on the psychology of Locke rely on some form of instinct or natural sense. Good is the object of this natural affection, and the moral motive or obligation is merely this affection itself. In contrast with both of these systems the Rationalist school asserts Good to be an idea of Reason, born neither of sense nor of experience. The motive to morality is a purely rational motive, for as soon as we conceive that a thing is good we know at once that it ought to be done. But here some distinction is necessary. Is the idea of good a complex idea or a simple one? The question serves to divide the ranks of Early Rationalists into two divisions. Let the opinion be held that good is a complex idea, and then the second question arises—What are the simpler ideas into which the idea of good can be resolved? It may mean 'fitness,' as Clarke supposed, or it may mean 'truth,' as was the opinion of the eccentric yet keen-witted Wollaston, or it may mean 'order,' as the Cartesian Malebranche imagined, or it may mean 'perfection,' according to the interpretation of the German dogmatist Wolff. In each case good is held to be a rational idea, but the reason which gave it birth can also analyse and expound it. Other writers, however, believe that good is an idea which is simple and irresoluble. To the question—What is good? no answer but a tautological one can be returned. Good is good, just as time is time, and space is space. We can give no further explanation of the two latter terms, neither can we of the former. Of these the best examples are Cudworth and Price. I shall attempt to illustrate these two varieties of the Rationalist school by taking Clarke as an example of the former division, and Price of the latter.

Dr. Samuel Clarke was a pupil of Newton, and an antagonist of Hobbes. The first fact explains the logical procedure of his ethical system; the second accounts for the unselfish character which his system assumed. In interpreting the idea of Good in a quasi-geometrical fashion, he desired to show at the same time its entire independence of selfish considerations. For Good means nothing but 'appropriateness' or 'fitness of relations'; and these relations being necessary and universal are far beyond and above the petty boundaries and narrow aspirations of a man's self.

The system is developed in the following fashion. The frame-work of the world in all its divisions, natural, spiritual, ethical, consists of certain *relations* which obtain necessarily and universally between things. Man cannot conceive anything without at the same time conceiving its relations to other things. The whole of these relations constitute truth; the knowledge of them is omniscience such as belong to the Eternal Mind, to whom all the relations of all things to all must have eternally been present. Now in the application of one thing to another, these different relations of things involve a consequent fitness or unfitness, appropriateness or inappropriateness. It is with regard to such fitness that the will of God always chooses, and this should likewise determine the wills of all subordinate rational beings. When a man is then called upon to act in a moral sphere, he is bound, so to speak, " to will fitness, and not unfitness." A good action is a fit or an appropriate action, want of fitness constituting evil. Because the relations are eternal, there rests an obligation on men's will separate from the will of God, and antecedent to any prospect of advantage or reward. It follows that wickedness is not only wilful, but actually absurd : it is an attempt to alter the necessary relations which obtain between things ; it is as if a man should attempt to alter the relation between numbers, to prove that 2 and 2 equal 5, or to deny that the three interior angles of a triangle are equal to two right angles. It is obvious, then, that the moral faculty in the judgment of Clarke is Reason, which either discovers or appreciates the necessary relations between things. If we ask the proper definition of Good, the answer will be 'fitness,' and right action will be the fit and proper application of one thing to another in accordance with these necessary and universal relations.

Three other characteristic attempts to resolve the idea of Good into simpler ideas may be cited. A contemporary of Clarke, Wollaston, defined morality as acting according to truth ; an evil act, therefore, being equivalent to a falsehood. Thus, the reason why a man should not break his wife's head is that it is a practical lie, a denial in action that she is his wife. Similarly, the murder of Cicero by Popilius was a falsehood, for Cicero had been his benefactor, whereas Popilius acted as though this were untrue. Malebranche, one of the early followers of Descartes, thought that good was 'order,' virtue being defined (in accordance with the metaphysical notion that 'we see all things in God') as love proportioned to the order of excellence observable in the realization of the divine ideas. Wolff, who was a disciple of Leibnitz, preferred the word 'perfection.' 'Bonum suitatis' (personal good) and 'bonum communionis' (common good) alike mean perfection, whether that of the individual or of the race. Of such explanations the criticism is obvious. They are illustrations of the *obscurum per obscurius*. For in what sense 'order' or 'perfection' or 'fitness' or 'truth' are simpler ideas than the idea of Good, none of these writers are at much pains to explain.

Shall we then fall back on the other view of these rationalistic moralists and assert that Good is a simple irreducible idea ? In this division, we cannot find a better example than the ethics of Price. Cudworth, indeed, is senior in point of time, but Cudworth is a Platonist, pure and simple, while Price is nearer the reconstructive problem, being, as I have said, a version of Kant in English dress ; or, if not that, at all events, the best representative of what is sometimes called Realism in Morals. Perhaps it would be true to say, that this realistic instinct is for Price an element of logical weakness, for the absolute character of ethics can never be proof against logical assault when founded on such a basis. But, right or wrong, the instinct was a generous one, and infinitely more worthy of sympathy than that of the Sentimentalists and Utilitarians of his time.

The immediate antagonist of Price was Hutcheson, who based, as we have discovered in preceding pages, his system on the psychology of Locke. With Locke, he seems to have assumed, that all primitive ideas were derived from sensation, and that the moral idea, therefore, emanated from the same source. We can resume the position of Hutcheson in the two affirmations :—

1. Our ideas of Good and Evil are simple and original.

2. Being simple and original, they must necessarily be derived from a sense.

But the first position does not entail the second, except to one who knows no other than the psychology of sensationalism. It was quite open for Price to accept the first assertion and deny the second; to believe in the simple, original character of moral ideas, without affirming their necessary dependence on sensation. He was thus enabled to impugn the logical conclusion which might be drawn from the position of Hutcheson,—that good and evil are relative to our sensitive constitution. For the verdict of our senses is distinctly relative to ourselves; in our affirmation as to the sweetness or acidity, or coldness or heat, of things we invariably express a relation to our own organism. If then morality is based on a sense, moral affirmations too must be relative to our organism. If they are thus susceptible of subjective variation, the old doctrine returns which the Sophist Protagoras expounded in ancient Greece, that man with his equipment of five senses, individual man with his particularity, his eccentricity and personal vagaries, is the measure of the world both of Truth and of Right.

It is thus that Price deems it necessary to preface his ethical doctrine by a psychological inquiry into the origin of ideas. Ideas, using the term in its broadest signification, may be said to emanate from two sources—from the sentient organism, and from the intelligent principle. According to Price, the difference between the two sources is this:—The first sees things as they appear to us; the second sees things as they are. The perceptions of sense, being modes of consciousness, must be of a nature different from their causes; the attributes, 'bitter,' or 'warm,' or 'red,' represent the effect produced upon us by things, and give us no inkling of what things are in themselves. We cannot argue from sensation in us to quality in the external object. On the other hand, such ideas as 'substance' and 'cause,' 'time' and 'space,' represent, not the effects produced on us by things, but what is truly objective and real. Now, to which of these two classes do the ideas of Good and Evil belong? If sense alone be the source and origin of knowledge, the doctrine of æsthetic feelings, or moral taste, seems the only available one. But such ideas as time, space, and cause, are not derived from sense, or any manipulation of sense by experience or association; they have their birth in the intelligent principle which thus vindicates its claim to be a veritable source of ideas. If Right and Wrong are qualities of actions, of objects; if they have some character of reality truly belonging to them, and truly affirmable of them, then they must emanate from the Intelligent principle, not from Sensation. Morality has its source in the Reason.

Such, then, is Price's position as opposed to Hutcheson. But we must attempt to define with more precision his place in the Rationalist ranks, by discovering the interpretation he gives of moral ideas as ideas of reason. For ideas of reason may be of two kinds. They may be creations of reason in the sense of 'mental forms,' or 'pure forms of our own mind' —the ways in which our understanding envisages things, the aspects under which we are forced to consider them. Thus we might attain to laws which would hold good indeed for every intelligence as such, but would not therefore necessarily be the laws of the eternal world. In our idea of Cause, for instance, it may be a law of our own mind, that when we are conscious of a sequence of impressions, we call the antecedent the Cause, and the consequent the Effect; but it need not therefore follow, that there is a real objective relation in the natural world, or a real productive agency in what we call Cause. Is it in this sense that Price speaks of ideas of reason, or is it in a second sense of the term according to which ideas of reason may be conceptions of real objective facts, though those real facts may be invisible, and imperceptible to sense? Now if Good was a rational idea only in the sense of being a mental form, it would not be an absolute independent objective reality, immutable and eternal. It would only hold good in relation to intelligence as such, and we should have replaced a sensational relativity of ethics by a relativity more subtle and refined indeed, but not less deserving of the name. Price, with his passion for moral Realism, as disciple of Cudworth, who was a Platonist, and of Plato himself, who was the first of Realists, prefers to make ideas of Good and Evil conceptions of real facts, not discernible indeed by sense, but lying patent and open to reason. Good and Evil are absolute eternal realities in Nature; laws, truths, and essences, which Reason in man is able to apprehend.

Price's system can, in point of fact, be formulated in four propositions. (1.) Moral determinations must in every case be referred to the intellect. (2.) Morality is absolute, not relative. (3.) Morality is immutable.

(4.) Good and Evil are what they are, in entire independence of God's will. The last is a position which is common alike to Cudworth, Clarke, and Price. Price adds, that this is not derogatory to the Divine Nature, for just as there are attributes of the Deity, which are independent of his Will, as Immensity, Power, Wisdom; just as Truth is independent of the existence of Mind; so too is Good independent. Morality does not depend on the Will of the Deity, though of course, it may be resolved into the Divine Nature.

Two or three obvious remarks occur to the mind with regard to these somewhat crude Rationalistic theories of morals through the outlines of which we have now passed. They arise by a perfectly proper and natural reaction from the selfish system of Hobbes, and that psychology of which Locke was the founder, with its exclusive dependence on the functions of sense. In opposition to both these schemes the Rationalists lay stress on the paramount importance of the reasoning faculty, which not only in their opinion affords a true version of the reality of things, but also conclusively disproves the unnatural predominance of selfish feeling. If reason be the sovereign faculty in man, it can never acquiesce in the abandonment of so important a sphere of human activity as ethics to the dominion of æsthetic emotion or sentimental faculty. Nor yet will it lightly accept that view of the Self which makes it an isolated and grasping atom,—every man's hand against his neighbour—*homo homini lupus*—and the other details of that picture of selfish humanity drawn by Hobbes and Mandeville.

Despite, however, the fact that such systems are animated by a noble regard for the better elements of human nature, there are undoubtedly points in these rationalistic schemes which invite logical criticism. Let us glance in the first place at a criticism of Professor Sidgwick in the *Methods of Ethics*.[1] To him these philosophical intuitionists, as he calls them, afford the best examples of 'sham axioms' in morality. They expound principles which immediately command assent and which are self-evident, merely because they are tautological. Most of them can be reduced to a principle of this sort; that it is right to do that which, in a certain department of life, and under certain circumstances and conditions, is right to be done. The criticism is no doubt effective as against Wolff's explanation of Good as 'Perfection,' or of Malebranche's and Clarke's similar employment of the terms 'Order' and 'Fitness.' For such explanations as these appear to give an information, which on further inquiry turns out to be no information at all. But, on the other hand, it is to be remembered that if we start with a hypothesis that Good is an *à priori* idea of reason, it is absurd to ask for a definition other than tautological of that which is so clearly maintained to be an intuitive conception. As we found in the account of the system of Price, the conception Good is held to be on the same level as Time and Space, and if we cannot define Time and Space except in identical terms, no more can we expect to define Good. There

[1] Book III. c. 13.

is also the further consideration, that much of the importance of moral conduct lies in the definition, not of what Good is, but of the circumstances under which, and the time when, it must be done. And it is just in the determination of these points that these moralists would assert the activity of reason and the power of intellectual calculation, rather than of the vague instinctive impressions of sentiment and feeling.

Another point, however, is of more importance. There can be no doubt that moral action depends very largely on the effective vitality of certain emotional states, which should be duly explained, and to which their proper importance should be ascribed. "Pure intelligence," says Aristotle, "has no moving power;" and, however clearly we may know the right, it is a far cry from the right knowledge to the right action. It is just this interval between the right knowledge and the right action, which is the sphere of emotional and volitional impulse—the sphere which no moral system can afford to neglect under penalty of being wholly speculative and infertile. Now Rationalist writers are, as a rule, deficient in the psychology of emotions, and the result is that several important admissions somewhat inconsistent with the main position have often to be made. Listen, for instance, to the following admissions of Price:—"In contemplating the actions of moral agents, we have both a perception of the understanding and *a feeling of the heart.*"[1] The first element his system can explain; the second is left without due emphasis in his theory. "It is only," he continues, "superior

[1] 'A Review of the Principal Questions in Morals,' c. 2.

K

beings which can discover virtue by the understanding." It follows that the majority of men are moral without the use of the understanding, an admission which is fatal to the logic of his system.

Yet, here again, something must be said on the other side. Morality is an absolutely stationary and unprogressive thing, unless a free play of thought is allowed even round those central doctrines on which it rests. If it is in this way stationary and unprogressive, it can only be strictly appropriate to that stage of society in which these doctrines were first formulated in their rigid and unbending form. The doctrine of ethical realism is especially liable to such a doctrine of stationariness and want of progression, just as it too must accept the consequence of placing the Divine Being in a purely external and objective relation to the eternal verities of right and wrong, and thus depriving us of one of our best indirect proofs that the conception of the Deity is necessary for morals. But though this may be the weakness of a crude rationalism, a more matured system will rather lay stress on the progress of morality as one of the best evidences of its foundation in the reason. If humanity advances, and the conditions of life are changed by the introduction of new elements which largely react on the fundamental doctrines of ethics, then it is clear that only when rationally understood and rationally applied can moral rules have their true significance. That virtue is knowledge, and conversely that knowledge is virtue, is, as Professor Jowett remarks in his *Plato*, a truth which in the history of ethics is ever being lost and ever being rediscovered. Formulated long ago by Socrates and

Plato, it was lost by the school that succeeded the death of Aristotle; rediscovered by Cudworth and Clarke, it was lost again in the philosophies of Shaftesbury and Hutcheson. Once more, it was set in its true light by the moral genius of Kant, however much its true significance has been obscured in the contemporary schemes of Scientific Ethics. For the truth is, that morality belongs to that creative and paramount Reason which science seeks to explain as the latest development of materialistic atoms and energies, but which vindicates its reality and its supremacy by the imaginative power with which it is able to form a theory of its own origin. Man is above nature, because it is due to man that we have a theory of nature.

BOOK II
CRITICISM.

§ 1. EARLY UTILITARIANISM.

[John Locke, 1632—1704: 'Essay on the Understanding,' Book I. c. 3, 4; Book II. c. 21, 28.—David Hume, 1711—1776: 'Enquiry concerning the Principles of Morals.'—David Hartley, 1705—1757: 'Observations on Man' (1749).—William Paley, 1743—1805: 'Moral and Political Philosophy.'—Jeremy Bentham, 1747—1832: 'Introduction to the Principles of Morals and Legislation' (1789).—'Deontology' (a posthumous work) arranged from his MSS., by Sir. J. Bowring, 1834.]

THE age of criticism is one of lassitude in creative effort: an age of provisional hypotheses and intellectual suspense. Speculation has had its rebuffs and discouragements: in its emotional youth it framed its day-dreams and built its airy castles; but now it is content to limit itself within the region of the familiar and of the trite; it prefers to analyze and to wait. The ancient founts of inspiration are run dry, which used to overflow the country with wayward currents; but there is an admirable artificial canal, and a well is sunk according to the most approved scientific methods. Indeed, the natural springs had their disadvantages: the water has been mingled with mud and has often had a brackish taste. There is much value in filtering-beds.

In the history of modern ethics Utilitarianism illustrates such an age of criticism. In the first place, there is the judicial attitude with regard to the source of ethical ideas. When a man sees the diversity of the theories which seek to explain this source, he begins to ask himself whether there is a moral faculty at all? Is the question relating to the origin of moral conceptions in reality different from that which asks for the moral criterion? In what sense can the morality of an act depend on the motive? Can we ever weigh in critical balances the relative value of motives? Moral sense, moral instinct, the practical reason,—are not these all mere abstractions, mere names? Not such shall be the ethics of scientific method. We will not be concerned with any supposed innate faculty which must be taken on trust, and about which, because it is innate, no further inquiries must be raised: nor shall we make our moral theories flow from the requirements of any presupposed doctrine, whether theological or political. But we are to approach the data of moral action in the same spirit in which science approaches the phenomena of the natural world : we are to tabulate, to classify, and to arrange such facts and data according to the methods of science, and to make our generalizations strictly depend on the due use of observation and experience. And if from this point of view the position of Utilitarianism is essentially negative and critical, it is equally so in its acceptance of provisional explanations. For no one, except in a lukewarm age, could be content with an analysis of duty which resolves it into utility. It is like the attempted reconstruction of water from hydrogen and oxygen without the electric spark. The later forms even of the scientific ethics are inclined to replace utility by social health and welfare, and no one has more severely criticised the utilitarian principle of Bentham and Mill than Mr. Herbert Spencer.

Utilitarianism has its earlier and its later forms, as it appears in the eighteenth and in the nineteenth century. In its earlier form it is illustrated by the writings of Hume, Hartley, Paley, and Bentham. The more recent writers on Utilitarianism in the nineteenth century are Austin, James Mill, John Stuart Mill, and a few others, mostly contemporaries. It will be the easiest method to exhibit the characteristics of early utilitarianism if we lay stress on the points which contrast it with the egoistic hedonism of Hobbes. For in one sense the utilitarian scheme was developed out of the lower form of selfishness. In another sense it avoids the imputation of undisguised hedonism by certain important extensions of the principle of Hobbes. The steps which serve to convert egoistic into universalistic hedonism (to adopt the phraseology of Professor Sidgwick) may be thus exhibited.

There is first a change of terms. The end of human action is declared to be not Pleasure, but Happiness and Utility—terms of vaguer and therefore more honourable import. It was further explained that by this Happiness was intended, not personal happiness, but the happiness of others as in some way included in, or deduced from, our own. Again, allowance was made, at all events by some writers, for the existence of originally sympathetic, and therefore unselfish, feelings. But the most important addition consisted in the adoption of the theory of the Association of Ideas to explain the moral feelings which could not be immediately resolved into calculations of utility.

The first three points were brought out in various ways by the speculations of Locke and of Hume. Locke, though not primarily an ethical writer, adopts a general position on moral questions, which is wholly allied with Utilitarianism. He does not believe in the existence of innate practical principles;[1] he resolves the free action of the will into the pressure of the greatest present uneasiness,[2] and decides that good and evil are nothing but pleasure and pain, together with the causes of pleasure and pain.[3] Hume, in the first section of his 'Enquiry,' does not exhibit the characteristics of utilitarian thought, for he hesitates between Reason and Sentiment as sources of moral determinations. But more explicit declarations are contained in the second section. When we praise a humane and benevolent man, the point on which we most insist is the happiness to society, arising from his actions. It follows that utility forms a considerable part of virtue, and is one source of the approbation which it receives. In the third section, Hume proves that the sole foundation of the merit of justice is its public utility. And in the fourth section he finds the same basis for the virtue of chastity. Then follow admissions that humanity and benevolence are ineradicable elementary feelings of human nature; while in the second Appendix Hume

[1] Essay, Book I. c. 3.   [2] Book II. c. 21.
[3] Book II. c. 28.

rejects with scorn the notion of Hobbes that benevolence is merely disguised self-love. But the great advance in the genesis of the utilitarian theory was made by Hartley, whom J. S. Mill calls " the father of Associationism." As the adoption of the theory of Associationism is an important point, it is necessary to treat it somewhat in detail. The law of the Association of Ideas is the name for the theory that sensations, impressions, and ideas, which enter the mind together, are united so indissolubly in the mind by a species of mental chemistry, that not only does one idea call up the others, but also the resulting idea appears simple and single instead of a complex of various elements. Ordinary instances of this undoubted mental law occur every day of our lives. A picture is seen in a particular room, and whenever seen is found to suggest invariably to the mind a certain train of thought. What is the explanation of this phenomenon? Merely that a particular train of thought was in the mind at the time when the picture was first seen, and the association once made is so strong that the sight of the picture will always recall the train of ideas. To use this law of Association in the service of Utilitarianism was a stroke of genius on the part of Hartley, for which he has received unstinted praise. The only motive of action was, in his opinion, primarily a selfish one. The problem then is, how from the basis of originally selfish motives to explain the obviously unselfish character of so many moral acts. The obstacle is surmounted by the device of the Association of Ideas according to the following fashion. The sight of suffering in others awakens in the mind of the child a painful recollection of his own sufferings, which parents, by appealing to the infant imagination, still further strengthen. The suffering of others becomes associated with the idea of personal suffering, and so is engendered the feeling of compassion. Benevolence and justice are associated in our minds with the esteem of our fellow-men, with the reciprocity of favours, and with the hope of future reward. They are loved at first solely for these results; owing to trains of association they are finally loved for themselves. Virtue becomes peculiarly associated with the idea of pleasurable feelings; it is soon loved independently of, and more than, these. Let us take a very good instance of the power of Association, an instance of which utilitarian writers are especially fond; the passion of Avarice. Money in itself possesses nothing that is admirable or pleasurable. It is, however, the means to procure many objects of our desire, and hence it becomes associated in our minds with the idea of Pleasure. It is therefore loved for itself: its acquisition is now desired as an end, not as a means, and the miser will forego all pleasure to retain his gold. So is it, according to the utilitarian contention, with virtue itself. Virtue is a means of procuring many blessings, and becoming thus associated with the idea of pleasurable and useful results, it comes finally to be recognized as an end in itself, and indeed the one and only end of life. It is the same with what we call Conscience. It is not, indeed, as Hobbes rashly imagined, immediately constituted by self-love, but self-love is the remote cause of Conscience. The moral sense is generated out of simple feelings of self-interest by long trains of associations. Such is the ingenious psychological analysis, which serves to explain how mankind, starting with purely selfish aims, can end by developing into self-sacrificing heroes, or self-annihilating martyrs.

Utilitarianism, though the term is of later origin, is now definitely formulated as a moral system. It then appears in a somewhat incongruous and repellent form in Paley, the utilitarian theologian, and in a strictly logical form in Bentham, the utilitarian jurist. Paley's well known chapter on 'the Moral Sense' in the first book of his *Moral and Political Philosophy* strikes the key-note of his position. It is a long argument to disprove the existence of a moral instinct, which, in the opinion of the author, can not be distinguished from prejudices and habits. For, in the first place, there is no such thing as an uniformity of moral code amongst nations; whatever approbation or disapprobation there may be, being due to particular fashions and institutions which have grown out of the local circumstances in each case. In the second place, it is matter of common experience that moral rules vary according to circumstances, *e.g.* the obligation of a promise, or veracity. In the third place, no instinct is possible without an idea of the actions to be approved or disapproved; and we are not born with any ideas of the sort. All three considerations are fatal to the theory of a moral instinct. What, then, is Virtue? It is here that Paley attempts in somewhat odd fashion to unite his utilitarianism with his theology. For there is no single criterion of virtue, but a double criterion. "Virtue is the doing good to mankind," that is one side, but the other side must also be included—"in obedience to the will of God, and for the sake of everlasting happiness." This double or treble criterion is naturally and conveniently elastic. For the explanation of morality becomes not simply Utility, but includes a Divine standard and a Divine sanction. It follows, then, that the obligation that is laid upon us to be virtuous (*i. e.* to secure human happiness and utility) is the knowledge that we are in the hands of a Divine Governor of the universe, who will reward us if we conform to his will and punish us if we rebel. "A violent motive" is thus secured for virtuous action in the rewards and punishments of a future life. So that the criterion of virtue is utility + the will of God: the moral sanction (the penalty in case of disobedience) is God's power to punish: and the condition, the *sine quâ non* of morality, is the belief in the revelation of God's will, and in God's ability and will to reward and punish in a future life. Unless we believe in a revelation, there is no sanction of morality.

Bentham, on the other hand, is totally devoid of the theological interest which is so conspicuous in Paley. Paley makes, as we have found, an appeal to Scripture, to revelation, and to God's will, simultaneously with an appeal to utilitarian considerations. Bentham appeals to utility alone. Bentham considers, indeed, that Religion may furnish a sanction to morality, but it may be perverted to a wrong use. If Asceticism, for instance, be preached as the ideal life in the name of Religion, the State may intervene. It may consider acts which are thus contrary to its interests, despite their supposed religious sanction, as offences. So clearly does this logical utilitarian keep to the main civic and social interest to the

exclusion of theology. For the rest, it is due to
Bentham perhaps more than any writer that utilitarianism as a definite moral scheme, has such clear
and sharp edges. Virtue, he tells us, when applied
to actions, simply means the tendency to promote
happiness and to prevent misery.[1] For " Nature
has placed mankind under the governance of two
sovereign masters, pain and pleasure. It is for them
alone to point out what we ought to do, as well as
to determine what we shall do. On the one hand,
the standard of right and wrong; on the other, the
chain of causes and effects are fastened to their
throne.—In words a man may pretend to abjure
their empire, but in reality he will remain subject
to it all the while. The principle of utility recognizes this subjection, and assumes it for the foundation of that system, the object of which is to rear the
fabric of felicity by the hand of reason and of law.
Systems which attempt to question it deal in sounds
instead of sense, in caprice instead of reason, in
darkness instead of light." There is no uncertain
or ambiguous tone in Bentham's ethics: there is
none of that process of softening down the harder
features, which we shall afterwards find in J. Stuart
Mill's contributions to the system. No proof must
be required of the principle of utility: it is an
axiom, a moral postulate. Morality means nothing
more nor less than the steady direction towards the
pleasurable, the steady avoidance of the painful.
Moreover, the psychological analysis on which Bentham founds his system is more elaborate perhaps

[1] 'Principles of Morals and Legislation,' chap. i. 'The Principle
of Utility.'

than that of any other moralist on the same side. Pleasures are classified, pains are classified.[1] The connection between ethics and politics is drawn out with consummate skill.[2] The so-called disinterested feelings are shown to be complex results of the Association of Ideas, or else deprived of any element of self-sacrifice; and the Moral Faculty, by an analysis into Prudence, love of Reputation, with some slight influence attributed to Benevolence and Religious feeling, becomes a broken reed, piercing the hands of the disinterested moralist.

Bentham's table of 'Sanctions' may be added as a characteristic portion of his system.[3] Moral sanctions are in Bentham's view, four "sources of pain and pleasure whereby men are stimulated to act right," viz. the physical, the political, the moral, and the religious. The physical sanction is, of course, that supplied by nature herself—pain and disease, or joy and health. The religious sanction is due to the Divine Being either in the present or in a future life. The political sanction is all that proceeds from the ruling power of the state—roughly speaking, the penalties of law. The moral sanction (or popular sanction, for the terms are not distinguished) is the force of public opinion. Every moralist, it must be supposed, has the right to give his own definition of the terms he uses; but we may be pardoned, if we still desire to know in which category to place the moral sanctions. For Bentham's four classes are all external, they come upon the individual from the outside with undoubted yet arbitrary force; and his own instinctive acceptance of the sanction is left

[1] *E. g.* chap. v.   [2] Chap. xvii.   [3] Chap. iii.

unexplained. Yet, if there be a moral sanction properly so-called, it must be subjective and internal, something which springs from the man's inner personality, expressed in feeling, of which words like 'sense of responsibility' and 'remorse' are significant. Moral sanction explained as the popular sanction or public opinion, still leaves the contented Epicurean unvisited in the privacy of his own home. "Populus me sibilat : at mihi plaudo ipse domi."[1]

[1] Hor. Sat. I., i. 66.

§ 2. LATER UTILITARIANISM.

[James Mill, 1783—1836: 'Analysis of the Human Mind,' chaps. xvii.—xxiii.—John Austin, 1790—1859: 'Province of Jurisprudence Determined.'—John Stuart Mill, 1806—1873: 'Utilitarianism.'

THOUGH there is nothing especially valuable in the contributions of the immediate predecessors of J. S. Mill to the science of ethics, there are yet one or two points in which they either consolidated the defences or strengthened some of the outlying buttresses of Utilitarianism. The characteristic of James Mill was a certain almost brutal frankness of logical consistency, not without its value in exhibiting to the eyes of opponents the bare bones of the utilitarian scheme, but which had to be obliterated in great measure by the softer counsels which prevailed with his son. Two points especially may be noticed in James Mill's treatment of ethics. The first is the resolute way in which the various sanctions of morality are reduced to a single sanction, popular opinion, or the fear of blame and praise from contemporaries. The second is the equally trenchant and cold-blooded analysis by means of which Conscience, though admitted to be a fact, is resolved into a keen apprehension of personal pleasures and pains. For James Mill had that excess of logical faculty which, however admirable in a being who should be wholly intellectual, is yet found to be either too sharp or too obtuse to gauge the complicated elements which constitute the moral and social life. Exaggerated logical analysis always tends to reduce to a single principle, with a wholly unnecessary violence, that complex phantasmagoria of effects which does not admit of such drastic methods. The same spirit which dictated the resolution of the many laws of mental association into the one principle of contiguity is found to preside over the so-called simplification of the moral sanction which exchanges the four classes of Bentham for the single sanction of the popular voice.[1]

Austin, in the first five lectures of his work, adds one or two considerations which are worthy of notice. "There is a misconception prevailing," he tells us, "about Utilitarianism, which, because it proposes as its end the well-being of mankind, reviles it as essentially a selfish theory. The mistake here is the supposition that utility is a theory of the motives of actions. It is nothing of the sort; it is a theory of the consequences and results of actions, or at all events their tendencies." Nothing could be clearer; but it is still open to us to ask whether an ethical system ought not especially to concern itself with motives. In J. S. Mill's *Utilitarianism* a fine distinction is drawn between motive and intention. The intention has to do with the morality of an act but not with the motive, though the latter has a good deal to do with the disposition of the doer.[2] A colourless word like 'intention' appears to be designedly employed to

[1] 'Analysis of the Phenomena of the Human Mind,' ch. xxiii. Cf. Preface, note 35, and J. S. Mill's 'Utilitarianism,' c. iii.
[2] Mill's 'Utilitarianism,' p. 26.

mediate between the opposite theories of *motives* and *results* of actions. But Austin does more than clear up the real nature of the ethical system which he expounds. He is ready with answers also to objectors. If we venture, for instance, to object to his theory that according to it we are forced to go through a difficult if not impossible calculation of the consequences of an act, Austin replies that we forget that there are such things as rules, empirical it is true, yet wholly satisfactory so far as they go, because inferred from the general tendencies of actions. If we still ask how it is possible to know *all* the consequences of actions, we are told that our ignorance is largely due to the slow progress of ethics as a science. It is only gradually being formed as an inductive science by a series of generalizations and a long course of experience: while for this true but tardy science of ethics many other modes of treatment, mostly deductive and *à priori*, have been mistakenly adopted.

We can now pass at once to the text-book of Utilitarianism in the nineteenth century, which bears the name of John Stuart Mill. Perhaps the first characteristic which strikes us is the refined and softened form in which the ethical doctrine appears as compared with the logical rigour of both Bentham and James Mill. We find in it a full admission of the existence of disinterested sentiments, though we are left doubtful whether they are to be traced ultimately to a self-regarding source or are assumed to be instinctive and innate. There is the recognition that pleasures differ in kind and not only in degree, a recognition which the stricter and perhaps more logical form of hedonism can never bring itself to make.

And there is, lastly, the ample use of that plausible and quasi-philosophic device—the association of ideas—which explains with so little shock to common sense the origin and growth of conscience. For the utilitarianism of the younger Mill is that of a second generation; and while inventors of a strikingly novel theory find a certain exhilaration in the very novelty of the radical doctrines which they espouse, their successors, who have to bear the brunt of much continuous criticism, are generally forced to admit into their system many elements derived from their adversaries.

Mill's 'Utilitarianism' contains four chief points: (1) the defence of Utilitarianism against objections; (2) the sanctions of Utilitarianism; (3) the proof of which the principle of utility is capable; (4) an exemplification of the analysis of moral notions in the treatment of Justice according to an utilitarian standard. Some of these points are not important for our immediate purpose. The analysis of justice,[1] for instance, may be passed over in a very few words. Mill's contention is that the idea of justice is grounded in law (*jus*), and that all that is moral in the sentiment of justice is due to notions of expediency and utility. Even that energy of retaliation which is inspired by injustice, is explained by the consideration that injustice threatens the most important and most impressive kind of utility, viz. personal security. The analysis, however, is not very satisfactory or very adequate. According to Mill, for instance, it may be just to disobey the law (p. 65), and yet justice has its origin in conceptions of law (p. 70). The fact is that justice, in the customary and conservative sense,

[1] 'Utilitarianism,' c. 5.

requires to be supplemented by an ideal conception or conceptions: the due performance of contractual relations must continuously be rectified by a tacit acknowledgment either of the right of every man to freedom, or the principal of the due requital of desert.[1]

Nor need much time be spent over Mill's defence of Utilitarianism[2] which covers ground tolerably familiar in modern times. The standard of utility being assumed to be not the agent's own personal happiness, but the greatest happiness of the greatest number, Mill proceeds to defend his principle against a primary objection that it is pitched in too low a key for humanity. It is quite true that men can do, and have done, without happiness. But according to the general position of this ethical school, self-sacrifice is not good in itself, but solely as a means to diffuse happiness over the world, an aim than which there can be none higher or more moral. If an opposite objection be made that the principle is too high for humanity because we cannot always hold before ourselves the general interest of society, the answer is that the pursuit of such an ideal is becoming more and more the test of modern progress.[3] Thus the general conclusion is reached, that in the conflicting circumstances of life, not only the best, but the only guide, is Utility.[4]

The other two points I have mentioned, are of greater significance. What are the sanctions of the principles of Utility? Obvious external sanctions there are of course in abundance: there are the pains

---

[1] Sidgwick's 'Method of Ethics,' Bk. iii. c. 5.
[2] 'Utilitarianism,' Chaps. i. and ii.
[3] *Ibid.* pp. 19, 24. [4] *Ibid.* p. 31.

and pleasures we are likely to experience from the verdict of Public Opinion, which is naturally anxious that its utilities should be secured : from Nature which visits with certain punishment any infringement of the law of that great human utility—health : and from God, who cannot be conceived to have any other end in view than the happiness of the world which he has created.[1] But when all these external sanctions have been allowed their full weight, Mill has to admit that the ultimate sanction of morality must be an internal one, must consist, that is to say, of a *feeling* of some sort. This feeling is clearly the very essence of what we mean by Conscience. What is Conscience ? It is not—so Mill tells us—an intuitive, an innate principle, but a growth, a product : it has grown to be what it is, educed and developed out of all kinds of heterogeneous sentiments—sympathy, love, fear, the recollections of childhood, self-esteem. Feelings of Remorse are explained as the result of the great effort it requires to break through all this incrustation of feeling which has encircled the primary elements of Conscience.[2] But if we ask what these primary elements are, if we trace Conscience back to its barest and most primitive form, we shall find the residual element in all this emotional accretion to be nothing but the consideration of utility, of expediency, of the line of conduct which is most likely to secure pleasure and obviate pain. The real support of the Utilitarian Philosophy, Mill adds, is found to consist in the Social feelings of mankind :[3] for men cannot conceive themselves otherwise

[1] 'Utilitarianism,' chap. iii.   [2] *Ibid.* p. 41 *et foll.*
[3] *Ibid.* pp. 46 and 50.

than as social beings, which explains why the welfare of Society is the great end and aim of all action. But whether Sympathy, on which the social sentiments are based, is, or is not, an instinctive feeling, and whether, if it is instinctive, it does not form a better core and heart to Conscience than the perception of utility, Mill is never at much pains to explain.

But why is happiness desirable? Why is it the great end of life? Why is everything else only desirable as a means to this end? These are the questions which remain, and to them Mill addresses himself in the fourth chapter of *Utilitarianism*. The answer is not very satisfactory: indeed, if one may venture to accuse a great writer on Logic of illogicality, there appears a most awkward hiatus between premisses and conclusion. For, says Mill, there is in reality no proof that happiness is desirable except that each man individually desires it.[1] Because each man, then, desires his own happiness, the general happiness is to be made an end of life, which is as much as to say that because each man is persistently selfish, therefore the general interests of society will be secured. The experience of children at a meal, or of a litter of puppies at the trough, points to a different conclusion. The rest of the chapter is concerned with showing that although men have other ends in life which they desire, such as virtue and power, these are to be explained as results of that inversion of means and ends, which is illustrated by the vagaries of the Association of Ideas. The possession of health,[2] for instance, is clearly not an end of human activity, but only a means. It is only useful

[1] 'Utilitarianism,' p. 53.   [2] *Ibid.* p. 54.

because it enables men to produce results which are beneficial in many ways to the human race. But because the idea of health is associated with these useful results, it becomes for the confirmed valetudinarian the sole end of life, an end which judicious gluttony and skilful doctors are to enable him to achieve. The usual illustration from the phenomena of Avarice then follows:[1] and the general conclusion is reached, that "to desire anything except in proportion as the idea of it is pleasant, is a physical and metaphysical impossibility."[2]

On this utilitarian adaptation of the law of the Association of Ideas, so far as it is applied to the explanation of virtue, I will make but a single remark. If the pursuit of virtue as an end of life really rests on a confusion between means and ends, if virtue be in reality only the means to happiness, and men are wrong-headed enough to invert this relation, then the increase of intelligence should enable us to clear ourselves from this logical error. As knowledge widens, and the use of logic becomes a normal habit rather than a painful discipline, we ought to be able to estimate virtue at its proper worth, and subordinate it to that happiness which is the only rational end of human activity. The courses of human history and the development of the civilization of a people prove an opposite conclusion. Growth, progress, improvement of all kinds increase in a nation, in proportion as men learn to estimate virtue above happiness, and find in self-sacrificing industry the only secret of national welfare.

[1] 'Utilitarianism,' p. 55.   [2] *Ibid.* p. 58.

§ 3. CONSIDERATIONS ON UTILITARIANISM.

THE system which professes as its motto 'the greatest happiness of the greatest number' has an undeniable attraction for many minds. Partly owing to the simplicity of the test which it proposes, partly to the inductive character of its method and its sympathy with modern scientific procedure, it has been more extensively fashionable in the nineteenth century than any other system. At the present day its position is attacked on two sides, for not only has it been exposed to the steady antagonism of Rationalistic and so-called *à priori* systems of ethics, but it has found a successor in the same lines of experimental inquiry, which, in the hands of Mr. Herbert Spencer and Mr. Leslie Stephen, threatens to lay somewhat violent hands on its acknowledged progenitor.

Let us first take some of the points in which Utilitarianism seems to give a satisfactory explanation of the problems which it discusses. When we approach the consideration of human action from the political and social side, the utilitarian view is perhaps the only practicable one. The happiness of the greatest number appears to be the only possible aim for the political and social philosopher. Indeed it has often been urged—sometimes as praise, sometimes as blame—that the utilitarian principle has a conspicuously political character, and Helvetius tells us "la science de la morale n'est autre chose que la science de la législation." For this there is the sufficient reason that Utilitarianism studies the consequences of action to the exclusion of everything else ; action as it were viewed from the outside, as it affects other people, a truly social point of view. But the question remains whether, if ethics is to be distinguished from Sociology or Political Science, it should not be concerned with the interior aspect of action—action, that is to say, viewed in connection with the principle and motive which animates it. To the interior principles and motives of action, however, no consistent Utilitarian ever professes to address himself.

There is, of course, no doubt in any reasonable mind, that the moral precepts which aim at Happiness, and those which aim at Right, cover much the same ground, and lead to much the same results. But though Happiness and Right may be co-extensive, it has yet to be proved that they are identical, and that the ordinary distinction which men draw between expediency and morality rests on unscientific grounds. We may further grant that questions of casuistry, questions of conflict of duties, are best settled by an appeal to Utility ; there is no better test than experience of the consequence of actions to decide the issue when duties collide. If a patriot, for instance, has to decide between his duty to the government under which he lives, and his duty to his own views and aspirations for his country, no better solvent for his doubts can be found than considerations of Utility and the happiness of the greatest number. But it must also be admitted, that there are virtues, the sacred and authoritative character of which is destroyed by the explanations of utilitarianism. The sentiment of Justice, for instance, is very clumsily and inadequately explained; the virtues of Honesty, Chastity, and Veracity, are more powerful before the analysis into Utility comes than after it. Neither Mr. Mill, nor Mr. Sidgwick, nor Mr. Stephen, can persuade men that the whole merit of self-sacrifice is its usefulness, and that where such a result is wanting it is so little of a virtue as to be almost a crime. A man will not consent to be killed rather than tell a lie, because the practice of telling truth is on the whole useful to humanity; nor yet will a forlorn hope march to certain death, because military discipline is good for the world.[1]

But it is time to take some specific points in the indictment to be drawn up against Utilitarianism. I shall touch on the more philosophical objections first before proceeding to those which have been urged on practical popular grounds.

The first of these turns on the unfortunate ambiguity of the word Happiness. What constitutes Happiness? Is it meant to indicate something different from and higher than Pleasure? No, the answer sometimes is, not if Pleasure be interpreted in the largest sense—pleasure of mind, sensibility and intellect, as well as pleasure of body. But then the further question arises, Are we to admit a difference in pleasures? Can pleasure so far as it is an emotional satisfaction differ except in degree? Do pleasures differ in kind as well? The most refined and softened form of Utilitarianism asserts that

[1] Cf. Jowett's 'Plato;' Introd. to Philebus.

pleasures do differ in kind; other forms more strictly scientific, though perhaps less cultured, refuse to admit the distinction. These difficulties have arisen in great part from the modern development of the system. In Bentham there was more thorough consistency than is to be found in Mill, for he perhaps would not have refused to call happiness merely pleasure, and would have denied that pleasures differ except in degree. Now, however, we are told that happiness includes the happiness of others as well as our own, includes, that is to say, an objective state of good as well as a subjective feeling; and Mill clearly affirms that pleasures differ in kind, which, from the utilitarian psychology, must mean that certain actions to which these pleasures are relative are already stamped as higher and lower, better or worse,—that is, are already morally qualified,—before pleasure, the supposed test of morality, comes in at all. For it is, surely clear, that if we do not admit any higher criterion than pleasure, we cannot find in the mere pleasurable emotion itself any other distinction than that of quantity.

Another difficulty occurs, in the proof of which this principle of utility is capable. The conclusion is that the general happiness is desirable; the proof of this conclusion is that each one desires his own happiness. We are then required to believe that universal benevolence is in some way proved out of individual selfishness. If each one of us is desiring what he deems to be most pleasant for himself, it is tolerably obvious that his mental attitude hinders rather than aids him in working for the general happiness. Hobbes saw clearly enough that if you start with the supposition that men are selfish, you must constrain men into working for the common good by some external authority, and the more powerful the authority the more completely is the general happiness secured.

Nor is it very easy to understand, if we analyze the greatest happiness principle, what it is exactly intended to imply and involve. The greatest happiness principle can be either a rule for public guidance or a rule for individual conduct. If it is the first, the alleged right principle of public policy is the distribution of the greatest amount of happiness among the greatest number according to the rule that everybody is to count for one and nobody for more than one. But can this mean that the criminal is to have as much as the virtuous? Is happiness something which can be cut up into parts and be handed round like cake at a tea-feast? Both suppositions are impossible. Or are the material aids to happiness to be equally divided? But this would clearly not produce the greatest happiness. And if the right answer be that the conditions under which each may pursue happiness are to be as far as possible equalized, this is nothing else but the much more commonplace assertion that equity must be enforced. Shall we then say that this principle is to be taken as a rule for individual conduct? In that case it either puts before us a perfectly impossible ideal, viz. that everybody should be working for some one else's happiness (which leaves benevolence without any field of action, because somebody must be selfish if benevolence is to be possible); or else this principle means nothing but the maintenance in our individual conduct of what we call equitable relations. It is thus that Mr. Spencer, whose criticism[1] I have been paraphrasing, declines to accept in its vague form the maxim that we must work for the general happiness.

A fourth and still more serious objection turns on the account which Utilitarianism gives of the growth and development of moral ideas. For, according to these writers, each man has to learn his morality experimentally, and ethical ideas are ever to be developed anew with the birth of each individual. The school is so afraid of what it calls the fallacy of innate ideas, that it falls into the opposite fallacy of misunderstanding progress and the gradual education of the human race. It is impossible to conceive that humanity during the many years in which it has been learning to be more moral, is unable to transmit from age to age certain formulated moral ideas. In knowledge each generation does not begin afresh: it has the heritage of the discoveries of its ancestors on which it may found additional discoveries of its own. Is morality alone to be begun by every generation afresh, or is it not rather true that for us, at all events, a moral conscience is innate, however much it may have gradually been evolved out of the experience of past generations? Utilitarianism appears to assume that there is an uniform man, a colourless sheet of paper, or primitive atom, upon whom all qualities are imposed by the circumstances under which he is placed. Further, according to this doctrine, society is an aggregate built up of the uniform atoms called men. Each of these desires happiness, and so happiness is regarded as a kind of emotional

[1] 'Data of Ethics,' pp. 221, *et seq.*

currency capable of being calculated and distributed in lots; and conduct is immoral or moral according as it diminishes or swells the volume of this hypothetical currency.[1] The fundamental error here is the inability to understand the value of time, the meaning of development, and the innateness of certain tendencies of character; to which must be added the misunderstanding of the true nature of society which is in many senses a living or growing organism, and not a concourse of independent atoms.

There are some other philosophical objections which connect themselves with the psychological and metaphysical basis on which Utilitarianism is reared; but I prefer to pass to the more popular, practical objections which have their birth in those ordinary feelings, and that ordinary experience which have more weight than some philosophers are inclined to allow them in the establishment of moral doctrines.

In the first place it is not too much to say that the 'popular consciousness' to which it is sometimes given to break through the cobwebs of analytical ingenuity, is clean against Utilitarianism. Nothing is more clear to unsophisticated minds than the distinction between what is *expedient* and what is *good*. We do not venerate the man, who when called on to do some act of heroism, is found to be calculating whether on the whole such an act will be useful or disadvantageous. The degrees of virtue and vice do not correspond with the degrees of utility, or the reverse. It is more natural, despite what the Utilitarians say, to call self-sacrifice noble than to call it useful, and no martyr would ever have gone to the

[1] L. Stephen, 'Science of Ethics,' pp. 359, *et foll.*

stake if he had stopped to reckon up the benefits to society which compensate the pain to himself of a death by burning. The fact is that acts of self-sacrifice and heroism are almost insuperable difficulties to the Utilitarian, for they are, more often than not, the reverse of beneficial to humanity at large, being due to a mistaken, foolish, and wrong-headed enthusiasm. And yet there are qualities about such acts which we instinctively admire, and to which with perfect appropriateness we apply the names 'noble' and 'good.'

Again, according to the Utilitarian system, virtue is not primarily an end, but only a means. It is only by long trains of association that men get habituated to look upon it as an end, because it is connected with the one and only end, happiness. To this we may repeat the objection alluded to before as the 'paradox of Hedonism,' that to do a virtuous act because it makes us happy, is just the way to lose the happiness. The pleasure of virtue is one which can only be obtained on the express condition of its not being the object sought. Theologians tell us that the practice of Prayer has a very beneficial influence on him who offers it, but it is probable that if a man prays solely to gain this reflex influence without any belief in the Being prayed to, the beneficial effect will be missed altogether.

There is, further, an absence of *universality* about the standard of happiness, which appears almost fatal to the ethical system in which it appears. We are told, that the happiness which is the end of morality, is the happiness of others as well as of ourselves. But what happens when they collide?

How are we to estimate the proportions in which each of the two happinesses is to be satisfied? How much of the happiness of others must I take to be equivalent to the loss of my own? Or again, an act which causes happiness to one person may cause unhappiness to another. What am I to do then? Am I to calculate which of the two persons is more worthy to have his feelings consulted? And how am I to estimate the worth, except on the basis of another ethical standard than the Utilitarian?

Several other difficulties centre around those elements of 'moral obligation,' 'moral sanction,' and 'conscience,' which are the strong points of the opposing system. Let us take Conscience, for example. Conscience, says Mill, is a gradual growth, arising from primitive considerations of utility, and developing into all kinds of disinterested sentiments and feelings. But all these sentiments and feelings are merely *apparently* disinterested, the only scientific element of conscience being that it is a record of experiences of Utility. Now, we are accustomed to call Remorse one of the effects of conscience, but Remorse, according to the Utilitarians, is only sorrow that we have made a mistake, not agony that we have committed a sin. Besides, there is undoubtedly more pain than pleasure in the possession of a Conscience, which makes one doubt whether on the test of expediency, it would not be more helpful to the happiness of men if they did not possess that undesirable inward monitor.

It is only another way of looking at the same set of facts to ask what is the personal obligation to morality which Utilitarianism can substantiate. It is enough, probably, for ordinary men that sanctions are to be found in public opinion, or in religious scruples. But there are logical or illogical maniacs, who nurse themselves in solitary lives, and repeat to themselves that they do not care for public opinion, that they do not feel the sanctity of religion, that they prefer seeking their own gratification by breaking the ordinances of the Decalogue. What is to be done with such men? They can hardly be confined in mad-houses, for they are, after all, only balancing their own pleasures against the pain caused by public opinion, and deliberately preferring the former. Is it not clear that Utilitarianism cannot bring to bear any individual personal sanction to make men moral when once the standard of morality has been described as happiness? The fact is, that to promote in every way human happiness may be a counsel of perfection, but hardly seems to offer any ground for a theory of moral obligation. 'You ought,' and 'you had better,' are fundamental distinctions in human thought, and when such distinctions exist, the burden of proof rests on the Utilitarians to show why it is wise to efface and unsettle them.

Once more. The explanation given of morality by Utilitarianism appears to be absolutely unhistorical. The great benefactors to mankind have not thought that they were adding to the happiness of the world, but elevating its moral nature. The best men have seldom been the happiest. The ideal personage of Christendom is called 'The Man of Sorrows.' It is quite true that the lives of all great men have been pre-eminently useful, but the question is whether that was the end they set before themselves, or whethe if they had believed in Utilitarian principles, the result would ever have been attained. To ordinary feelings Utilitarianism inverts the proper relations of ends and means, and confuses consequences with motives. Utility was not the intention of these great men's lives, but the consequence : <u>virtue</u> was not the means to an end of happiness, but rather the <u>only end</u>, with the attainment of which were united such happiness and satisfaction as only a great life can feel.

BOOK III.

RECONSTRUCTION.

CHAPTER I.

KANT. (1724—1804.)

['Foundation for the Metaphysic of Morals' (1785).—'Critique of Practical Reason' (1788).—'Metaphysic of Morals' (1797).]

§ 1.

IN the divisions which have been made of ethical systems, Kant must be included amongst the Rationalists. To him, too, as well as to Cudworth, and Clarke, and Price, Reason is the sovereign element in Morality, the parent of all moral distinctions, and the source of all moral obligation. The ideas on which ethics as a science reposes, such ideas, for instance, as the Freedom of the Will, the Immortality of the Soul, the Existence of God, are ideas of Reason constructively working in a realm which is wholly its own. But the very possibility of this construction in ethics, and the fact that the active force is Reason, are points which in the Kantian ethics require explanation. How, in the first place, is the ethical realm distinguished from the kingdom of logic and speculative knowledge? How, in the second place, can ideas of Reason, essentially *à priori*, be exhibited as possessed of real and true validity? In these questions is centred the earliest of the difficulties which surround the student of the two Critiques of Reason. For the issue of the office of Reason in the two spheres appears to be totally dissimilar. According to the earlier Critique, the ideas of Reason are baseless, if not self-contradictory. According to the second, the ideas of Reason form the irrefragable basis, the undeniable presuppositions of Moral Science. Can it then, we ask, be the same essential faculty whose work is destructive in Logic, and constructive in Ethics?

What is the difference between the sphere of Knowledge and the sphere of Practice? For this difference will explain and justify the two antithetical conclusions. In knowledge, and the acquisition of experience, the mind is, as it were, subject to an alien element, and it is only by means of an increasing intercourse with this alien external sphere, that the borders of knowledge are increased. But this does not hold true in the realm of ethics. The mind, so far as it is practical, is free from the control of an outside world. In moral activity, the mind of man deals with a sphere which is absolutely its own. It can lay down laws for itself untrammeled by the instigations of sense: it can listen to the voice of reason in entire independence of sensuous motives, because the true seat and home of morality is that inner self-consciousness and veritable personality of man, which Kant calls the true or noumenal Ego. Let us put the matter in a different way. When we are speaking of the activity of Reason in the acquisition of knowledge, the subject with which we are occupied is one relating to the knowableness of things. The conditions of knowledge, the part played by sensible experience, the functions of the understanding, the office of the reason, the limitations of the free synthetic power of the mind—these are the subjects to be discussed. And the conclusion forced upon us is, that in the acquisition of knowledge, we are ultimately conditioned by the limits of experience in the widest sense of the term. To the question whether Reason is adequate to an *à priori* knowledge of things, the answer must necessarily be 'no.' We cannot construct an ideal world of our own, because this ideal world is shattered at the first contact with reality. But in the moral sphere this is exactly what we can do, and what we must do. We can construct an ideal world of our own, because the subjects of our inquiry lie entirely within the province of consciousness. For what are the questions with which Morality is concerned? The motives which make us act, the springs which effect our volitions, the office and importance of the Will, the laws which reason lays down for us to conform to, the awe, respect, and reverence which the moral law entails, the stringent and imperative character of duty—all these are questions of an internal sphere, lying within the four corners of our own spiritual activity. However little, then, we can trust Reason divorced from experience in the construction of Knowledge, we can entirely give ourselves up to Reason when dealing with moral problems, because here we are superior to and above the phenomenal world, constructing a world of our own by the aid of that reason which works in us, and in all intelligent beings. To the question whether

Reason is adequate to an *à priori* determination of the Will, the answer must necessarily be 'yes.' The practical reason is capable of influencing the Will purely from its own self, and we can therefore trust the ideas of the practical reason with implicit and unquestioning confidence.

A few words of explanation are necessary as to these ideas of Reason, which are found to be of such unequal validity in the spheres of knowledge and morality. In the *Critique of Pure Reason*, the essential question which Kant propounded to himself was one relating to the conditions under which knowledge was possible. Mathematical knowledge was possible under the condition that the sensibility possessed two *à priori* forms—Space and Time. Physical Science was possible under the condition that the understanding possessed twelve categories, of which Substantiality, Casuality, and Reciprocity are examples. Metaphysical or ontological knowledge was possible under the condition that there were certain ideas of the Reason capable of the same valid application to objects as the forms of the sensibility and the categories of the understanding. But could the latter condition be realized? For in the case of mathematics and physics, knowledge was rendered possible by the interaction of two factors; one emanating from the *à priori* synthetic activity of the mind, the other from the manifold but chaotic possibilities of the external world. Experience demanded the interaction of these two factors, and the forms of the sensibility and the categories of the understanding were valueless, except in relation to, and as constructive of, a 'matter,' coming as it were *ab extra*. But the ideas of the Reason rested on a different basis. They were, so to speak, free constructions of mental activity,—an activity which demanded no other factor, alien and external, to supplement its own intrinsic value,—disembodied creations, called into life by the restless energy of Reason, which was for ever seeking the unconditioned. If experimental knowledge, then, demanded the interaction of a subjective and an objective element, the ideas of reason must be something outside of, or different from, experience and knowledge. From the same cause they must, in the constitution of our knowledge, be wanting in validity. They might possibly regulate it; that is, they might furnish the guiding clue and ideal end which knowledge was always in search of, but they could not enter into the field of experience, and become the known, the explored, the familiar. Whether, then, knowledge seems to demand an idea of Self, as the absolute subject of all our mental states, or an absolute World as the totality of objects in *rerum natura*, or the idea of God, as the absolute subject-object, and necessary presupposition of all knowledge and all being,—in each case we must distinguish between a regulative and a constitutive validity. Regulative the ideas of Reason might be, constitutive they could not be. From the point of view, therefore, of logic and knowledge, the ideas of Reason were deprived of all speculative value.

It is precisely these ideas which are of paramount value in the realm of ethics. For ethics depend on three postulates: the Freedom of the Will, which is none other than the absolute existence of an uncaused activity: the Immortality of the Soul, which is another version of the real existence of an absolute Self: and God, which is the final, consummate Idea lying at the basis both of knowledge and existence. In what sense morality is dependent on these three ideas we must now proceed to consider.

We start with the idea of Duty, for this is an absolutely unique phenomenon which distinguishes ethics from every other science. By a law of duty is meant something which can neither be questioned nor disobeyed. It is what Kant calls "a categorical imperative," meaning thereby to contrast it with hypothetical imperatives which can be both questioned and disobeyed. The hypothetical imperative is couched in the following terms:—"If you want to get this or that, you must do so and so," *e.g.* "if you want to enjoy yourself you must preserve your health." "If you want to make money you must exercise self-control." Hypothetical imperatives, then, relate to ends of pleasure, happiness, profit, and expediency—ends which are given in experience. But the moral imperative has no hypothesis about it; it is a categorical imperative. It does not put before us a certain result as dependent on a certain condition, but its formula is, "you must act thus," without any further proviso. No expediency or happiness comes in to act upon the Will; there is the law standing by itself, sublimely masterful in all its naked simplicity.

What are the consequences which flow from this conception? In the first place this idea of duty proves that Reason solely by itself can influence the

Will; for there is no question here of external motives. It is Reason alone which issues its commands—that self-determining reason which is identical with the Will, or the absolute Ego. In the second place, if the Will can thus lay commands on itself it must possess perfect autonomy. "Thou canst, for thou shouldst," says Kant; for to tell a man he must, is to pre-suppose that he can, or in other words, the absolute character of duty implies the freedom of the Will. In this conception of duty we see the difference between the autonomy of the Will and the heteronomy of the Will. The Will laying command on itself, is the Will as autonomous; all other conceptions of duty involve the idea of the Will as heteronomous — as ordered by something external to and outside of itself. For instance, we have found some moralists bringing forward certain principles of happiness as known in experience to act on the Will. This happiness may either be the material well-being of the body, or the moral well-being of the soul; but in either case this is to lay upon the Will of man injunctions to act, derived as it were from the outside. The Will is ordered to act in order to secure happiness—an external and arbitrary principle. So, too, we have other moralists who appeal to certain ends which they call perfection, or to a certain revealed Will of God. In such systems Reason says to the Will, "You must so act as to achieve perfection," or "You must so act as to carry out the Will of God." Here, again, we have heteronomy of the Will, for the Will is ordered by some ends outside itself. But in the true conception of duty, it is Reason alone in its pure exercise which influences the Will—the self-determining reason, which, as we have before seen, is the Will commanding itself.

The three formulæ of right action which Kant details as the supreme ordinances of Reason exhibit the essential character of ethics both from an objective and a subjective standpoint. Objectively considered, that act alone can be considered moral which is done with full consciousness of the relative claims of other members of the social body. Subjectively considered, the moral act is that alone which finds its motive and principle in the deepest grounds of the rational self, which is the act of a man's veritable personality, or of that common universal element which is at the heart of all life, intellectual or physical. The formula of right action from the first point of view will be couched in terms expressive of the claims of humanity upon the self. "So act as to use humanity whether in yourself or others always as an end, never as a means." "So act that the maxim which guides your volition may be capable of being made law universal." But the internal aspect of right action must reveal its dependence on the universal and absolute reason itself. "Act according to the idea of the will of all rational beings, legislating supremely and universally." In such a formula is brought into prominence the conception of the self-determining reason which moves alike in all human beings as the one absolute legislator.

Can, however, such abstract formulæ serve as guides or test of action in the concrete difficulties of human life? Some simple instances will reveal the value of these principles, and will perhaps suggest the limits of their applicability. A man is tempted to commit suicide. In such a case he is proposing to treat humanity in himself as a means, viz. in order to secure relief from suffering. He is therefore transgressing the formula of right actions which tells him to use humanity always as an end, never as a means. Or again, a man is tempted to avoid the acknowledgment of a debt. He very likely may escape detection in so doing; but let him suppose for a moment such an action to be made law universal, according to the formula of right action, and he at once stands convicted. For if every one treated a loan in similar fashion, neglecting to pay when he could escape detection, the result would naturally be that no one would lend, and public security would be destroyed. Or, once more, suppose a man tempted to tell a lie to escape some temporary embarrassment. Let him bring such an action to one of the tests before mentioned. Let him think of the will of all rational beings legislating supremely and universally. If it were once laid down as a part of such supreme and universal legislation, that a man could tell a lie to suit his convenience, life would become intolerable and impossible. In such fashion, acts within the normal sphere of duties can be proved to be subject to the abstract formulæ of morality. It must, however, be granted that such a resolution of the difficulties of life savours somewhat of a logical *tour de force*, that ordinary utilitarian tests are, if not in themselves preferable, at least more easily applied, and that the possible conflict of duties is inadequately provided for. On the other hand, there can be no doubt that our conception of ordinary duties is both purified and exalted by being brought under the exhibition of some ideal principle; that the duties of life require, in logical analysis, the prior idea of Duty itself to explain their validity, and that the belief in the moral order of the universe acquires thereby greater force and authority. Such, at least, is Kant's notion of the proper treatment of ethics. To those who find it strange and fanciful, as well as to those who find it unpalatable, the Kantian *Critique of Practical Reason* has nothing further to say.

If we further ask a question as to moral motives, the answer of Kant is, that there is but one motive,— respect, awe, or reverence for the moral law. Nor must we look upon a moral motive as an instigation of sense, or as emotional or sentimental. The reverence for the moral law is not a mere feeling, not a pathological state; it is a settled attitude of the man's whole nature. It is only when an act is done out of reverence for the moral law that it becomes truly moral. If it is done because it gives pleasure to do it, it may possibly accord in its results with the moral action, but it is not in itself moral. So stern and unbending is the character of the moral law. A single instance will make this clear. Assuming that the Christian maxim, "Love your enemies," is made the guiding principle of a man's action, it is clear that, according to Kant's vigorous standard, such action is not strictly moral. For to do good to an enemy because you love him, is to do a benevolent action because of a natural inclination prompting it. Therefore, according to Kant, however much an act may accord in its results with morality, it is not in itself moral, for the only moral act is one done out of respect for the moral law. Or take another Christian maxim,—the rule which bids us do as we would be done by. The dictating motive here is clearly the hope of reciprocal favour, or else an appeal to the sense of justice. The malefactor might turn it against his judge, the servant against his master. The maxim, therefore, which guides the volition is not properly a moral one, because in such cases the action is done in order to secure a future good result for the agent, not out of reverence and awe for the bare moral law itself.

We can resume the characteristics of moral action, which have been thus unsystematically indicated under the three following heads :—

1. The moral value of an act lies not in the object, but in the principle which guides the volition. Here the question a man should ask himself is, whether he is acting according to the idea of his will, and all other rational wills, legislating supremely and universally, and out of reverence for the moral law: or whether he is guided by the intention to secure definitely good results for certain persons, or a certain society, or for himself.

2. An action has no true moral value, unless done in the absence of the natural inclination prompting to it. Here a man should ask himself, Am I acting because it gives me pleasure so to do? Am I benevolent and philanthropic because, on the whole, benevolence and philanthropy will either give me a pleasure, or save me from pain? For in these cases my action may be *useful* to humanity, but it has no real moral value.

3. Duty is the necessity for an action out of respect for law. And here, once again, a man should ask himself whether such a respect for the moral law is an ephemeral feeling, a fugitive emotion, or whether it denotes a fixed and habitual attitude of his whole nature, as subservient to the law of moral obligation.

If we look back over the ground we have traversed, we shall see that all the foregoing deductions proceed on the supposition that in morality man's will is free. Except on such a supposition as this, it would be neither possible to formulate a great law of duty which is authoritative, categorical, and exceptionless, nor to indicate even in outline the formula of right action as that which is done in accordance with an universal legislation of reason. But there are other postulates which the science of ethics presupposes. In the opinion of Kant such a science can only be built on the foundation of the soul's immortality and the existence of God. The *Dialectic of Practical Reason* is intended to make these points clear.

Reason, we have found, influences the will purely from itself. But it does more than supply the motive power; being essentially the faculty of construction, it proposes, as in logic so too in ethics, a certain ideal, towards which human experience is for ever pointing, although it may be incapacitated for its fulfilment. In ethics it sets before human beings an ideal of consummate or perfect good. The various ends we strive for at single moments of our lives are so many different goods, conditioned by one another and controlled in various ways by our several circumstances in life. But Reason, over and above these goods, demands a yet higher perfection, a good which is absolutely unconditioned and supreme, and which fulfils the requirements of what the ancient moralists called τὸ κυρίως ἀγαθόν, or *summum bonum*. This *summum bonum* can be nothing but the union of the greatest virtue with the greatest felicity. There is here a combination of two distinct elements, which together are to form the highest good at which man can aim—Virtue and Happiness. In what way are these two elements related to each other? Can we conceive them as only different aspects of one identical thing? Are they respectively the convex and the concave sides of the same arc? If we analyse the one, do we necessarily come to the other? Many moralists have believed in such an analytic relation. The Stoics, for instance, thought that if Happiness were analysed it would be found to be at bottom nothing but Virtue; while the Epicureans, reversing the relation, supposed that an analysis of Virtue would lead to the discovery that it only meant Happiness. But such opinions are too paradoxical. It is impossible to bring Virtue and Happiness to a common denominator, for the two notions are too widely dissimilar. The real relation, then, must be a synthetic one; in other words, a relation of cause and effect. Either virtue must cause felicity, or a life of happiness must bring in its train a continuous pursuit of virtue. Alas! experience gives the lie to each of these suppositions in turn. Virtuous we may be, now and again, but not, therefore, necessarily happy. Fragmentary glimpses of happiness may come within the range of our vision without making us thereby virtuous. A jarring discord seems to exist between the two elements in our *summum bonum*, and the peacemaker cannot be found, at all events in the phenomenal sphere. But it is just the fact of this discord which makes it necessary for us to suppose a realm other than the phenomenal, to serve as the true home for morality. For reason craves an union of the two, and understanding assures us that in the world, as we know it, virtue and happiness fall asunder into irreconcilable antagonism. Yet if there be such a thing as morality for creatures like ourselves endowed with a sensitive frame, which craves, if not for enjoyment, at least for freedom from pain, there must be an inner home of the spirit—a super-sensuous sphere, or as Kant calls it a 'noumenal' sphere, where happiness is raised above the accident of circumstance, and virtue is secure from the incessant interruptions of sense. Observe, however, the postulates for morality that our demand involves. Supreme or consummated virtue demands the eternal existence of the soul, for only in an eternity of progressive efforts can we reach that ideal virtue which is our aim. Supreme happiness, on the other hand, demands the supposition that a God exists with masterful control alike of nature and its events, and of the moral world and its laws, who because supreme over both can combine them in transcendental union—in other words, can give us, if we are moral, a perfect felicity. Such a consummation, devoutly to be wished, is necessary if the moral edifice is to be duly crowned. Virtue is mulcted of its sovereign rights if there be no God to reward, and no eternity to render possible a ceaseless practice of morality.

It is thus that we are enabled to see the dependence of ethics on three essential principles. The possibility of the moral law postulates the existence of free will in man. The possibility of perfect virtue postulates the immortality of the soul. The possibility of perfect felicity postulates God. But Kant will not allow us to misunderstand the nature of these three principles. They are not, it must be remembered, dogmatic conclusions of logic, but practical postulates, that is, necessary presuppositions of morality. For Kant's logic had led him to the conclusion that the three ideas of reason are speculatively incapable of proof. We cannot prove by stress of logic that the soul is a spiritual unit, any more than we can prove that there is such a thing as free causation, or such an absolute being as God. And yet these are the three ideas which are the necessary foundations for ethics. It is this contrast between the conclusions of logic and ethics, which forms so fatal a chasm between theoretical and practical certainty. Freedom, immortality, God, are declared to be not speculative certainties but moral postulates. Knowledge is not extended by such ideas, but ethics is rendered possible. They are truths of the inner life of man, when eyes and ears are shut, and his soul is at home within its unconquerable spiritual realm. In the common light of day they fade, when reason is confronted by a world not its own, and is subject to conditions which it has not itself created. But a real advantage, Kant adds, is secured by the darkness in which these principles as speculative dogmas are involved. For morality cannot, under such circumstances, have impure motives. A man cannot be moral because he either fears God's punishments or courts his rewards. Such issues are too doubtful to act on his will. But in this speculative darkness he can do right in the only moral way—out of respect and reverence for the moral law which reason has ordained.

§ 2.

THE Kantian system of ethics presents certain features on which criticism has always fastened. For in many respects it appears to be formed in contravention of the ordinary moral sentiments of humanity; while in others, where the conclusions are less paradoxical, if it does not violate the convictions of practical men it at least wounds their sensibilities by degrading eudæmonism as an end of life. The most salient points which invite consideration may perhaps be resumed under three heads. (1.) The Doctrine of Free Will. (2.) The Formulæ of Right Action. (3.) The Conception of the Absolute Character of Duty. To these points may be added the systematic tendency which is observable in Kant towards a doctrine of Subjective Idealism, which from the historical point of view serves to connect him in the development of thought with such men as Fichte and Jacobi.

1. The ethical postulate of Free Will depends on

a distinction which is constantly appearing in the Critique of Practical Reason. It is that which in Kant's judgment serves to separate man as he exists and is seen in the world of nature, from man as he is in himself. In the former aspect man is the subject of science, a being whose actions conform to the natural laws of Cause and Effect, the last link, it may be, in a great series of developing organisms, whose physical nature is explained in ultimate analysis as compounded of cells and molecules. In the latter aspect the word 'man' has an entirely different connotation. He is to be regarded as a spiritual unit, one element in the hierarchy of intelligences, a being endowed with all the attributes of power, independence, and authority; superior to the chain of antecedents and consequents which constitute the natural world, because in a certain sense it is due to his mental activity that there is such a thing as Nature at all. Now, as the subject of morality, man must be considered from the point of view of a noumenon; so that while the sciences of biology and anthropology regard man in his phenomenal aspect—man as he is and appears in the world of sense and of nature—the student of moral philosophy has to change the point of view, for he discovers that the problems of moral activity are insoluble without the assumption of man as a rational free agent in the world which underlies the appearances of sense. Kant is always bringing in this distinction in order to extricate himself from the difficulties of his own logic. Logic had conclusively proved that when Reason attempted to set up ideas of its own, without recourse to experience, it fell into antinomies and paralogisms. As soon, however, as it is discovered that morality is based on ideas of Reason their damaged validity has to be reconstituted by the severance between man in a phenomenal sphere and man in a real sphere. Logic proves that in the world as we know it there is an absolute discord between virtue and happiness, while yet it is the union of virtue and happiness which Reason seeks as the *summum bonum*. Here, again, the distinction between the two spheres comes in. The harmony we desire between morality and felicity only holds true of the spiritual world. Once again, when the inexorable demands of logic seem to force us to believe that man is not a free agent, that the so-called Freedom of the Will is a metaphysical figment, Kant steps in with the distinction between a world in which man is subject to the laws of nature and a world to which by his reason he belongs where the law of duty is built up on the postulate of freedom. "A rational being," says Kant in the *Foundation for the Metaphysics of Morals*, "has two points of view from which he can regard himself, and recognize laws for the exercise of his faculties, and consequently of all his actions. First, so far as he belongs to the world of sense, he finds himself subject to the laws of nature: secondly, as belonging to the intelligible world under laws which being independent of nature, have their foundation not in experience but in reason alone. . . . When we conceive ourselves as free we transfer ourselves into the world of understanding as members of it, and recognize the autonomy of the Will with its consequence—morality."

Can we say, however, that such a distinction in

any way meets the difficulties which encompass morality? For morality involves a series of acts done here and now: these acts are phenomenal, being done in a phenomenal sphere: in other words, they belong to the ordinary world of experience. Therefore so far as our everyday actions are concerned, we can have, on Kant's showing, no Free Will. What serves it, then, that we can repeat to ourselves the conviction that we have Free Will in some transcendental fashion? What profit is it to us as hoping, fearing, struggling creatures, in a world of experience, particularity, and phenomena? Such a solution serves rather to mock at our difficulties than to solve them, to beguile us with an idea of freedom, while it deprives us of its reality. It rests, indeed, for its defence on a conviction which is ineradicable in most men, that they are something higher than their circumstances and bodily needs, than all that their mundane existence is and amounts to; but such a theory of a two-fold aspect of man is always open to the suggestion that the world of experience is at all events something we can see and handle and be sure of, while the other so-called intelligible world can only be taken on trust, is seen only by the eye of faith, and has been proved to be the parent of many mystical delusions.

It is easy to urge such criticisms. It remains, however, to notice that the only possible solution of this much-vexed question is forced by the nature of the case to proceed on much the same lines which Kant indicated. No man of practical sense is a fatalist: no logician is a libertarian. Between these two extremes some middle course has to be found which can allow for such determinism as may render possible a science of social man, and yet can allow of such self-sufficiency as the rational understanding craves. We may say that a man's actions flow from his circumstances *plus* his character; but it must not escape our notice that the term 'character' at once introduces a metaphysical conception. We may say that a man is so far responsible for what he does as to justify the Penal Code of the State, but the expression 'responsibility' leaves us face to face with the old problems. We may say that acts necessarily flow from motives, and even from the preponderant motive, but it will have to be allowed that a 'conscious' motive is something wholly disparate in connotation with what we mean by a physical antecedent. The forces, it is said, do not affect man blindly, for he makes them a part of himself. Or, in other words, the possession of Consciousness seems to lift men in some strange way out of the natural world. All these dicta by which the old difficulty of Free Will is sought to be explained are themselves, if analysed, nothing but affirmations of the Kantian distinction. In any discussion of the question it appears necessary to distinguish between two points: the relation of motives to actions, and the relation of a man to his motives. Let it be granted that the relation of motives to actions is on the same plane with the relation of physical antecedent and physical consequent. But the other relation—the relation of a man's personality to his motives,—introduces another question which can only be met and answered by metaphysics. Will it be said that a man is nothing but the motives which act on him? And how, then, can we explain the fact that within the same lifetime motives act on a man with different force? The man himself has changed, we say. But what has altered the relative strength of motives? Can they be conceived to have the power to augment and decrease their own volume? If not, there must at least be a reaction of spiritual agents on preponderant motives, and the possibility of such reactions is the very point to be explained. "There is," said Kant, "a noumenal Ego, and there is a phenomenal Ego." There are certain sides which a man shows to the outside world, and there is a certain face which his inner personality turns to the Absolute Reason.

2. The formulæ of Right Action, as they are described by Kant, are so phrased as to appear especially liable to misconstruction. An obvious criticism attaches to their abstract character which is instinctively felt to be out of harmony not only with the complexity of human circumstances but the concrete application of moral rules. "So act as to use humanity always as an end, never as a means." Could there be anything more baffling than the conception of humanity as an end in itself?[1] Such humanity as we know is composed of a number of individual units with mutual relations, which serve to connect them together, and with certain claims upon ourselves either of actual service, or at least of sympathetic feeling. These claims distinctly include some merely subjective non-rational wishes. According to Kant's position, subjective non-rational wishes can never furnish us with proper ends for moral activity.

[1] Cf. Sidgwick's 'Method of Ethics,' p. 363 (1st edition).

"So act that the maxim which guides your will may be fit for law universal." Here again, difficulty surrounds the conception of this universal and formal legislation. For the formula includes the idea of duty for duty's sake, which by analysis can easily be resolved into the process of willing the bare form of Will.[1] Now let us suppose a man trying to act in this fashion. "There is nothing," says Kant, "so good as a good-will." But what is to be the object of this Will? It must will something, some act to the exclusion of other acts. But such a particular act is in the region of the sensuous, the particular, the empirical. But the principle on which, according to Kant, we ought to will, must exclude all sensuous, particular, and empirical elements. When once these are excluded, only the bare form of Will remains, or in other words, the effort of the Will must be to give force and effect to an abstraction. But here again a fresh difficulty occurs. To realize in this sense means to render concrete, and an abstraction that is once rendered concrete ceases to be an abstraction. To will, then, the bare form of Will, is to perform the well nigh impossible feat of destroying that which is the object of activity, of rendering concrete that abstract, which once rendered concrete loses all its ethical value.

Such arguments appear forcible exercises in logic, but they are of the same value as the corresponding arguments which can be urged against the Kantian categories of the Understanding. When Mill asserted that the disproof of the Kantian category of causality, was the fact that the ancients believed in Chance, he gained much the same verbal triumph.

[1] Cf. Bradley's 'Ethical Studies,' p. 131.

It is quite clear that different views have been held as to the Uniformity of Nature; it is quite true that men have included very different kinds of agency under the general appellation of Cause. But it is a question whether either of these two facts in reality impairs the value of the doctrine that makes the uniformity of nature, as well as the law of causation, depend on an *à priori* law of the understanding whereby phenomena are connected by the synthesis of cause and effect. It is obvious, for instance, that Chance, by Aristotle, was envisaged as itself a cause, and that our Aryan forefathers in the mythologic age reduced the world, as they knew it, to uniformity by the supposition of animated beings as causes. So when we are told that the disproof of Kant's categorical imperative is furnished by man's habit of finding the contents of the law of duty in utilitarian considerations, we seem to apprehend that such a criticism proceeds on an entirely mistaken estimate of Kant's analysis of ethics. According to Mr. Lewes, the capital mistake of Kant was to confuse a question of *psychogeny*,—of the growth of mind, in other words,—with a question of *psychostatics*, —the analysis of the mind as a statical entity. The criticism is capable of an easy retort, for the confusion may be due to the critic rather than to the author of the system. In the *Critique of the Practical Reason*, at all events, we have expressly an analysis of ethical activity on the formal side. The problem is to enunciate not all the elements which enter into the conception of duty, but the formal ones; those, for instance, which may serve to distinguish a dutiful act from a benevolent, or from an expedient act. How else can such elements be distinguished except by the admission that duty on the formal side postulates a notion of universality? "Quod semper quod ubique quod ad omnibus"—the formal character of truth has just the same elements. Expediency differs with the individual. Benevolence varies with its objects, and the circumstances under which it is practised. The essential nature of duty is that it transcends these relative individual characteristics. If it also assumes an abstract form, this is nothing more than could be expected from the logical analysis of an universal idea. What is it we desire to get from a philosophic treatise on ethics? Is it the empirical rules of daily practice? Then we must turn elsewhere than to the *Critique of the Practical Reason*, which is concerned with the analysis of the logically prior notion of Duty itself.

3. But further difficulties are found in the authoritative character of duty when viewed in the light of a possible conflict of duties. Kant, it is said, fails to recognize the possibility of such collision: he does not admit of circumstances in which a man may have to choose between two duties, and sacrifice one to the other. If once an absolute and categorical imperative were infringed, it would cease to be what its name implies. Unfortunately, the experience of men is full of such collisions. You must never tell a lie; but there are circumstances in which a man may have to tell a lie. It is quite right to speak falsely to a brigand, a burglar, a cut-throat. Ordinary morality says, "I don't call that a lie," thus instinctively qualifying the duty of truth-speaking by a higher duty—viz. the preservation of life. So,

too, with many other of the provisions of the decalogue which are held to be rightly infringed under certain imperative circumstances.[1]

Here again, the question turns on whether we are demanding a practical treatise on the conduct of life under trying circumstances, or a formal and logical analysis of duty. Let us ask, for instance, more narrowly, how ordinary morality excuses such violations of the laws of ethics. In these collisions of duty it will be said, the rule is that a duty must never be sacrificed except to a higher duty; never sacrificed, for instance, to an inclination, a sensuous appetite, or a selfish wish. But this account of the matter itself reveals under a new form the absolute character of duty. In certain arduous circumstances of life, it requires much careful consideration to discover what our duty is. This is all that the criticism amounts to. That the duty once found must be rigidly performed, would be affirmed by the most Jesuitical of casuists. So that it would appear that the law of ethics requires that duty as such shall never be infringed, which is what a fair interpretation of Kant's doctrine affirms to be his view. In other words, if we regard the matter from a logical aspect, there can be no such thing as a collision of duties, though from a practical point of view, there may be collision between dutiful acts. In such matters the doubt is concerned with the exact action to which the term 'dutiful' is properly applied. There is no shadow of question concerning Duty itself. An abstract analysis of ethics must always appear wanting in life and actuality to

[1] Cf. Bradley's 'Ethical Studies,' pp. 141—143.

those who are immersed in the daily struggles and temptations of existence. But the value of such an analysis can only be doubted by one whom Plato would describe as unconsciously and traditionally moral, ἄνευ ἄνευ φιλοσοφίας ἀρετῆς μετειληφότα.[1]

In one respect, indeed, the Kantian doctrine is open to a charge to which we shall have to refer presently. But that affects the system as a whole, and is concerned with the historical place it fills amongst reconstructive schemes. It is easy for us, who view the matter from the vantage-point of a century of thought, to say that Kant was too subjective an Idealist, or to assert that the Thing-in-itself,—the unknown x which represents the absolute antithesis of Spirit,—exercised too overpowering an influence over his speculation. But such points become patent when we are regarding the transition from one speculative system to another, and must not affect our judgment of the intrinsic value of the system, which first gave the cue to all subsequent attempts at reconstruction. For myself, I do not care to do injustice to a noble and symmetrical work of art, by insisting on the commonplace criticisms, which any facile historian of Philosophy would be eager to urge. There are systems of Philosophy, just as there are human characters, which ought to be judged by their strongest and not by their weakest features, and with regard to which the opinion of the ordinary expert is just that which is most valueless. For the system is reared, just as the character is formed, by some masterful touch of

[1] Plato, Rep. 619.

genius, and its central worth and essential nobility are too fine to be weighed in the scales of merely logical acumen. The becoming attitude is one rather of appreciative admiration than captious criticism; and however much it may be necessary for the purposes of historical synthesis to weigh and contrast advantages with drawbacks, it is a shallow judgment which does not end by admitting that our weights and balances leave the primal and intrinsic value both of the genius which inspired, and the work which was executed, absolutely unimpaired and uniquely singular.

I desire, then, in connection with Kant, to refer to one or two points which appear essential to a constructive system of ethics. I say nothing in this reference, of the resolute assertion of the Freedom of the Will, which many have selected as a crowning characteristic of Kant's moral views; although it might well be maintained that a belief in the power of his own personal initiative, as it is one of the earliest convictions of a strong man, so also it is the one which he will last of all and most reluctantly part with. Nor need anything further be said of those wide and far-reaching formulæ of Duty, which serve to bind all humanity into one corporate commonwealth of moral units; although even so unimpassioned a critic as Professor Sidgwick has allowed himself to get eloquent over them. Nor yet need the importance of Reason, as supreme moral faculty, be again insisted on, although it has been the object of these pages to suggest that this is the significant mark which distinguishes the real from the spurious in moral schemes. But the attempt may fitly be made to connect some of those principles which were before laid down somewhat dogmatically, with the fuller treatment which they receive at the hands of Kant.

It was asserted, that the question with which Moral Philosophy is concerned, is the elucidation of the word 'Right,' rather than 'Good,' and the reason assigned was that the main interest for the moralist is man's attitude towards alternative courses of action, and not primarily at all events the results of given acts. It is only another way of stating this principle to assert that morality is a question of motives rather than of results. This is, of course, a direct and categorical denial of the Utilitarian thesis, according to which the business of the moralist is to explain Good as general utility, and to estimate action by its (useful) results. But, as distinct from other sciences, Ethical Science, we maintain, must begin from the side of the internal consciousness,—must begin not from objective data, scientifically analysed, but from the springs and impulses of action, discovered by self-reflection. From this point of view, directly we approach ethics from this interior and intimate standpoint, the question of 'motive' becomes of paramount importance. Let us, however, hear Kant on the matter. The moral value of an action, he will tell us, lies not in the intention of it, but in the maxim which determines it,—not in the object, but in the principle of volition. For our wills are capable of being influenced by the bare form of law, even before the full content of such law may be apprehended. Now the bare form of law is otherwise expressed in the fact, that I live under a law of obligation, a law of duty. The particular specifications which enter into my present duty, may be, and must be, controlled by experience and a knowledge of results. But the moral character of my action is determined by my acknowledgment of that great 'I must,' which we call the Law of Obligation. If I acknowledge that I, together with others, am subject to this Law of Obligation, then am I moral, and if every act is performed under the deep and abiding conviction that I live under such a law, I have vindicated my claim to belong to that spiritual world of reality which is over and above the changeful and perplexing phenomena of sense. In other words, then, morality deals with certain internal elements,—with that inner side of volition which we call 'motive,'—rather than with volition as outwardly expressed and rendered concrete in a given act. A moral scheme, the whole end and purpose of which is to purify the ethical consciousness, which in consequence lays stress on a man's character and motives as distinguished from the useful or felicific quality of his actions, is to this extent a truer and more adequate account of those phenomena of human nature which render it a subject to morality.

Ethical science, which must not disdain to answer the most elementary questions, must provide a satisfactory reply to the question, "Why must I be moral?" In other words it must provide a personal and individual sanction for doing right. It is no answer to this question to refer a man to the practice or the habits of others; to the voice of society which always champions the party of the respectable; or even to the ordinances of Nature which are sometimes found "to be on the side of the angels." For a man may in turn disregard any and every sanction which comes upon him as it were from the outside. He may be too reckless to care for the physical sanction; too selfish to be affected by the voice of public opinion; too much of an *esprit fort* to be alarmed by pictures of another world. Is he, therefore, to be freed from the obligation of being moral? Seemingly so, unless we can exhibit to him the existence of a necessity which shall not affect him from the outside, but shall be part and parcel of his own nature—a law under which he lives, not as a member of a social commonwealth nor even as partner in a Christian faith, but as a single individual spiritual being. Such a necessity may be called 'Conscience,' as Butler called it, or 'Moral Sense,' as Hutcheson called it, or 'Categorical Imperative,' as Kant called it. But the point to be insisted on is, that unless it is shown to belong to the essence of a man's nature, there can be no personal obligation to morality. Judged from this point of view, how inadequate are some of the explanations of ethical systems! Why must I be moral? Hedonism answers, 'because otherwise you will violate a physical sanction,' albeit that experience tells us every day how little the voluptuary cares for the threats of outraged nature. Utilitarian schemes, with some hesitation, appeal to a social sanction, and have to admit, at the same time, how little coercive force the voice of public opinion at present possesses. The sanction of scientific ethics is to be found in a great law of evolution, in natural selection, in the survival of the fittest; and the majority of human beings have passed their lives in complete ignorance of what these terms mean. But every man knows, at all events in a rudimentary form, the phenomena we designate by such terms as Repentance, Remorse, Desire for Reformation, and if a moral system is unsuccessful in placing such phenomena on a philosophic basis, it may safely be held to have failed in its mission. Such failure, at all events, does not attach to the Kantian system, despite its abstract terminology and its bristling array of technicalities. The Categorical Imperative, the Law of Duty, the Autonomous Will which lays commands on itself—these are, however disguised, the ordinary and commonplace experiences of the moral life.

There is another point in which Kant boldly challenges the creed of the world and of science. Morality is in his view ultimately created by a Self, which is above the conditions of time and place, and independent of the phenomena of the natural sphere. There is no more characteristic point than this whereby to exhibit Kant's antagonism to the so-called sciences of ethics which are produced in our country. For Utilitarian schemes as a body desire to study the phenomena of moral action in the same way as other phenomena, to analyse them by the same scientific methods, and to arrive inductively from them to the generalizations called moral laws. The procedure of Evolutionists is similarly to regard man himself as the last term in a series of natural productions, whose activities, whether in ethical practice or in other modes, are conditioned by those natural laws which have throughout regulated the process of development. The system which

Kant formulated is the direct antithesis of both of these. He will not apply induction to moral data, nor will he make moral laws dependent on an inquiry into the tendencies of actions. Still less will he regard morality as the gradual development of conduct in the history of animate life. But his system of ethics is deductively established—deduced from the veritable existence of a real self which serves for him as the necessary presupposition of all morality. Are we, therefore, to call him unscientific? To many minds this will undoubtedly appear the right verdict. Many critics have held (as, for instance, Lange in his *History of Materialism*), that while Kant's Logic has indeed effected a revolution comparable to the astronomical discovery of Copernicus, his ethics may safely be discarded just as we discard the metaphysics of a Descartes. Perhaps Kant was wiser than his critics; perhaps he wished to preserve the unique character of moral phenomena. For directly we approach the problems of Right and Wrong, we seem to discover how little any solution of them which treats them from an external point of view, as phenomena of time and space, appears to satisfy the requirements of philosophy. The moral life is to such an extent the antithesis of the natural life, that it appears to involve the supervention of some higher force. Not only is the animal life controlled by the human, but the human life itself is in morality controlled by what, for want of a better name, we call the spiritual self. If Kant's division between the phenomenal and the real self was an attempted explanation of the mysterious authority of the moral law, so far at least he would appear to have understood the essential problem of ethics. If such a doctrine be Mysticism, it is the Mysticism of every thinking man when he is alone with his past failures and his future hopes. For then he is in the world of ideals; and while to frame ideals is impossible, except to a Self which is above the accidents of circumstance, morality, which is the creation of that Self, is nothing but the determined attempt to secure what should be, rather than what is.

CHAPTER II.

THE SUCCESSORS OF KANT.

§ 1. JACOBI AND FICHTE.

It still remains to attempt to determine the position of the Kantian Ethics in the history of the evolution of moral thought. Reconstructive the system may be admitted to be, for it aims at the regeneration of Ethical Science on the basis of self-consciousness. Morality, as the creation of the Ego, is now securely founded against the criticism of empirical philosophy, whether expressed in the form of Utilitarianism or Scientific Ethics. But it represents the work of Reconstruction in an early stage: and it may well be that certain elements of weakness or inconsistency are included, which may be brought out by subsequent controversy. Is there any advance on the position of Kant made by his successors on the same reconstructive lines? If so, in which direction are such advances possible? It is these questions which must now be answered.

The broad features of the Kantian philosophy recognize an elementary distinction between Things-in-themselves and Phenomena. In the analysis of sensible perception there is the manifold, the chaotic data which are the material, and the laws of the

Sensibility which are the formal element. The interaction of the two give us 'objects' in a primary sense, though we find subsequently that to the formal element must be added the categories of the understanding. Phenomena, then, are due to forms of the sensibility *plus* categories of the understanding on the one side : on the other they demand the 'material' supplied as it were from the outside. The necessity of this outside material is obvious : for it is really this which finally disposes of the claim of the Ideas of the Reason to substantial validity. If we ask why the Ideas of the Reason are invalid, the answer is, that they are constructed in independence of experience, and experience demands the sense-given material as well as the mentally-supplied form. If we ask Kant whether the Ego could create both form and material (so that Things-in-themselves would cease to be the unknown antithesis to the laws of our mind) Kant answers emphatically in the negative. No doubt need be felt on this point, for it was the subject of an express declaration made by Kant himself on August 7th, 1799, in opposition to Fichte. (Intelligenzblatt, Allg. Litt.-Ztg., No. 109, 1799.) Thus the supposition of the outside Thing-in-itself is for Kant necessary to knowledge ; any other view, getting rid of the empirically-given material, produced on him, he declared, 'a ghostly impression.' But if this be the case, the discord between the spheres of knowledge and morality remains for ever insoluble. The Ideas of the Reason in the speculative sphere will always be valueless (except as regulative), while in the practical sphere they will still be fundamentally necessary. We shall have to set up a sort of competition between the Speculative Reason and the Practical, and decide in arbitrary fashion that to the latter must be ascribed supremacy. (Kant, Ros. and Schub. viii. p. 258.) If in knowledge there is to be recognized a necessary but wholly unknown and incalculable factor supplied by Things-in-themselves, then the ideas on which morality is based can never become articles of a creed, but only practical postulates.

Let us look a little closer at the analysis of sensible perception. There is 'the manifold' on the one side: the forms and categories lying ready on the other side. A certain affection of the senses takes place, through which we receive the material element of perception. Whence does this affection of the senses come? To what is it due? From phenomena, or from things-in-themselves? Let us suppose it comes from phenomena. But phenomena are only representations of our minds. Therefore, the origin of our representations is due to the action of our representations on our senses. Therefore it would appear that representations can affect us before they exist, and that there were ideas before there were ideas. But this is nonsense, and hence one of the two alternatives (the one supported by J. S. Beck in his 'only possible standpoint'[1]) is disposed of. Shall we say then that the sense-affection comes from Things-in-themselves? This is undoubtedly the view of Kant, but it is exposed to a peculiar difficulty. For in that case, Things-in-themselves stand in a causal relation to our sense-affection.

[1] 'Einzig möglicher Standpunkt aus welchem die kritische Philosophie beurtheilt werden muss.' Riga, 1796.

But the causal relation is by Kant declared to be wholly subjective, causality being one of the categories of the understanding. Therefore Things-in-themselves, which stand wholly apart from such subjective forms as Time, Space, and Causality, yet seem to stand in a causal relation to the temporal and spatial affection of the senses in perception.[1] There are only two ways of escape from this dilemma. Either it must be asserted that Time, Space, and Cause are objective realities existing in *rerum naturâ*, in the realm where Things-in-themselves exist—a supposition which is quite impossible for Kant or any Kantian to make: or else starting from the subjective character of Causality, we must conclude that this supposed relation of Things-in-themselves to our sensible affection is itself subjective, and that, therefore, the Ego, in a sense, creates the opposition between object and subject. But if so, the dread unknown noumenon becomes harmless: being itself due to the activity of the Ego, it ceases to prevent the Ideas of Reason from being valuable in knowledge, and therefore serves ultimately to reconcile the work of Reason in the spheres of Knowledge and Morality. If Kant stopped short of such an ultimate development of his own principles, Fichte is, perhaps, justified in appealing to "the holy spirit in Kant" as doing better service to the cause of truth than that thinker's individual personality had done.

In similar fashion, Kant, as the inaugurator of a new reconstruction in ethics, might well be understood

[1] Jacobi: Ueber David Hume, Werke, Vol. II. p. 301 (1787): cf. Schulze : 'Œnesidemus' (1792).

to have suggested rather than worked out the conception of a self-determining Reason in morality. This reason, which lays commands on itself, which in undisturbed autonomy gives out the edicts which become the comprehensive formulæ of right action—is it the Reason of the individual? Is the inner and veritable personality of a man (the Noumenal Ego) the source and author of morality? And how then can Kant escape the charge of having formulated a certain relativity of morals—not, indeed, in the ordinary sense of the term, but in one quite appropriate and applicable? For ethics become, indeed, relative to the individual, though to the intelligible character rather than to the phenomenal and variable elements. The only escape from such a charge would be to lay stress on the universal character of intelligence as such, so that if ethics be the creation of Reason, Reason must be understood as possessing a common fund of principles acknowledged by all humanity. Thus gradually we slip into the conception of an universal Reason, an absolute and world-ordering Intelligence, in order to avoid the imputation of introducing contingency into moral laws: and by the same process, we have enlarged the Subjective Idealism belonging to the system of Kant into the Objective and Absolute Idealism of his successors. A parallel development is found in the gradual enlargement of the term 'Experience' in the history of the English philosophical school. Experience, as understood by Locke and Hume, was the experience of the individual: in J. S. Mill we are never quite certain whether it is entirely individual: but Spencer and Lewes leave us in no doubt in the matter. Experience has become universal—the developing experience of the whole animal series. Thus do the forces of continual criticism and the exigencies of an adequate explanation of mental phenomena serve to widen the ground-plan of a theory. Such enlargements, moreover, are often an affair of the century. While individualism was the characteristic of seventeenth and eighteenth century thought, the nineteenth century is especially prolific in universal conceptions. The evolution dogma of Darwin, the 'Humanity' of Comte, the synthetic and absolute self-consciousness of the German idealists, are obvious examples.

The subjective individualism of Kant reveals itself in many ways to those who have begun to accustom themselves to think from the side of the universal; and in almost all cases, acts prejudicially on the constructive wholeness of his ethical system. Morality, it has been seen, rests on immortality of the soul as one of its necessary postulates: and Kant proceeds to draw out a sort of objective proof of its necessity. The soul can only approximate to its ideal of Virtue in a series of progressive efforts. This progressive advance is made through an infinity of steps. The soul must therefore have an infinite life. But how 'a series of progressive steps' is to be understood in a real world, which lies beyond the notion of Time and Space, Kant fails to explain. Such conceptions as 'progression' and 'advance' must be strictly relative to a world which we explain by the *à priori* form of Time, and can have no meaning in a suprasensible world. But, further, if an indefinite progression of individual steps really amounted to infinity,

infinity would not be an unity but an arithmetical practice in addition, and it would rather be negative than positive. A magnified and non-natural man does not satisfy our idea of God: we cannot take the qualities of a limited individual, and supposing the qualities enormously exaggerated, flatter ourselves with the notion that we have imagined the Deity. In just the same way we cannot take an infinite addibility of moments to be the equivalent of eternity. The truth is, that, starting from the individual lifetime with its appropriate conceptions, we can not conceive immortality at all. It is the inalienable prerogative of the universal, but it cannot be reached by an indefinite elongation of the individual. In this matter, Kant's subjective individualism stood him in bad stead. All the so called objective proofs of immortality suffer under an incurable defect, for they seem to imagine that an objective certainty is superior to a subjective certainty. As Fichte says: "Should any being whatever, contemplating its existence in time, declare at any moment of that existence, '*Now* I am eternal'—then on that very account it could not be eternal."[1] In other words, immortality stands out of all relation to the moments of time.

But perhaps, the most unfortunate instance of Kant's tendency is to be found in his treatment of the third ethical postulate—the existence of God. Because the *summum bonum* of the individual is the union of the greatest virtue with the greatest felicity, we have, therefore, to presuppose a Deity

[1] Fichte's 'Recension des Œnesidemus.' 'Literatur-Zeitung, 1794. Werke,' i. 23 and foll.

who can unite the two elements, and who can therefore give a man happiness if he be virtuous. Can there be a clearer or a bolder statement, that God exists for the sake of an individual's happiness? Why Duty, which is declared by Kant to be unselfish in this world, should suddenly become selfish in the next world, and demand happiness, is not explained. Yet this is not all. The undignified position to which the Deity is thus relegated, can only be partially excused by that inveterate desire to find happiness, if not in this world, at all events, in the next. The aspirations of the individual soul are, it is true, buoyed up on the idea of happiness: but none of such aspirations contain in themselves anything especially God-like, nor can they be made to evidence the existence of God. Morality in itself is a better proof of God: and no one has exceeded Kant in his divorce between Morality and Eudæmonism. Yet here in the presence of the most sovereign idea, Kant will allow the eudæmonistic cravings of an individual soul to be a measure of Godhead. No wonder that Heine, with characteristic levity but ready wit, declared that Kant had resuscitated the Deistic corpse for the sake of his poor old servingman, and out of fear of the police, as a sort of farce after the tragedy.[1] Yet even old Lampe, with his stern matutinal summons 'Die Zeit ist angekommen,' might prefer an argument founded on his devotion to his master to one which based itself on his predilections for happiness.

But how is the Universal, which thus seems the necessary complement to, or ground-work of, the

[1] Heine: 'Sämmtliche Werke,' v. 204.

individual and subjective Ego, to be found? This was the problem left to his successors by both the analytic and synthetic elements in Kant's *Critiques*. The partial reconstruction effected in the *Critique of the Practical Reason*, had to be supplemented, the destructive analysis of the *Dialectic of the Pure Reason* had to be obviated, by some further advance in philosophic thought. Jacobi and Fichte in different ways undertook the task; the first by shrinking back from the logical path; the second by resolutely following it to its close. Jacobi inaugurated the Philosophy of Faith, Fichte the doctrine of the autocratic Ego; but the Faith philosophy had but few followers, while Fichte directly led on to the constructive systems of Schelling and Hegel.

The decisive turning-points in philosophy seem often to have similar features. There are always two ways of meeting criticism, of which the first in time is usually the method of rhetoric and emotional fervour, while the second slowly works out its course by a deeper speculation. When Hume's *Treatise* and *Enquiry* first made their mark on the literary public, the school of Reid and common sense began by pouring out the vials of rhetorical commonplace: but it was left not to his countrymen, but to a German, to appreciate the extent of the revolution which Hume had caused. As it was in the days of Hume, so was it in the days of Kant. The analogue of the school of Reid is furnished by the system of Jacobi, just as Fichte and his successors represent the attempt at a deeper and more thorough-going analysis. The interest, however, of Jacobi's position is greater than could possibly be aroused by the blank negations of common sense, for in some shape or other, the invocation to Faith to heal the breaches of destructive analysis seems to correspond with the native instincts of the human intelligence. It is on these instincts that Jacobi plants himself. So far as logical demonstration goes, there can be no other consistent system of philosophy than that of Spinoza, but the imperative needs of the human spirit can never be content with Pantheism. Carry the chains of causal nexus as far as you please, you will never get any link to connect the world as a whole with an author outside the world. The sphere of the conditioned can by no *salto mortale* be overpassed; logical demonstration is confined to the inter-dependent series of phenomena, and the only issue is to recognize in the Kosmos at large the sufficient ground of its existence. But a man who acquiesces in such Spinozism, deliberately forfeits the jewels in the crown of humanity, and silences the voices of his heart. What does the pure intuition of a rational soul reveal to us? It reveals to us the suprasensible quite as clearly as our senses reveal to us the world of nature. No object, in point of fact, can possibly move us with immediate conviction of its truth more forcibly than do those ideas of the beautiful and the good, which the inner mental vision beholds. So, too, do we apprehend God, not indeed by the understanding, but by Faith; for God has given us a spirit by which to be conscious of his presence—a spirit which bears witness of God's presence in the heart. It is true that Jacobi does not always use this confident language. He allows that a consistent Spinozist can not be out-argued; he asserts that

Fichte's very different view of the Deity was logically correct. But he will not be enslaved to the logical understanding, believing it to be the prerogative of humanity to see with the soul objects which only reveal themselves to that sacred organ. It is thus that in language which reminds us of St. Paul's admission of the conflict between the Law and the Gospel, Jacobi explains that he is a heathen with the understanding, but a Christian with the spirit. "There is light within my heart, but when I try to bring it into the understanding, it is quenched. Which illumination is the true one, that of the understanding, which reveals clear shapes with an abyss behind, or that of the heart, which sends rays of hope upwards, but can not fill the gaps in logical knowledge?"

There is no man who does not know something of this cry. It is the pathetic language of a man whose intellect is strong enough to destroy, but not strong enough to build, who sees the discords which logic makes in unreflecting beliefs, and can not trust his reason to heal the wounds which it has itself inflicted. But, once brought to an impasse, it is folly in a man to throw away the light which has guided him hitherto, as though darkness could yield the consolation of concealing the obstacle. It is, however, of more importance for our purpose to observe that in reality the position of Jacobi is not a whit in advance of the Kantian: there is a difference in the names, and that is all. What for Kant is an antagonism between ideas of Reason, speculatively considered, and ideas of Reason, practically considered, is for Jacobi an antagonism between the understanding and the heart. Nothing is altered or gained by the change of expression. Reason is made neither more or less real by being called Faith: and Faith itself is on Jacobi's own showing only a word to cover the absence of definite knowledge. So, too, did Plato use the mythus to conceal the gaps in scientific demonstration.

Fichte represents in two definite stages of his philosophical system the only possible lines of advance on such a position. The first of these connects itself with the Kantian idea of the supremacy of the Categorical Imperative of Duty: the second leads on by a natural and consistent development to the imposing Transcendentalism of Hegel. In what aspect can we envisage the Absolute? How can we be sure that behind the individual subjectivity of a single rational intelligence, there lies the vast eternity of the Universal? The first answer is furnished by the existence of the Moral Order. Here History as well as Ethics is our testimony. In the progress of Humanity, in the story of developing Civilization, in all the pages which record the steps by which tribes are welded into a nation, and a nation grows from subordination to conquest, there is traced in outline the ideal Moral Order, which in one sense is the background and underlying reality of each changing picture, and in another sense is the Divine End, to the realization of which the whole creation travaileth and groaneth. To which must then be added the presupposition of Ethical Science as it affects the individual unit. Without such a moral order, there is no meaning in Conscience and Responsibility, no interpretation of the conception of

Good, no authoritative agency in the idea of Duty. Fichte is very clear on this point: "It is not at all doubtful," he says,[1] "it is rather the most certain of all things, nay more, it is the ground of all certainty, and the only absolute, objective truth, that there is a moral order in the world; that every individual has his definite place in this order, and that his labour is reckoned upon: that his destiny, in so far as it is not occasioned by his own conduct, is the result of this plan: that no hair of his head can fail, no sparrow can fall without it: that every true and good action prospers, and every bad action fails: and that for those who truly love goodness, all things must work together for good." The essay from which the above sentences are taken, Fichte published as an introduction to Forberg's paper 'On the Definition of the Idea of Religion.' The whole tendency of that article was to deprive the idea of Religion, as ordinarily interpreted, of any substantive value: for Forberg declared it to be at least uncertain whether there existed a God or no: and Fichte, as a consequence of his participation in the article, suffered for many years under the imputation of an atheist. It is accordingly quite clear that the meaning of Fichte in the essay is not that the existence of the Moral Order implies the existence of God as its cause: but rather that the Moral Order *is* God, and that we mean nothing else by the conception of God. Ethics lead us, indeed, to an Universal, but that universal is not to be hypostatised in any anthropomorphistic fashion, but must be regarded

[1] Fichte: Ueber dem Grund unseres Glaubens an eine göttliche Weltregierung. 'Philosoph. Journal.' 1798.

as an abstract logical or metaphysical principle, which has also its concrete exemplifications. "The living and operative moral order is itself God: we need no other God, and can comprehend no other."—"No one who reflects a moment, and honestly avows the result of his reflection, can remain in doubt that the conception of God as *a particular substance* is impossible and contradictory; and it is right candidly to say this, and to silence the prating of the schools, in order that the true religion, which consists in joyously doing right, may come to honour."

However elevating such a conception, the Absolute, envisaged as moral order, has its defenceless side. It is no argument against it to say that many nations have had their religion and their views of God, and never attained to the conception of a moral order, because in this reference we are not speaking of men's conscious acceptation of the principle, but rather of the implicit necessity of the principle in order to explain the phenomena of ethics. But the position itself is peculiarly exposed to attack from the Pessimistic analysis of life. If it were provable or proved that life exhibits an order indeed, but not a moral order, then the ground is cut away from our feet. It is the effort of Schopenhauer and von Hartmann to exhibit the world as the theatre of the activity of a Will, which is non-moral; in Schopenhauer's theory the Will is a blind, enormous agency, ceaselessly rushing into life, and by the energy of its volition, causing unspeakable misery; in von Hartmann's view, the Will is united with Idea, but the Idea is not anything more than the affirmation that the Will knows what it is doing, and has, in the present world, no authority over the unceasing urgency of the Will. In either case, Moral Order in Fichte's sense there is none. The Absolute, to which we rose through the idea of ethical obligation, has crumbled away, or else is replaced by the savage and terrible conception of an Absolute, which is irrational.

From such attempted reconstruction, Fichte passed in his 'Sun-clear Exposition,' and his 'Way to the Blessed Life,'[1] to a more excellent method. Instead of God as the equivalent of the Moral Order, we pass to the conception of God as the necessary foundation of all Knowledge and Existence. Especially in the last of these two treatises, are found the culminating point of the Fichtean speculation and the real importance of a thinker, who has perhaps been too hastily accused of Subjective Idealism, and whose fame has been somewhat unfairly obscured by the reputation of the Hegelian System. In the 'Way to the Blessed Life,' the outlines of an Absolute Idealism are traced with a fervour of religious emotion which has in some measure eclipsed the real philosophical value. Here, if anywhere in Fichte, the reconstruction is complete and final. Only when it is maintained that the individual, however real (and every infraction of that reality is a sin against ourselves), is necessarily dependent on the Universal, can the adequate solution of the moral problem be gained; for morality has a double face,—on the one side it is the duty of *the individual*, on the other it is the evolution of *the Absolute Duty*.

[1] 'Sonnenklarer Bericht an das grössere Publicum über das eigentliche Wesen der neuesten Philosophie' (1801); 'Anweisung zum seligen Leben' (1806).

There is no particular mysticism in such a conception; it is only the imperfect expression of it in language which can justly incur such a charge. It is, for instance, clear enough that for me, as an individual, no act which I deem it right to do, can gain the necessary validity of a Duty, unless there be something higher than my own reason to fix the absolute standard. In ordinary practice we shrink from justifying our actions except in reference to some higher judgment. We appeal to the verdict of a public opinion, or to the common principles and usages of our nation, or to a vast body of antecedent authority. By a closer analysis of our ethical ideas, we give up each of these canons and standards, because they are arbitrary in the first place, and themselves need justification, and because, in the second place, we seem to find within ourselves a deeper ground of Reason. But if we try to envisage this as our own reason, the effort fails. We make the distinction between our everyday rationality, and the better Reason within us, and it is to the latter that we have recourse as ultimate source of ethical judgment. This 'better Reason within us' is, if we examine it, *not* individual, for we appeal to it with confidence as that which unites us and other individuals, as a common fund of ethical principles. If it be not individual, it must be universal, and the analysis by perfectly legitimate steps of logic has led us to the recognition of a Moral Universal, as underlying and explaining our ordinary ethical judgments.

The steps in the analysis of knowledge are in complete parallelism with those in the analysis of ethical judgments. Here, again, the individual intellectuality needs the support of an universal intellectuality, in order that the progress and validity of knowledge may be comprehensible. The common consciousness of mankind recognizes a great outside Kosmos, the gradual communion with which enables knowledge to advance. We learn by getting closer to this external world, by subordinating ourselves in patient industry to the incoming of the messages of Nature. Then ensues the fatal scepticism involved in the discovery that such a patient and submissive attitude is impossible. We are always reacting on our environment: we know, by sowing ourselves and our own modes of cognition broadcast over the field of our study. Thus knowledge is our own creation, and not the pale reflex of the objective reality. Is it, however, the creation of the individual mind? Is Nature made by ourselves? Is the world born again at the birth of every consciousness? Such a doctrine of subjective individualism is as impossible in knowledge as we have found it to be in morality. There must be some Absolute to which all individual consciousnesses are commonly related, so that my world is also yours, and our world the common property of all thinking intelligences. If my knowledge grows, and advances on parallel lines with that of others, no explanation of such a fact is possible except that which acknowledges an Absolute. The spider-like propensity of evolving everything from oneself died with the death of its ablest exponent, Christian Wolff. In its room there comes the conception of an Universal of Thought and Life—not alien from us and remote, like the Nature of the Materialists, but instinct with a spirit like our own spirit, though vaster, grander, and eternal. By the gradual communication of its nature to ours are the narrow limits of our knowledge widened, and the ideal of a perfect knowledge dawns for us, because that on which we depend is already perfect. Call it God, or the Universal, or the Idea, it matters not: once let it become realized by us, and we have shuffled off the mortal coil, and already breathe the larger air.

I am aware that such a conception appears to many minds too unreal and shadowy to be seriously entertained; I am also aware that the real difficulty begins with its application to the concrete development of thought. In Fichte himself we have in the *Wissenschaftslehre* all the paraphernalia of exposition, whereby the Ego posits in distinction from itself a non-Ego, theoretically positing the Ego as determined by the non-Ego, and practically positing the non-Ego as determined by the Ego. But I am not here concerned with the details—which probably every metaphysician would draw out differently—but with the general principle. Fichte is doubtless open to criticism: especially in the way in which he envisages that Absolute, to which so tardily he had arrived, for he is inclined to regard it rather as an empty abstraction, figuring at the beginning of the process, than as the ideal goal of development, full of concrete contents. But, however taken, and with whatever stumbling effort, the step had been made from subjective to objective and absolute Idealism, and thereby Fichte had vindicated his kinship with the progressive advance of thought. For as Goethe says,[1] " All eras in a state of decline and dissolution are subjective:

[1] Eckermann's *Conversations of Goethe*, vol. i. p. 416.

on the other hand, all progressive eras have an objective tendency." The time had come when the more worthless elements in the Kantian critiques were to be abandoned, and those which had an eternal value (the categorical imperative of Duty and the synthetic unity of apperception) were to be taken up, assimilated and transcended in the metaphysics of the Future.

§ 2. SCHELLING AND HEGEL.

THE further development of Idealistic Philosophy is concentrated in the two names of Schelling and Hegel. It is not, however, possible within short limits to define in any adequate way the essential characteristics of their advance upon Fichte and Kant. All that can be attempted here is the briefest sketch of the difference in metaphysical problems which was caused by the two systems respectively of Objective Idealism and Absolute Idealism. The obvious task which devolved upon a successor to Fichte was the maturer criticism of the Absolute,—how much it meant and what it entailed. From the strictly ethical standpoint it makes all the difference whether that Absolute which all systems of rationalistic morals must ultimately accept as their starting-point be interpreted as an empty abstraction or an ideal full of concrete contents. The shortest description of the work of Schelling and Hegel respectively is that the first attempted to find room within the Absolute for a philosophy of nature; while the second, recasting the conception of the Absolute, found its best and amplest interpretation in the evolution of history.

Schelling is perhaps not so much a philosophic as

a literary genius. Possessed of a style which is incomparably superior to that either of Kant, or Fichte, or Hegel, he is in his intellectual development at the mercy of every fresh philosophical movement which temporarily arrests his attention. In his speculative creed he is a very Proteus of changing dogmas. He begins with Fichte, to whom in rapid succession come Spinoza, Leibnitz, and Jacob Böhm, and his final issue is in the direction of a vague and nebulous mysticism. All his studies are done before the public,—a fact which makes him interesting perhaps as a man, but proves that he failed to be the systematic metaphysician which it was Hegel's ambition to become. For Hegel was, on the contrary, possessed, to adopt his own words, 'with the labour of the notion.' In various fields of study, especially the department of religious history, he tested the value of his dialectical method before he made it the corner-stone of his system. The result is, that though he began to study Kant after Schelling was already famous, his *Phenomenology of the Spirit* marks a decisive departure from the position of his predecessor, and contains fully formed that doctrine of the developing idea which critics have agreed to call Absolute Idealism.

Multiform as the phases are of Schelling's philosophic creed, for us their importance is concentrated in the systems known as Nature-Philosophy and the Philosophy of Ideality.[1] Despite such universal touches as Fichte was able to give to his principle of the Ego, it remained true that the principle itself

[1] Cf. 'Vom Ich als Princip der Philosophie' (1795), 'Natur philosophie' (1799), and 'Identitätsphilosophie' (circ. 1802).

was too subjective, too narrowly idealistic; for in any scheme which strives to interpret the reality, not only of what we are, but of what we know, nature will not be dismissed as simply non-Ego. It is not enough that it should be treated as that which in some way starts in opposition to the Ego, and thereby excites its activity. We desire to have it proved to us that that which is the subject matter of science and the world of knowable things possesses an existence of its own, if not wholly independent and original, at all events endowed with a relative independence and originality. To make a philosophy of nature was the most original and the best work of Schelling, for the nature which seemed to Fichte to stand in some purely negative fashion over against the omnipresence of the Ego, is, as he himself found, not only necessary to knowledge, but necessary also to morality. It was the field of moral exercise, that which brought the volitional freedom of the subject into direct contact with those various obstacles, to surmount which in turn was the goal of the ethical career. If the universal could not contain within itself this objective element it had only a partial vitality and a reality which was not commensurate with the problems to be explained. Nature-philosophy hence becomes Schelling's great achievement, especially as the Nature which he expounds is described as the visible analogon of the Spirit.

The next step is an obvious and a necessary one. If both Ego and non-Ego form two corresponding realities, what is to be the nature of that Absolute which is to comprehend and combine them? If it is in any sense to form the meeting-point between the two opposed sections, it must be greater than either: it must transcend and resolve them into a higher unity. But from that point of view the two complementary sections must be partial, limited, and therefore unreal. If such an alternative be accepted we are not far from the position of Spinoza. The other alternative is to envisage the Absolute not so much as the higher reality, but rather as the indifference-point between objective and subjective—a purely negative description, but one which seems alone to meet the conditions of the enquiry. Thus we get the Identity-philosophy, where Schelling, led seemingly by the pressure of his own logic, can find no other definition of the Absolute, but one which reveals it in its blank emptiness, or as Hegel wittily puts it, as the night in which all cows are black. For if the Universal on which life and thought and morality depend, be not full-crammed with contents, more bountifully rich and more absolutely real than all we know or do, it is that worst form of philosophic abstraction of which Plato's 'idea of the good' is the most notable example—an ideal which is vacant, a goal in which there is nothing to aim at, an empty orb which contains neither light nor heat. Moreover, the organ whereby the Absolute is apprehended, is not ratiocinative construction, but a sort of intellectual intuition, which Kant declared to be impossible, and which tends to become the denial of all philosophical method whatsoever.

The difference between Hegel and Schelling is primarily a difference in character. The brilliant Schelling, who was wont to signalize each new departure in philosophical study by a new volume, in which consistency with the old opinions was not sought for so much as artistic elaboration of the newly-found system, contrasts in every way with the patient laboriousness of a man like Hegel, who attempts to complete his philosophy after years of study 'in a single piece,' and whose sentences are wrung from him by intense and concentrated travail of the spirit. It is like the difference which separates Butler from Berkeley, or to use a more notable and a more customary comparison, which divides a Plato from an Aristotle. Hegel himself was quite conscious of the contrast between himself and his predecessor, and in the Introduction to his *Phenomenology* (1807) he criticises the Identity-philosophy in a series of weighty and significant illustrations. For it is one thing to make all knowledge and morality depend on an absolute: it is another thing to show throughout the details of an elaborate system the character of such dependence. It suited perhaps the artistic temperament of Schelling to believe in an intellectual intuition; it was left to a later thinker to exhibit all that 'labour of the notion' by which alone the universal could be established. Hence possibly some of the bitterness which certain critics have discovered in Hegel's references to preceding thought. They appear to indicate, not a pent-up indignation, but rather an essential difference of temperament such as made Aristotle an admirable critic except when he was criticising Plato.

The change in the respective standpoints can be summarized under three heads. Schelling established a sort of equipollence between nature and spirit—a balance of antithetical departments, which he sought, with however little success, to resolve into the blank indifference of the universal. But Hegel's idealism is not of this pattern. To him spirit is out of all proportion to nature, or as he himself expresses it, it 'overlaps every way.' Thus a return is made to the original standpoint of Fichte—so far at least as Fichte's relation to Schelling is concerned. It is significant from this point of view to find that a philosopher like von Hartmann, who is professedly concerned with the introduction of materialism into philosophy, proclaims himself on the side of Schelling rather than on that of Hegel. The followers too of Schelling had carried out his nature-philosophy to the utmost verge of fanciful analogy. Even in Schelling's own case, as Hegel himself remarks, "the parallelism between subjectivity and objectivity worked out to such instructive lengths as 'Understanding is electricity,' or 'The animal is nitrogen,' is as unbearable as the repetition of a conjurer's trick when once the secret is learned."[1]

Hegel's dialectical method is a second point of decisive importance. Just as Fichte spoke of thesis, antithesis, and synthesis, so Hegel believed that the universal progress of all rational thought lay through position, negation, and resolution into a higher unity. Begin with any notion you please and it will be found by no means to stand alone, but will carry with it its own negation. Positive thus being contrasted with negative, and negative with positive, we move to a higher plane of thought where both are seen to be partial abstractions, issuing from the more exalted

[1] Hegel, *Phaenomenologie*, Vorrede. Werke, II.; and Seth, *From Kant to Hegel*, p. 69.

standpoint in a truth which embraces all lower departments. Even in Kant's series of categories, some hint is found of this dialectical movement. But he seems to have stumbled upon it by accident without connecting it with the other parts of his system. The highest exemplification of such a triple movement is to be found in the relation in which the science of Logic stands to the doctrine of Nature, and both are related to the philosophy of spirit. For the Absolute is firstly pure immaterial thought; then it is externalized or alienated into the infinite atomism of time and space; while in the third place it returns again from such temporary exile, resolving the externalization into a higher thought, which is now conscious of itself as Absolute Spirit. Such evolution of the notion is both necessary and spontaneous. That A carries with it, as it were in its own bosom, not A, in order that it may develop into a higher A, is a capital doctrine of Hegelianism; and he, to whose intelligence such evolution does not commend itself as indubitably necessary and spontaneous, is stumbling on the very threshold of the Hegelian Creed.

But from a historical point of view, as well as from an ethical platform, the value of Hegel's advance is measured by the fuller connotation given to the Absolute. In the philosophy of earlier stages, where any distinction was drawn between the seeming and the real, between the sphere of sense and that of reason, between the phenomenal and the noumenal, it always seemed as if the first department, which was theoretically deficient in value and reality, was nevertheless the one most full of vitality and important contents. The Absolute, the *Ding-an-sich*, the universal, which was held to be the sole foundation of life and truth, was exactly that which was most shadowy, unsubstantial, and meaningless. And naturally so, for when we try to postulate something to serve as the timeless *prius* of the world, such a conception eludes our grasp by its very denial of all the attributes which convey any meaning to us. Hegel transformed the notion of the Absolute. It is not *some one thing*, vaguely defined on the borderland of dreams, but it is the whole rich contents of the world which is slowly developing before our eyes. It is development, evolution, growth, progress: it is the process by which pure thought externalizes itself in nature, and wins its way back again to self-conscious spirit; it is the world's history in all its departments, fulfilling the divine order of things. To us, who live in a world of Time, such an absolute is only discovered piecemeal, here a little, there a little, line upon line, precept upon precept; but from the side of the universal, viewed 'sub specie æternitatis,' it is one completed kosmos, which ever was from the beginning.

It is easy to see how such a conception, immeasurably superior to the 'indifference-point' of Schelling, enlarges the ground-plan of history. Hegel himself worked it out in many partial studies long before he formulated it in the Phenomenology, and set the conclusions of a collective history in the framework of a vast metaphysical scheme. In Switzerland and in Frankfort, it was religion and history which he perused rather than philosophy: and manuscripts of a *Life of Christ* and a *Critique of Positive Religion* attest his belief that the religious consciousness was "the bearer of all human culture." But in Ethics also, such a conception serves at once to raise a system of bare formalism into a living and articulated development of the moral consciousness. That Ethics is not completed at a stroke, nor yet fallen like the image of Diana straight from heaven, but slowly worked out by all those in whom Reason fulfils the commands of an ideal order—such is the magnificent postulate which Hegelianism involves. The task of Constructive Ethics is to go through the step-by-step process of this development, while yet it acknowledges the Absolute, as in itself total and complete. Thus God is at once beginning and end, cause of the Moral order, and fulfiller of the moral Ideal, the author and finisher of our ethical faith.

CHAPTER III.

Scientific Theories.

[Herbert Spencer: 'Data of Ethics.'—Leslie Stephen: 'Science of Ethics.'—(Henry Sidgwick: 'Methods of Ethics.'—W. K. Clifford: 'Lectures and Essays.'—Fred. Pollock: 'Essays in Jurisprudence and Ethics.']

It is an old criticism on moral philosophy that it is unprogressive. In one sense, indeed, it appears eternally so; for the successive works on ethical questions which are produced in our own country leave the reader—generally in the last chapter—face to face with the old insoluble problems. That which has been, that it is which shall be; the stringency and obligation of duty, the character of the moral intuition, the necessity for man to be moral, conscience, free-will, responsibility, remorse—the familiar facts appear once more, painted once again in their old colours, or else temporarily disguised in make-shifts, through the rents of which the antique lineaments are yet visible. Unprogressive indeed is moral philosophy in this sense; for the querulous demand for something new is itself illegitimate. There is no new light, no new revelation, unless the lines of humanity are to run in different channels. A critical and unbelieving generation seeketh for a sign, and there shall be no sign given to it, save that which was given to Socrates and Buddha and Christ. But if, abandoning the idle quest for a novel morality, we look at the gradual development of the moral code, and the extent and variety of the relations to which morality is applied, we are struck with the immensity of the progress of ethics. For, in truth, there is nothing so sensitively receptive as moral philosophy, nothing which is so quick at assimilating and adapting new material. Every fresh acquisition in science—science physical, biological, and psychological—has left its mark, for good and for evil, on ethical speculation. The readiest question which men ask in the presence of some new conception is—What is its bearing on conduct; what is its value for the illustration of human duty? And the first answer, often misconceived and generally superficial, is taken as condemnation or confirmation of the novel truth. From this point of view, the progress of ethics has run parallel with the progress in scientific knowledge, and the one set of doctrines has its natural and inevitable consequence in the other.

It is necessary to bear in mind the striking vicissitudes of moral philosophy, in order to understand the present aspect of ethics in England. Already Mill's Utilitarianism has grown 'somewhat musty,' and the 'greatest happiness' principle possesses an almost archaic sound. Mr. Herbert Spencer's 'Data of Ethics,' and Mr. Leslie Stephen's 'Science of Ethics'—to take two prominent examples from contemporary literature —move on newer ground. Nothing could be more significant, from this point of view, than Mr. Spencer's acute criticism of the 'greatest happiness' principle,[1] which, in the first half of this century, was accepted

[1] Referred to before, p. 159.

as the greatest discovery of English ethics. It needed only one more step to have conducted Mr. Spencer out of the ranks of 'universalistic hedonists' altogether. If he had examined the psychological basis on which the theory rests, he might have discovered that inasmuch as the self of man is not exhausted by the enumeration of any or all of its sentient states, it is for ever impossible to make a sentient satisfaction the end of life. The pleasure is attained, the happiness secured, but yet the man is not satisfied. Why is this? Because the sequent feelings and emotions of man form a series which cannot be summed. The self, which is something more than the series of its feelings, vindicates its own reality by a divine dissatisfaction, after every successive pleasure or happiness is secured. For the only ends of a rational human life must be fixed by the reason, and therefore moral aims can never rest on the foundation of sense or feeling.

From such views as these, however, Mr. Spencer is debarred not by such psychology as that which forms the basis of most utilitarian and hedonistic schemes, but by his scientific presuppositions. It is time to return from merely collateral considerations to the main ideas which serve to distinguish the ethics of our own day from those which were formulated in the early part of our century and in preceding times. What, in point of fact, are the greatest scientific ideas of our age? For, in accordance with the principle with which we started, we are likely to find that they cast their shadow on ethical speculations. Can we point to any thoughts sufficiently far-reaching and commanding to be able to dominate man's ordinary notions and practical affairs; to intrude their influence in every contemporary speculation; to be, as we say, "in men's mouths and in the air?" There are at least two which have attained sufficient importance to be mentioned in this reference—the great scientific law of Evolution by survival of the fittest, and the formation of the science of Sociology or Social Physics, with all the historic and philosophic postulates which it presupposes. And it is curious to observe that while Mr. Spencer's 'Data of Ethics' is dominated, as we should expect from the author of *The Synthetic Philosophy*, by the first conception, the influence of the second, though of course to be traced in Mr. Spencer's work, is specially observable in Mr. Leslie Stephen's 'Science of Ethics.' Mr. Spencer makes moral philosophy a department of biology: Mr. Stephen makes it a department of sociology. Both would be equally firm in declaring that no intrinsic difference separated ethics from all other branches of science. Both would deprecate with equal earnestness the introduction into the subject of any *à priori* ideas of reason or metaphysical notions of the unique character of self-consciousness.

In March 1860, a Titanic scheme was propounded of works to be issued in periodical parts by Mr. Herbert Spencer. The series was to begin with 'First Principles,' with its two divisions of the unknowable and the knowable, to proceed to the 'Principles of Biology' in two volumes, the 'Principles of Psychology' also in two volumes, and the 'Principles of Sociology' in three volumes, and to end with the two volumes of the 'Principles of Morality.' Of this enormous programme, the greater portion is now completed; the so-called 'Data of Ethics' standing as a first instalment of the 'Principles of Morality.' The whole of this scheme is intended as an exhibition of one vast conception, which serves as a focus in which are gathered and concentrated all the rays of thought in different departments. This conception is the great modern scientific idea of Evolution. According to Professor Huxley, the only complete and methodical exposition of the theory of evolution is to be found in Herbert Spencer's *System of Philosophy*.

What is the law of evolution? It is necessary to get some general expression or definition of it before we observe its special application to the problems of ethics. The fundamental principle is the persistence of energy. Natural objects change, adopt new forms, transform themselves, die out—in a word, develop, simply for the reason that energy in nature never dies. The formula of the law runs thus: "Progress consists in the passage from a homogeneous to a heterogeneous structure." The law of all progress is one and the same—the evolution of the simple into the complex by successive differentiations. If we ask why progress should run always in this direction—from the homogeneous to the heterogeneous—the reason is twofold. In the first place, if a body is in a homogeneous condition it is unstable; "homogeneity is a condition of unstable equilibrium;" or, in more simple language, a state of uniformity is one which cannot be maintained. A familiar illustration is furnished by the scales. "If they be accurately made, and not clogged by dirt or rust, it is impossible to keep a pair of scales equally balanced. Eventually one scale will descend and the other ascend; they will assume a heterogeneous relation."

Or, again, "Take a piece of red hot matter, and, however evenly heated it may at first be, it will quickly cease to be so; the exterior, cooling faster than the interior, will become different in temperature from it; the lapse into heterogeneity of temperature so obvious in this extreme case, takes place more or less in all cases."[1] The second reason for this direction of progress is, that every active force produces more than one change; every cause produces more than a single effect. The multiplicity of resultant effects naturally converts homogeneity into heterogeneity. If a body is shattered by violent collision, besides the change of the homogeneous mass into a heterogeneous mass of scattered fragments, there is a change of the homogeneous momentum into a group of momenta heterogeneous in both amounts and directions. "Of the sun's rays issuing on every side, some few strike the moon; these being reflected at all angles from the moon's surface, some few of them strike the earth. By a like process, the few which reach the earth are again diffused through surrounding space; on each occasion such portions of the rays as are absorbed instead of reflected, undergo refractions that equally destroy their parallelism." For these two reasons—that homogeneity is a condition of unstable equilibrium, and that every active force produces several changes—the law of evolution may be defined as a process, during which "an indefinite incoherent homogeneity is transformed into a definite coherent heterogeneity."

[1] H. Spencer, 'First Principles,' p. 402; chaps. xii.—xviii. of Part II. should also be consulted. In more popular form, cf. 'Essays' (London, 1861).

How may the action of this law be illustrated? In many spheres—in the world's growth, in the growth of individual organisms, in the growth of social organism, in the genesis of science, in psychology. For instance, in the beginning (so geologists tell us) our globe was a mass of matter in a state of fusion, and was, therefore, of homogeneous structure, and of tolerably homogeneous temperature. Then came the successive changes into heterogeneity, into mountains, continents, seas, igneous rocks, sedimentary strata, metallic veins. The law holds good equally of organisms. Fishes are the most homogeneous in their structure, and are one of the earliest productions on the globe. Reptiles come later, and are more heterogeneous. Mammals and birds, which are produced later, are still more heterogeneous. Man is the most heterogeneous of all. Or, once more, let us limit ourselves to the case of man alone. The multiplication of races, and the splitting up of races amongst themselves, have made the species much more heterogeneous. The Papuan has very small legs, resembling in this the quadrumanous kind; while in the case of the European, whose legs are longer and more massive, there is more heterogeneity between the upper and lower limbs. Another example of the progress in heterogeneity is furnished by the subdivisions of the Saxon race itself, which has within a few generations developed into the Anglo-American variety, and the Anglo-Australian variety. Perhaps, however, a still clearer example of the operation of the law can be found in the development of the social organism. A society of savages is an aggregate of individuals, who all hunt, fish, go to war, and work; or in other words, it is homogeneous, every individual executing the same functions. Then comes a differentiation between the governing and the governed, while in the governing power are still united religious and executive functions. Other differentiations lead to our present conditions of heterogeneity; Church gradually dividing itself from State, and the actual political organization consisting of numerous subdivisions in justice and finance, in executive and deliberative powers.

But how can such a purely natural law of progress be applied to the solution of moral questions? The answer can be partly seen in the difference which Mr. Spencer draws between the scientific ethics and the system which in historical order was its immediate predecessor, Utilitarianism. Both have at least one point in common. If the question be raised as to the end of life, both agree in calling it happiness. "No school," says Mr. Spencer,[1] "can avoid taking for the ultimate moral aim a desirable state of feeling called by whatever name—gratification, enjoyment, happiness. Pleasure somewhere, at some time, to some being or beings, is an inexpugnable element of the conception. It is as much a necessary form of moral intuition as space is a necessary form of intellectual intuition."

It is true that Mr. Spencer proves elsewhere that space is not an intuition, so far as the race is concerned, but an experimental discovery; and if we care to press the analogy here drawn we might assert that pleasure too was an experimental discovery—a thesis which would effectually disprove the view that

[1] 'Data of Ethics,' p. 46.

the primary object of activity was pleasure. But we are not here concerned with captious and minute polemics, and the important point is to discover wherein utilitarianism is by the later system proved defective. The defect is this—that though it recognizes the fact that some lines of action conduce to happiness, it does not determine how and why they do so. "The view for which I contend is that morality properly so called—the science of right conduct—has for its object to determine how and why certain modes of conduct are detrimental and certain other modes beneficial. These good and bad results cannot be accidental, but must be necessary consequences of the constitution of things; and I conceive it to be the business of a moral science to deduce *from the laws of life and the conditions of existence* what kinds of action necessarily tends to produce happiness, and what kinds to produce unhappiness. Having done this, its deductions are to be recognized as laws of conduct, and are to be conformed to irrespective of a direct estimation of happiness and misery."[1] Mr. Spencer's ethics, then, propose to put Utilitarianism on a thoroughly scientific basis, to deduce morality from the larger laws of life. This is Rational Utilitarianism.

The result may be seen in a much more effective analysis of 'conscience' (p. 123). Mr. Mill, in his *Utilitarianism*, traces the growth of conscience from successive accretions of sentiment derived from all sorts of sources, round one or two primary impulses, mostly selfish in their character. But the process is limited to the individual's life-time, and the solution

[1] 'Data of Ethics,' p. 57.

in consequence always appears paradoxically inadequate to the problem to be solved. The latest scientific schools have the incomparable advantage of the conception of time, to eke out the possible deficiencies of the analysis. If what we now know as conscience has been slowly developing throughout the history of the human race, and of animate life, the indefinite number of unrecorded years appears somehow to answer to the conditions of the problem. For to us, at all events, born in a modern age, conscience is an *a priori*, an intuitive fact, however much it may be proved to be *a posteriori* from the point of view of racial experience.

> ἅπανθ' ὁ μακρὸς κἀνἀρίθμητος χρόνος
> φύει τ' ἄδηλα καὶ φανέντα κρύπτεται,
> κοὐκ ἔστ' ἄελπτον οὐδέν.[1]

From such a standpoint, ethics can only be the science of conduct—conduct as depending on conditions of life, physical, biological and physiological. Ethical conduct is a part of conduct at large, its chief characteristic being that conduct which has a definite purpose. And conduct can only be understood by regarding the evolution of conduct. How, then, does conduct evolve? It passes through three stages. In the first of these we have such continuous adjustment of acts to ends as serves to prolong and intensify individual life. In the second, we have such acts as prolong and intensify the life of the species, *i. e.* race-maintaining conduct, not only self-maintaining conduct. In the third, we have such acts as not only avoid giving injury to others, but are designed to

[1] Soph: Ajax, 646-8.

help and promote the interests of others. Therefore perfectly ethical conduct involves peace and industrial co-operation. "Conduct gains ethical sanction in proportion as the activities, becoming less and less militant and more and more industrial, are such as do not necessitate mutual injury or hindrance, but consist with, and are furthered by, co-operation and mutual aid."[1]

The question, however, still remains—how is ethical conduct to be exhibited as conforming to the general law of evolution? Inasmuch as ethics is a part of general science, it must have data derived from the various departments of science. It must have (*a.*) physical data; (*b.*) biological data; (*c.*) psychological data; (*d.*) sociological data.

(*a.*) What is the physical aspect of ethics? Adopting a physical standpoint, and viewing conduct objectively as a series of acts, it will be found that an advance in rectitude of conduct means an increase in coherency, an increase in definiteness, an increase in heterogeneity. That is to say, a man is more moral in proportion as he co-ordinates his actions more effectually towards definite ends, and has many interests and occupations. A man is thus less moral as a bachelor than when he has marital, conjugal, and paternal duties ('the addition of family relations necessarily renders the actions of the man who fulfils the duties of husband and parent more heterogeneous than those of the man who has no such duties to fulfil,' p. 70). Lastly, his conduct is better when it tends to a "moving equilibrium between external and internal forces, between waste and corresponding

[1] 'Data of Ethics,' p. 20.

repair." So that the conclusion from such a point of view would hardly be caricatured by the assertion that a man is more moral in proportion as he is longer lived.[1]

(*b.*) What is the biological aspect of ethics? Strictly speaking, it is this. A man must develop all his functions and maintain a balance of functions. Now it is found that pleasure is the concomitant of a normal function, pain the concomitant of a deranged function. Therefore a man must follow the lead of his pleasures, accepting these without hesitation as his guides, inasmuch as the evolution of organic life has proceeded on the lines of helpful pleasures and harmful pains. But this Mr. Spencer acknowledges to be an ideal. Men are imperfectly adapted to their social environment, and their social environment is imperfectly adapted to them. When, however, humanity has ultimately provided itself with a completely adjusted social state, it will be found "that actions are only right when they are immediately pleasurable; and that painfulness is the concomitant of actions which are wrong" (p. 99).

(*c.*) What is the psychological aspect of ethics? This at once leads us to the development of the moral consciousness, the genesis of the idea of duty. There are two elements in the idea of duty, of which the first is authoritativeness, and the second coerciveness, and the problem is to see how these are respectively developed. Taking as our definition of psychological life the adaptation of certain correlated internal states to certain correlated external states, acts, or events, it is easy to see that as mind evolves the adaptation will grow more complex on both sides. The feelings on

[1] Cf. pp. 73, 74.

the one side will grow less immediate, more representative, more complex, in order to suit chains of acts and events less immediate, more complex, more future. In the average of cases the result is that ultimate satisfactions are preferred to more immediate ones, and a notion of greater authoritativeness is attributed to them. Now it is of the very essence of the idea of duty that it should consist in the control of present feelings by future ones ; and because ultimate consequences are preferred to immediate ones, the feelings connected with the ultimate become more authoritative than those connected with the immediate. 'Authoritativeness' is thus explained. But how does the sense of 'coerciveness' arise ? It arises simply through association with external positive sanctions. In the development of humanity, feelings and actions are controlled, first, through fear of the chieftain or king (political sanction) ; then through fear of the voice of public opinion (social sanction) ; then through fear of Divine punishment (theological sanction) ; only lastly does a man restrain and control his actions by regarding their intrinsic effects, and then he falls under the moral sanction. So that the sense of obligation is attached to the moral sanction only through association with positive external sanctions. Finally, however, as a man becomes really moral, he does and forbears simply out of regard for the intrinsic effects of his acts. Pleasures surround the right performance, and therefore the notion of duty as obligation disappears, because it becomes pleasant for him and natural to do right. "The sense of duty is transitory, and will diminish as fast as moralisation increases" (p. 127).

(*d.*) What is the sociological aspect of ethics? The fact that man is a social being is so important a factor in the ethical problem, that 'the necessitated modifications of conduct have come to form a chief part of the mode of conduct.' From the sociological point of view ethics is nothing but a definite account of the forms of conduct that are fitted to the associated state. But it makes a great difference whether the state with which we are dealing is one of habitual or occasional war, or one of permanent and general peace. Yet, unfortunately, we are living in a state halfway between the two, having not fully abandoned the first, nor heartily espoused the second. Hence our perplexed and inconsistent morality, for we are forced to accept a virtual compromise between the moral code of enmity and the moral code of amity. If, however, we assume a social state, in which peaceful activities are undisturbed, the leading traits of a code under which complete living through voluntary co-operation is secured may be thus stated. "The fundamental requirement is that the life-sustaining actions of each shall severally bring him the amounts and kinds of advantage naturally achieved by them; and this implies, firstly, that he shall suffer no direct aggressions on his person or property, and secondly, that he shall suffer no indirect aggressions by breach of contract. Observance of these negative conditions to voluntary co-operation having facilitated life to the greatest extent by exchange of services under agreement, life is to be further facilitated by exchange of services beyond agreement; the highest life being reached only when, besides helping to complete one another's lives by specified reciprocities of aid, men otherwise help to complete one another's lives" (p. 149).

Such are, in main outlines, the ethics of evolution, which it appeared necessary to expound somewhat fully, if only that it might be understood how clearly it is the lineal descendant of Utilitarianism, and yet how ruthlessly it lays hands on its natural parent. For the sequence of empirical ethics has, in England, run through three stages; first, egoism, pure and simple, or, as it is called, hedonism; then utilitarianism; and, finally, what the author calls rational utilitarianism, or as it is better called—evolutional ethics. All three systems alike have accepted pleasure or happiness as the only test of moral action: all are exposed to the difficulties of the hedonistic calculus—the arduous enumeration of real pleasures. All have to accept, with the best grace they can, the hedonistic paradox that to gain happiness—the sole end of life—the best way is not to aim at it, but something else, and all must explain how it comes that happiness, which is so clearly the gift of expansive, imaginative natures, can be possibly acquired by logical, calculative, ratiocinative natures. But just as the psychology of Spencer and Lewes has taken the place of the individualistic psychology of Locke and Hume and Mill, with its larger notions of race-experience, and its wider faith in time, so, too, has the ethics of evolution in reality destroyed the narrow Utilitarianism of Bentham and Austin and James Mill, with its fuller views of the development of conduct and the genesis of the moral consciousness.

As to Mr. Spencer's scheme, however, two remarks may for the present suffice. In the first place, he, like the other scientists, passes over the chasm between conscious life and unconscious life, as though, in reality, no chasm existed. Yet, perhaps, the chasm is deeper, or, at all events, more deeply felt, in ethics than in biological and psychological science. All conduct, he says, is marked by the adaptation of means to ends: the unconscious adaptation of the acts of a beaver or a dog is the same in kind as that of a man working for some moral end. To unsophisticated minds the difference is not only enormous but absolutely incommensurable. For a man who consciously adapts his acts and his circumstances to some far-off Divine event is in reality fighting with his environment, fighting with his physical frame, fighting against Nature. And is the moral life, then, a development of the natural? Does not the single word 'conscious' so transform the adaptation as to remove ethics from the sphere of 'natural' life altogether? In the second place, it must always be remembered that evolution, whether it explains cosmical and biological phenomena, or whether it penetrates the world of thought and of history, never explains the primal cause. It is concerned with sequence in the form of a series, without a beginning and without an end. On this point Mr. Spencer is very emphatic.[1] So that if any philosophical student refuses to acquiesce in such an indefinite phantasmagoria of effects, if he seeks to find—say in ethics—the underlying cause which explains the evolution of conscience and moral consciousness, the path is left clear for him, so far as Mr. Spencer knows or cares. Nor need he even feel

[1] Cf. *inter alia*, 'Essays,' Vol. I. p. 58 (second edition, 1868).

that he has lost Mr. Spencer's sympathy in such a quest. For when it comes to distinguishing himself from Auguste Comte he does not hesitate to say (as against the positivist formula) that "the idea of cause will govern at the end, as it has done at the beginning. *The idea of cause cannot be abolished except by the abolition of thought itself.*"[1] Even when Mr. Spencer is not in a polemical attitude, he would hardly care to abolish 'thought itself.'

It is because in the sequence of empirical ethics, only the decisive turning-points are important, that no mention has hitherto been made of Professor Henry Sidgwick's valuable book, *The Method of Ethics*. On other grounds it merits a most careful criticism, and affords a most instructive commentary on utilitarian ideas. Mr. Sidgwick's position in the utilitarian ranks is, indeed, in many respects remarkable. He has too clear and logical a mind not to see many of the difficulties of the so-called Universalistic Hedonism. He feels, for instance, much of the absurdity of the hedonistic paradox that we can only attain happiness on the express condition that we do not aim at it.[2] He has some doubts as to whether happiness is intrinsically and objectively desirable, out of relation to the consciousness which, in reality, gives it all its meaning;[3] and in some of his concluding pages he honestly confronts the fact that Utilitarianism can only with the greatest difficulty (and, perhaps, hardly even so with this limitation)

---

[1] Cf. Spencer's 'Reasons for Dissenting from the Philosophy of M. Comte;' third edition, 1871.

[2] 'Method of Ethics;' first edition, pp. 130—133.

[3] *Ibid.* pp. 371, 372.

provide any stringent and obligatory sanction of morality which shall be binding alike on all men.[1] For in many ways ethics cannot exist without the assumption of a moral order of the universe, an assumption which, of course, can never be empirically proved. When Professor Bain came to review Mr. Sidgwick's book in *Mind*, it was exactly this point which appeared to him such a stumbling-block, and so fatal an admission (as indeed it is) for empirical ethics. But when we seek to estimate Mr. Sidgwick's position in relation to the school to which he belongs, it is at once apparent that the development of thought runs through Bentham, J. S. Mill, and Herbert Spencer, and leaves Mr. Sidgwick's speculations on one side. For just the point which marks the decisive advance from Utilitarianism to scientific or evolutional ethics is not ignored but discarded by Mr. Sidgwick. To the question whether moral ideas are gradually formed by a long course of years, by experiences of utility made in successive generations, he returns a negative reply.[2] And yet this is the characteristic note of later or rational Utilitarianism. Mr. Spencer has accordingly many criticisms to offer on Mr. Sidgwick's opinions, as, for instance, in the chapter headed 'Criticisms and Explanations.'[3] So, too, Mr. Leslie Stephen, in the preface to his 'Science of Ethics,' declares that "he differs upon many points from Mr. Sidgwick, and especially upon the critical point of the relation of evolution to ethics."[4]

[1] 'Method of Ethics,' first edition, pp. 470—473.
[2] Cf. esp. pp. 429—435.   [3] 'Data of Ethics,' pp. 150—172.
[4] L. Stephen's 'Science of Ethics,' Preface, p. vi. A clear statement of Mr. Stephen's views on preceding Utilitarianism will be found in 'Science of Ethics,' pp. 353—359.

In the last of Mr. Spencer's views of ethics we trace the influence of a so-called sociological science. To illustrate the curious importance of such an idea in contemporary ethics, we have to turn to Mr. Leslie Stephen's *Science of Ethics*, a notable and significant contribution to the solution of contemporary problems. Mr. Stephen leaves us in no doubt as to the ethical school to which he belongs. "My ethical theory," he says in his preface, "when I first became the conscious proprietor of any theory at all, was that of the orthodox Utilitarians. At a later period my mind was stirred by the great impulse conveyed through Mr. Darwin's *Origin of Species*. So far as ethical problems were concerned, I at first regarded Mr. Darwin's principles rather as providing a new armoury wherewith to encounter certain plausible objections of the so-called Intrusionists (Mr. Stephen probably means "Intuitionists"), than as implying any reconstruction of the Utilitarian doctrine itself. Gradually, however, I came to think that a deeper change would be necessary, and I believe that this conviction came to me from a study of Mr. Herbert Spencer's works. . . . I differ, however," he proceeds a few pages further on, "from Mr. Spencer in various ways. Mr. Spencer has worked out an encyclopædic system, of which his ethical system is the crown and completion. I, on the contrary, have started from the old ethical theories, and am trying to bring them into harmony with the scientific principles which I take for granted."[1]

The characteristic doctrine of the *Science of Ethics*, is the use made of the conception of a

[1] 'Science of Ethics,' pp. v, vi, viii.

'social organism,' and the employment of an abstract entity called 'the social tissue.' The heritage of M. Auguste Comte to his successors was the doubtful advantage of having founded a science of sociology as the modern science next in order of complexity to biology. The implication was that just as biology dealt with the laws and vital functions of a given organism, so sociology must deal with the functions of what was really an organism, though of course of a somewhat different and special kind. Society was an organism exhibiting activities and possessing functions which could therefore be treated organically, however little these might be incorporated in, or proceeded from, a single frame. The interconnection, or 'radical consensus,' of the social organism is to M. Comte a 'masterthought' in philosophy. It is only in organic systems, as he says, that we must look for the fullest mutual connection; the idea becomes the basis of positive conceptions, and it becomes more marked, the more compound are the organisms and the more complex the phenomena in question. It must, therefore, be scientifically preponderant in social physics, or sociology, even more than in biology, where it is so decisively recognized by the best order of students.[1] Hence it is that we can properly speak of Social Statics, or theory of the spontaneous order of human society, and Social Dynamics, or theory of the natural progress of human society, together with the celebrated,' Loi des trois États,' the unfailing sequence of theological, metaphysical, and positive periods.

The 'positive conceptions' of which this idea has

[1] Cf. Miss Martineau's 'Abridgment of Comté,' Vol. II. p. 80.

proved the basis are indeed curious. It has been fertile, for instance, in psychology, and so has produced Mr. Lewes' 'general mind,' which transforms sensations into perceptions, and is the parent of necessities of thought. "The distinguishing character," says Mr. Lewes, "of human psychology, is that to the three great factors, organism, external medium, and heredity, it adds a fourth, namely, relation to a social medium, with its product the general mind."[1] And now Mr. Leslie Stephens finds it equally fertile in ethics. Its latest offspring is the 'social tissue' to which the creation of morality is expressly due, for "morality is the definition of some of the most important qualities of the social organism."[2] "The moral law defines a property of the social tissue."[3] In a similar fashion the late Professor Clifford traced all morality to what he termed the 'tribal self.' "The tribal self learns to approve certain expressions of tribal liking or disliking; the actions whose open approval is liked by the tribal self are called right actions, and those whose open disapproval is liked are called wrong actions. The corresponding characters are called good or bad, virtuous or vicious." Probably, however (though it is difficult to be certain what is the exact meaning of such purely logical abstractions), Mr. Clifford does not mean precisely the same thing by "tribal self" which Mr. Stephens means by "social tissue." For instance, he declares that "we must carefully dis-

---

[1] Mr. Lewes's 'Study of Psychology,' p. 139; cf. 159—162, 169, 170.
[2] 'Science of Ethics,' p. 148.   [3] *Ibid.*, p. 168.

tinguish the tribal self from society, or the common consciousness; it is something in the mind of each individual man which binds together his gregarious instincts."[1] Here, then, is another illustration of the progress in English philosophy from individualism to a species of universalism. In psychology there is the change from Hume and Mill to Spencer and Lewes, the general mind taking the place of the individual, and evolving by means of accumulated experiences the so-called forms of thought. In ethics there is a double change. First, the progress from individual hedonism or egoism to utilitarianism or universalistic hedonism; secondly, a change from the individual judgment of what is or is not useful to the judgment of the social organism, or social tissue. The latter is the interval which separates Mill and the utilitarianism of our youth from Mr. Stephen, Professor Clifford, and the evolutional ethics of contemporary thought.

But is society actually an organism? Or does the parallelism between a body politic and a body individual (between the big letters and the small of Plato's *Republic*) amount at most to an analogy, and an analogy which may conceivably be misleading? Mr. Stephen appears to have no doubt on the subject. "Society," he says, "in fact, is a structure which by its nature implies a certain fixity in the distributions and relations of classes. Each man is found with a certain part of *the joint framework*, which is made of flesh and blood instead of bricks and timber, *but which is not the less truly a persistent structure.*"

[1] 'Clifford's Essays,' Vol. II. pp. 112 and 116.

"The social body is no more liable to arbitrary changes than the individual body." "A full perception of the truth that society is not a mere aggregate but an organic growth, that it forms a whole, *the laws of whose growth can be studied apart from those of the individual atom,* supplies the most characteristic postulate of modern speculation."[1]

It is curious to note that what Mr. Stephen regards with so light a heart as 'a postulate' is considered as at least an open and arguable question by so modern a speculator as Mr. Herbert Spencer. In his 'Essays,' Vol. I. p. 390 (2nd Edition), and more fully in his 'Sociology,' Vol. I. part ii. chap. ii., he thinks it worth while to go carefully through the points of resemblance and difference. The resemblances are four in number. Both social organization and living organism commence as small aggregations, and insensibly augment in mass. Both assume in the course of their growth a continually increasing complexity of structure. In both the parts gradually acquire a mutual dependence; while finally in both the life and development of the whole body is far more prolonged than that of any of its component elements. But the differences are also four. Societies have no specific external forms. The social organism does not form a continuous mass like the living body. While the ultimate living elements of an individual organism are mostly fixed in their relative positions, those of the social organism are capable of moving from place to place. And lastly, in the body of an animal only, the nervous tissue is endowed with feeling, but in a society all the members are endowed with feeling. It is quite true that Mr.

[1] 'Science of Ethics,' p. 31.

Spencer substantially agrees with Mr. Stephen's cardinal proposition, but he is fonder of the word 'analogy' in dealing with this subject than the strong term 'postulate.' To most minds, of course, the relation between the society and the individual appears to have great illustrative value; but the cardinal difference that there is no social sensorium (*i. e.* that in the one, consciousness is concentrated in a small part of the aggregate, while in the other it is diffused throughout the aggregate), has at least one most important consequence, as Mr. Spencer himself allows. In an individual body, clearly, the welfare of the whole has a value perfectly independent of the welfare of the units. But the case is not the same with the social body. The welfare of the aggregate is not an end to be sought independently. The society exists for the sake of its members, while in a real organism the parts exist for the sake of the whole body. "It has ever to be remembered that great as may be the efforts made for the prosperity of the body politic, yet the claims of the body politic are nothing in themselves, and become something only in so far as they embody the claims of its component individuals."[1]

From social organism we proceed to 'social tissue,' which is declared to be the primary unit upon which the process of evolution hinges, and the direct agent, therefore, in the production of morality. What is this social tissue? It is by no means easy precisely to formulate the conception. It appears to be a better piece of nomenclature than social organism, which is a vague term, and does not imply the same

[1] Spencer's 'Sociology,' Vol. I. p. 480.

loose kind of unity, or rather community. "The limits of social tissue are fixed not by its internal constitutions, but by external circumstances. It, therefore, is not analogous to the higher organism which forms a whole, separated from all similar wholes, but to an organism of the lower type, which consists of mutually connected parts, spreading independently in dependence (*sic*) upon external conditions, and capable of indefinite extension, not of united growth. The unity which we attribute to it consists in this—that every individual is dependent upon his neighbours, and thus every modification in one part is capable of being propagated directly in every other part" (p. 126). "The tissue is built up of men, as the tissue of physiology is said to be built up of cells. Every society is composed of such tissue; and the social tissue can no more exist apart from such associations than the physiological tissue can exist apart from the organs of living animals" (p. 120).

The social tissue then appears to represent the general material or all-pervading substance (the ὕλη or ὑποκείμενον, as Aristotle might say), from which the subordinate associations are constructed, and the conditions of its vitality require to be considered independently. "The social evolution means the evolution of a strong social tissue; the best type is the type implied by the strongest tissue" (p. 136). However vague may be the exact nature of the social tissue, whether it be an important or valuable conception, or an ingenious but wholly mythical abstraction, it holds a most intimate relation to morality, according to Mr. Leslie Stephen. For some of the most important qualities of the social tissue come to be defined by morality. "The process by which society has been developed implies that the most important characteristics developed in the individual by the social pressure correspond to the conditions of existence of the society. The moral law defines some of the most important characteristics so developed, and is therefore a statement of part of the qualities in virtue of which the society is possible. It is not an exhaustive statement, for other qualities may be essential; nor an absolutely accurate statement, for societies exist in which the morality varies within wide limits. But so far as it goes it must be an approximate statement of part of the conditions."[1]

So that the moral is, after all, the useful; the immoral is the useless; though, indeed, the qualification ought to be added, useful or useless to the social tissue. Nor is the qualification unimportant, for many consequences are involved. In the first place, morality is not evolved conduct, as with Mr. Spencer, because the welfare or progress of the social organism is something different from the activity of the social organs. In some sense or other, morality always implies action for the good of others.[2] And, in the second place, virtuous action is not estimated solely by consequences, but in relation to character and motive, because the social evolution tends to educe the higher type which spontaneously and instinctively obeys the so-called moral law.[3] Moreover, the direct reference to the social organism is enough to change Utilitarianism into the ethics of Mr. Leslie Stephen.

[1] 'Science of Ethics,' p. 148. [2] Cf. p. 170.
[3] Cf. 'Science of Ethics,' pp. 276—278.

There is no part of the *Science of Ethics* which is more worth diligent perusal than that which deals with the relation of the new criterion to the utilitarian criterion. Mr. Stephen is not inclined to spare his predecessors in moral philosophy. " He (the utilitarian) can only make an outward show of morality, and run up an edifice which looks like the everlasting structure, but falls to pieces at the first touch. He may call his code moral, but in fact it is a code which has neither permanence, nor supremacy, nor uniformity, nor unconditional validity.[1] But is, then, the new code so radically different from the old? Are not both based on experience? Do not both accept happiness as a test of morality? Mr. Stephen feels the necessity of grappling with this objection. He acknowledges (with a playful touch which comes almost with a shock of surprise, because, in this book, at all events, Mr. Stephen studiously conceals the lighter style to which he has accustomed us in some of his essays) that the new system is to many thinkers simply "the old dog in a new doublet."

What, then, are the theoretical deficiencies of Utilitarianism? "The tendency," he says, "of the Utilitarian, is to consider knowledge in general as conforming to the type of that purely empirical knowledge in which the experience of a former coincidence of two distinct phenomena is the sole basis for an expectation of a future coincidence. Carrying out this principle as far as possible, reasoning is essentially an association of ideas, and the association, though practically indissoluble in some cases, is regarded as always potentially

[1] 'Science of Ethics,' p. 139.

dissoluble. The logical result is atomism, or the reduction of every kind of organized system, whether of ideas regarded as existing in the mind, or of the objects external to the mind, and represented by the ideas, to an aggregate of independent units, capable of indefinite analysis in the mind, or being taken to pieces and reconstructed in reality" (pp. 359, 360).

The passage is a remarkable one, as indicating that reaction against individualism, which has before been noted as characteristic of modern scientific speculation. At last, science (or rather science as applied to mental and moral phenomena) seems to have discovered that there is a difference between the particular or the isolated unit, and the individual or the related unit, and it has been discovered that the individual is in some way the fusion of the universal and the particular, the particular universalized by its relations, and that, therefore, to understand the individual, we must start from the universal. For observe the application of Mr. Stephen's criticism to the purely ethical aspect. According to the assumptions of atomism, every man is like every other man, to begin with; the existence of uniform atoms being presupposed upon which circumstances then begin to operate. Therefore the difference between two men is solely due to the various associations which have acted upon them, and not to those innate tendencies of character which are suspected of an affinity to 'innate ideas.' We must suppose, in consequence, that there is a " uniform man, a colourless sheet of paper or primitive atom," upon whom all qualities are imposed by the circumstances under which he is placed. This is ethical atomism. Further, according to this doctrine, society is an aggregate, built up of the uniform atoms called men. Each of these desires happiness, and so happiness is regarded as a kind of 'emotional currency,' capable of being calculated and distributed in lots; and conduct is immoral or moral "according as it diminishes or swells the volume of this hypothetical currency." What, now, is the fundamental error of utilitarianism? It is the refusal to take into account the true nature of society, which is an organism, and not an aggregate of independent atoms. "The utilitarian argument would be perfectly relevant, if we could take each action by itself, sum up its consequences, and then generalize as to the actions of the class. But it is also true, that our judgments as to the effects of immoral conduct are very inadequately represented by this simple and direct process. We must take into account the existence of a certain social order, and of a corresponding character in the individual constituents. The consequences of immoral conduct can only be traced when we recognize the nature of the social structure, which again implies the existence of a certain stage of individual development, and neither of these is deducible from the properties of the assumed unit (an individual, uniform man)" (pp. 361—363).

The conclusions of such a criticism are obvious, and we need not trace them further. Briefly, the difference between the utilitarian and the evolutionist criterion is this, that the former lays down as a

[1] Cf. Mr. Spencer's criticism of the 'greatest happiness' principle referred to above.

criterion the happiness, the latter the health, of the society. Utilitarianism gives what may be called 'instantaneous morality,' not scientific ethics, because it neglects the conception of a slowly developing organism. "The importance of the distinction is illustrated in almost every important social discussion. We notice certain bad results. from a particular economical or social arrangement. The indissolubility of marriage inflicts hardship upon many individuals; let it be dissoluble in those cases. The importation of foreign products ruins certain manufacturers; let it be prohibited. We remedy the immediate evil by suppressing more obvious symptoms; but we often forget that we are dealing with a complex organism, and that the real problem involves innumerable and far-reaching actions and motives due to its constitution. We may be remedying the grievance of individual husbands and wives by lowering the general sanctity of family relations, and helping a particular class at the expense of the general efficiency of the nation" (p. 371 ; cf. p. 426).

Such is Mr. Stephen's admirable criticism of the utilitarian fallacies. The only wonder is, that having got so far, he does not perceive that he is even yet in the province of social physics, and has not reached the ethical realm, and that when he talks of the sanctity of certain moral ideas, he speaks of that which, on his assumption, is none the less due to experience, although it may be an enlarged and developed experience—the experience of the race, and not of the individual.

But few points remain in the *Science of Ethics*, which call for notice. Mr. Stephen once and for ever separates himself from the school of egoists and logical utilitarians, by affirming the original character of sympathy. "Sympathy," he says, "is not an additional instinct, a faculty which is added when the mind has reached a certain stage of development, a mere incident of intellectual growth, but something implied from the first in the very structure of knowledge" (p. 230). Sympathy, it would appear, is identical or conjoined with such intellectual action as is implied in the possession of representative ideas. "The sympathetic being," Mr. Stephen goes on to say, "becomes a constituent part of a larger organization, and therefore ceases to act simply on the prudential motive of the hedonists" (p. 257). The sympathetic being is not, therefore, the *same* being as the non-sympathetic, though acting from different motives (which is contradictory), but a different being with a different set of faculties (viz. the social ones), and he, apparently, has gained a fresh capacity (p. 263). The only difficulty is to see how sympathy, which is thus clearly affirmed to have grown, can yet have been implied from the first in the very structure of knowledge. For that, too, is dependent on certain forms or ultimate laws of intelligence, and yet these are the very things which are supposed to be evolved in the growth of knowledge.

It may possibly surprise the reader to see how Mr. Stephen solves the free-will problem. In the first place he resolves 'cause' into a continuous procession of effects. To this we have been familiarized by Mr. Lewes' discussion of the meaning of cause in the second volume of his *Problems of Life and Mind*. But then Mr. Stephen proceeds to a kind of solution which is hardly to be expected in one who calls himself a disciple of the experimental school. For he embraces a Kantian standpoint, which was by its author intended as an answer to the empirical assumptions of Locke and Hume. "The difficulty," he says, "is dispelled so far as it can be dispelled (for Mr. Stephen has his sceptical moods) when we have got rid of the troublesome conception of necessity as a name for something more than the certainty of the observer. When we firmly grasp and push to its legitimate conclusion the truth that probability, chance, necessity, determination, and so forth, *are simply names of our own states of mind, or, in other words, have only a subjective validity*, we have got as far as we can towards removing the perplexity now under consideration" (pp. 293, 294). An admirable conclusion; but if some audacious critic were to venture to assert that the troublesome conception of 'social tissue' was nothing more than the abstraction of an individual thinker, and had only a subjective and relative validity; that moral facts were what they were, and that no material difference is made to their concrete significance by relating them to social tissue, Mr. Stephen would probably feel that the time had come for more spirited and pointed writing than he has deigned to make use of in his present volume.

In the matter of 'associationism,' however, as applied to the genesis of moral ideas, Mr. Stephen has some trenchant things to say. The device of 'association of ideas' to eke out the assumption of utilitarianism was first tried by Hartley, whom Stuart Mill has so enthusiastically termed the 'father of associationism.' According to the general hedonistic position, all human action is ultimately interested and selfish. How, then, can the disinterested pursuit of virtue, so obvious in the best examples of morality, be accounted for? Easily enough, according to Hartley and Mill; for association of ideas explains how virtue was associated with the only real end of activity, viz. happiness, and then became transformed from means into ends, just as the acquisition of money is transformed from means to happiness into end of life by the confirmed miser. Mr. Stephen's criticism on this device appears to be unanswerable. "If love (or other moral sentiments) thus explained should prompt us to act in such a way as to sacrifice our pleasure for the good of others, we should be unreasonable in the same sense as the miser. We should be applying a rule in a case where it was plainly inapplicable, and using means for an end in a case where we knew that they would not produce that end. Association in this sense implies illusion; and the more reasonable we become, the more we should deliver ourselves from the bondage of such errors" (p. 378). Such a conclusion is not the least of the advantages we derive from the substitution of scientific ethics for the crude and paradoxical theories of the utilitarian morality.

There is nothing of much interest for the student of contemporary ethics in Professor Frederick Pollock's recently published essays. He has appended to his volume, which deals principally with questions of jurisprudence, four essays professedly dealing with moral subjects, but there is none of that solid work in them which is conspicuous in the author's work on Spinoza, and which the world has now a right to expect from any one who touches on so vexed and so arduous a field of controversy. Mr. Pollock is apparently, if we may judge from his essay on 'Ethics and Morals,' a disciple of the school of common sense: but he is also a utilitarian, and a firm believer in the application of the historical method to moral questions, although, oddly enough, he thinks (p. 359) that the utilitarianism of J. S. Mill or of Bentham was not empirical, or at all events not so empirical as Mr. Spencer assumes. He is troubled with many doubts, especially on two points; the bearing of scientific ethics on practical morality, and the relation of moral ideals to contemporary practice. And so it is not unnatural to find in his essays sentences which are not obviously consistent. He says, for instance (p. 276): "The ethical judgments of mankind are framed with regard to an ideal standard;" and on p. 370: "We do not want an absolute standard to guide us in the exercise of moral approbation or disapprobation;" and again on p. 271: "The ethical judgments of the community have no express mouthpiece. Our only tribunal is an ideal and abstract one; the practical judgment, as Aristotle saw long ago, must measure itself by the *imagined* judgment of the reasonable man." This is almost as baffling as to discover in Aristotle on what the ἀρχαὶ τῶν πρακτῶν are based. Or again, we read on p. 299, that "the most important motives and sanctions are those which *operate without being perceived*, and consequently are not expressed in popular theories;" while on p. 295: "A man of normal sight does not want optics to make him see;

nor does a right-minded man want ethics to make him know right from wrong." To judge by the last passage, it would appear either that right-mindedness is normal—which at least is open to doubt—or else that the right-minded man is not on the level of popular theories of morality, in which case he would certainly seem to have studied a science of moral optics. But, in itself, the sentence that the right-minded man knows right from wrong is on a par with Butler's famous reasoning that conscience is *naturally* superior, because, *in the nature of things*, conscience is above self-love and the instinctive appetites. On the whole, Mr. Pollock seems to doubt the value of scientific ethics, and to rest his faith on a version of moral sense or popular ethical judgments. Mr. Pollock, in fact, approaches ethics from the same point of view as Austin and Bentham. He is a student of law first, and of morality afterwards. There are many disadvantages in such approaches, but there is at least one advantage. Ethics undoubtedly derives from jurisprudence some admirable illustrations, and Mr. Pollock's technicalities of final jurisprudence, statical jurisprudence, and dynamical jurisprudence, serve him in good stead in his discrimination between absolute ethics, relative ethics, and casuistry.[1]

In works like Mr. Spencer's *Data of Ethics* and Mr. Stephen's *Science of Ethics*, the modern system of scientific morality may be said to be formulated. It remains, then, for us shortly to consider the position in which it stands, and to compare its presuppositions

[1] 'Essays in Jurisprudence and Ethics,' pp. 262—268.

and its conclusions with the opposite scheme, to which it bears the strongest contrast. For there can be little doubt that for us, in a modern day, there is no alternative except to embrace the scientific ethics, or some modification of the Kantian system. It is the old contrast between empiricism and rationalism which has run through all the history of moral philosophy, but the special form which the contrast has assumed has, of course, varied with the different generations. On the one side the changes have been rung on such systems as Cambridge Platonism, Moral Sense or Conscience, and Kantianism. On the other side, the ethics of empiricism have also had successive stages: a purely selfish system or hedonism, Utilitarianism in its earlier form, Utilitarianism in its later form, to which has now succeeded Evolutional Ethics with Spencer and Stephen. Which shall it be? Shall we begin with such conceptions as moral law, moral order, and a free and self-directing moral agent, or shall the method be to catalogue the tendencies of actions, to accept pleasure and pain as the ultimate test of good and bad, and to make morality the gradual creation of a slowly-evolving social tissue?

Let us begin by noticing a few points in which the novel ethics are either confessedly defective, or at least find considerable difficulty in explaining their position. Every moral system has to establish the sanctions of morality on a clear basis; but, unfortunately, the word itself is used in so many ambiguous senses that the substitution of weak, vague, and superficial sanctions for what is clearly and positively stringent and imperative, very often escapes detection. A sanction, in the proper sense of the term, means nothing more or less than a penalty incurred by the violation of a law. If a man systematically takes "every pleasure as it flies," he becomes liable to a physical sanction, or, in other words, pain, disease, or death. If he transgresses the known law of the land, he comes under the political sanction of legal punishment. If he defies the ordinances of society, he pays the penalty for his eccentricity in the social sanction of ostracism. But are any of these properly *moral* sanctions, moral penalties incurred by an immoral agent? Perhaps it will be enough to accept on this point the answer of Mill:—"The ultimate sanction of all morality is a subjective feeling in our minds"—in other words, the really moral sanction is an internal one, and not such external ones as pain, punishment, or social ostracism. "The internal sanction of duty is a feeling in our own mind; a pain, more or less intense, attendant on violation of duty, which in properly cultivated moral natures rises, in the more serious cases, into shrinking from it as an impossibility. This feeling, when disinterested, and connecting itself with the past idea of duty, is the essence of conscience."[1] Nothing could be more strongly or better expressed; only, after Mill has thus conclusively thrown us back on an internal sanction, he proceeds to deprive his sanction of all its force by showing that its disinterested character has really a selfish core, and that the virtue it bears witness to has risen by an irrational confusion between ends and means. Nor is Mr. Sidgwick more fortunate in

[1] Mill's 'Utilitarianism,' pp. 41, 42.

establishing an internal sanction of morality, as may be seen in the final chapter of the *Method of Ethics*. "I do not find," he says, "in my moral consciousness, any intuition, claiming to be clear and certain, that the performance of duty will be adequately rewarded, and its violation punished." If Utilitarianism, then, is unable to place the real sanction of morality on any clear basis, can we say that the scientific ethics are in this, as we have found that they are in many points, more successful? Let us listen to Mr. Leslie Stephen :—

"There is no argument in existence (to persuade people to do right) which, if exhibited to them, would always appear to be conclusive. . . . How can we argue with a thoroughly selfish man? By pointing out the misery he causes? If to point it out were the same thing as to make him feel it, the method might be successful. . . . Shall we then appeal to some extrinsic motive, to the danger of being found out, despised, and punished? But if for any reason the man is beyond the reach of such dangers, he may despise our arguments, and we have no more to offer. He may say—and, as it appears to me, may say with truth—'I shall personally get more pleasure from doing wrong than from doing right, and I care for nothing but my personal pleasure.' The first statement may be—it often is—undeniably true. Of the second he is the only judge." [1]

Nobody can accuse Mr. Stephen, at all events, of blinking the conclusion, or of not seeing the weakness of a hedonistic system. "The attempt to establish

[1] 'Science of Ethics,' pp. 429, 430.

an absolute coincidence between virtue and happiness is in ethics what the attempting to square the circle or to discover perpetual motion is in geometry and mechanics."[1] Can there be any better elucidation of the truth that, if one starts with the axiom that pleasure and pain are the tests of morality and immorality, there can be no sanction of morality at all? For surely the 'social tissue' can give no better sanction than the egoistic fibre. The difference between one and the other is only a question of degree, or rather one of time. Given a certain continuity of self-regarding activity, and by the course of nature there is educed a larger conception of self *plus* surroundings, of man *plus* his fellow-men, of egoism *plus* altruism. So that the only logical conclusion would appear to be that there is no personal internal obligation to be moral, but only at most a social expediency, with which, for want of a better substitute for a sanction, we must fain be content.

It is only another aspect of the same question to ask whether the existence of ethics does not require the assumption of a moral order of the universe, and whether such a moral order could ever be empirically proved. Let there be no misunderstanding on such a point. There is no hint here of some cut-and-dry system of transcendental metaphysics. The words 'moral order' are innocent of any reference to the evolution of 'the idea,' or any other Hegelian device of *obscurum per obscurius*. The question may be stated with the most absolute simplicity. The meaning of an expedient act, or a useful act, or a pleasurable act, is readily understood; for experience—the hourly and

[1] 'Science of Ethics,' p. 430.

daily experience of every man—testifies to its exact signification. It can be translated into its concrete equivalents with the most absolute ease, for twelve hours' ordinary existence furnishes us with a ready dictionary. But is the meaning of a dutiful act thus readily comprehended? Let us consider for a moment how much is involved. A dutiful act is one done in obedience to conscience. Conscience dictates in accordance with a moral law. A moral law is an ordinance relative to a general scheme of the government of the universe. I participate in that general scheme as a morally active being. Therefore I obey the law. By these steps the conclusion is reached that it is only because I am part of, and am an active participator in a general moral scheme that I am a subject of morality; and it is only because a dutiful act is a part of, and relative to, a general moral order of the universe, that it *must* be done at all. Or, to put the matter in a nutshell, How can I understand what a dutiful act is unless I start with an idea of duty? And if not, is my idea of duty in any sense empirical, or is it not, in a certain obvious sense, an *à priori* idea?

But let us listen to Mr. Sidgwick on the matter, who ought to be in such a case an unprejudiced judge. "The old immoral paradox, that my performance of social duty is good not for me but for others, cannot be completely refuted by empirical arguments: nay, the more we study these arguments the more we are forced to admit, that if we have these alone to rely on, there must be some cases in which the paradox is true. And yet we cannot but admit, with Butler, that it is ultimately reasonable to seek one's own happiness. Hence the whole system of our belief as to the intrinsic reasonableness of conduct must fall, without a *hypothesis unverifiable by experience, reconciling the individual with the universal reason*, without a belief, in some form or other, that the moral order which we see imperfectly realized in this actual world, is yet actually perfect. If we reject this belief, the cosmos of duty is thus really reduced to a chaos; and the prolonged effort of the human intellect to frame a perfect ideal of rational conduct is seen to have been foredoomed to inevitable failure."[1]

It is a pity that Mr. Sidgwick should have seen fit to alter this in a second edition of his work; it is a great point, nevertheless, that he should have even once left it on record. No more decisive condemnation of the empirical ethics has ever been framed even by its professed antagonists.

There is only one issue out of the dilemma. Either we must accept the dependence of ethics on certain *à priori* assumptions, and give up the empirical interpretations, or else we must utterly transform the conception of duty. The latter alternative is Mr. Spencer's device, and his sentence on the subject has already gained a striking notoriety. "The sense of duty is transitory, and will diminish as fast as moralization increases."[2] The implied conclusion is obvious. Morality, or as Mr. Spencer calls it with a view to its gradual growth, moralization, has only an accidental, and not an essential, connection with duty. Little wonder is it that Mr. Spencer should call the conclusion 'startling.' But if 'moralization' means an

---

[1] 'Method of Ethics,' p. 473. First Edition.
[2] 'Data of Ethics,' p. 127.

improved experience of the socially useful, it is obvious enough that the stringency and imperative character of duty is only an accident of its development. It began in supernatural terrors; it ends in natural expediencies. It had its rise in the imperious commands of some chieftain both in lifetime and after death; it has its issue in the discovery of the true happiness of society. But is there, then, no ideal morality the function of which is gradually to rectify the imperfect moral scheme of to-day and to-morrow? This leads us to another point, which, as it more especially concerns Mr. Spencer's 'Ethics,' is of some importance.

"A great part of the perplexities in ethical speculation," says Mr. Spencer, "arises from neglect of the distinction between the absolutely right and the relatively right. Scientific truths, of whatever order, are reached by eliminating perturbing, or conflicting factors, and recognizing only fundamental factors. When by dealing with fundamental factors in the abstract, not as presented in actual phenomena, but *as presented in ideal separation*, general laws have been ascertained, it becomes possible to draw inferences in concrete cases, by taking into account incidental factors. All this holds of Moral Science. In a chapter entitled 'Definition of Morality,' in *Social Statics*, I have contended that the moral law, properly so-called, is the law of the perfect man—*is the formula of ideal conduct*. Instancing questions concerning the right course to be taken in cases where wrong has already been done, I have alleged that the answers to such questions must be given *on purely ethical principles*. Ascertainment of the actual truths has been made possible only by *pre-ascertainment of certain ideal truths*. Similarly, then, is it with the relation between absolute morality, or the law of perfect right in human conduct, and relative morality."[1]

Sentences bearing more clearly the idealistic impress could not be written. Two formidable difficulties, however, remain. How is it that duty, which surely means the ideal conduct of a human being, can on this supposition be so unconnected with moralization as eventually to disappear? And how is it that Mr. Spencer believes that such absolute ethics as he here postulates can be conceived, even in some wild dream of fancy, as resting on the narrow empirical basis on which his whole system reposes?

For the truth is that, to understand ethics, we must first study the essential conditions of that consciousness which is over and above those sentient sequences which we call empirical knowledge. The self with which morality is concerned is not the self of empiricism, but that self in relation to which everything—nature, world, good, and evil—acquire intelligibility and existence. For what, even on Mr. Stephen's showing, is the essence of morality? It is not *to do* so and so or so and so, but *to be* so and so;[2] and that immediately points us back to the secret home of our spirit, the self which makes us and everything else what we and they are. Here, once again, the caution against the windy rhetoric of metaphysics is a criticism which can neither be

[1] 'Data of Ethics,' pp. 260, 268, 270, 271, 274, 277.

[2] Stephen's 'Science of Ethics,' p. 145. "Morality is internal. The moral law has to be expressed in the form 'Be this,' not in the form 'Do this.'"

justly urged nor plausibly maintained. In asserting that ethics is incomprehensible except on the supposition of an autonomous self, we can appeal to considerations which are unmetaphysical, and move on the common grounds of logic and reasoning. It is true that the ultimate foundation of the thesis is a piece of metaphysical analysis, which is probably distasteful to English 'common sense;' but there are many subsidiary arguments which are neither recondite nor ideal, and which make no excessive demands on common logical acumen.

Observe, for instance, what successive transformations the self can effect, according to Mr. Spencer. It is, first, the narrow self of an organism which is limited by the range of its own desires. In this stage its conduct is described as that continuous adjustment of acts to ends, which serves to prolong and intensify individual life. Then, under pressure, it is presumed, of an historical necessity, it suddenly includes within the circle of 'self' the life of its species, and displays race-maintaining conduct and not self-maintaining conduct. Then, finally, under a pressure which is never described or accounted for, it performs such acts as not only avoid giving injury to others, but are actually designed to help and promote the interests of others. No one can pretend that the stages here indicated are purely successive or simply 'natural,' for the second is the direct negative of the first, and the third is largely limitative of the second. If, indeed, the self is above natural laws, and can itself regulate or circumscribe their operation, the process becomes comprehensible; but if the self is a plaything in the hands of natural forces, what can be the solution of so strange a development? Either the evolution requires the helping hand of some extra-mundane force, which is the belief of those who recognize the continuous action of a deity, or else the self is capable of a self-realization in a manner not purely natural, because it is, as Kant would call it, a 'noumenal (*i. e.* supra-phenomenal) Ego.' Let us see how Mr. Clifford describes the process in the essay entitled 'The Scientific Basis of Morals,' where he is speaking of "the purpose of tribal approbation or disapprobation."

"It is necessary to the tribe that the pious character should be encouraged and preserved, the impious character discouraged and removed. The process is of two kinds—direct and reflex. In the direct process the tribal dislike of the offender is precisely similar to the dislike of a noxious beast; and it expresses itself in his speedy removal. But in the reflex process we find the first trace of *that singular and wonderful judgment by analogy which ascribes to other men a consciousness similar to our own. If the process were a conscious one*, it might, perhaps, be described in this way: the tribal self says, Put yourself in this man's place: he also is pious, but he has offended. *But the process is not a conscious one:* the social craft, or art of living together, is learned by the tribe and not by the individual, and the purpose of improving men's characters is provided for by complex social arrangements long before it has been conceived by any conscious mind."[1]

Can any careful reader understand the process which is here described? Can he conceive of a some-

[1] Clifford's 'Essays,' Vol. II. pp. 115, 116.

thing which is not conscious, which can yet form a singular and wonderful judgment by analogy? And further, which can ascribe to other men a consciousness similar to our own? An unconscious process, which can include other men's consciousness into our own and yet remain unconscious, is indeed a miracle which eclipses the wonders of a seven-days' creation. Is not the alternative which Mr. Clifford expressly rejects the only conceivable one, viz. that the process is a conscious one, and that the imperfect consciousness which exists in individuals gradually learns to know the perfect self-consciousness of which the divinely simple rule is, " Put yourself in his place ? "

Or let us take the conception of duty, which is, perhaps, the clearest point of difference between the rival systems of rational and experimental ethics. Duty, as understood by the Kantian system, is the law laid by a man's higher self (*i. e.* his reason) on himself. He has no option but to obey, unless he will cut himself off from all communion with the universal spirit which moves in him and all intelligences. Every recalcitrant attempt is attended by that haunting remorse, which is nothing else but the agony of feeling that he is a spiritual outcast, a moral pariah. How shall experimental ethics explain such an *à priori* conception? We have already seen the attempt made by Mr. Spencer. There are two elements in duty—authoritativeness and coerciveness. Authoritativeness is explained as the growth of a mental capacity to prefer the future in comparison with the present; coerciveness is explained as the gradual transference of sanctions from an external to an internal relation. Each of these is a very

T

difficult psychological process to understand, so difficult as to be almost hopeless. How is a mind, limited to experiences of successive conscious states, capable of so summing up its conscious life as a whole that it can balance what has yet to come with what is immediately present? And, even if the process were possible, are we a whit nearer to the conception of obligation? Still more difficult is it to comprehend how a mind, passively developing according to natural laws, can yet with conscious activity transform external sanctions into an internal law of itself; and yet, without such conscious power of translating outer into inner, the coerciveness of duty is wholly unexplained. For Mr. Spencer's two elements of duty are, in common language, the fact of moral obligation and the necessity of an internal sanction for morality, and both of these —both the fact and the necessity—remain as 'inexplicable surds' in the evolutional ethics. Nor is this all. For Mr. Spencer, as if to accentuate that wastefulness in Nature which the doctrine of evolution has put in such clear light, after all the laborious process of the growth of duty, mocks our difficulties by telling us that it is all of no use. Duty itself will disappear. The evolved man in his millennial stage will have got the better of the 'authoritativeness' and the 'coerciveness.' The rationalized human being will in this case, as in all cases of association of ideas, see through his logical errors, and hereafter live in peace.

But, perhaps, there are simpler considerations than these, which bear on the main issue. For instance, it is quite obvious that ethics must of necessity consist of two parts—a scientific part and a preceptive part; we must have, in other words, both a science and an art of morality. Every ethical writer must perforce agree that, besides the explanation of the validity and sanctions of the moral laws, there must be some attempt made to exhort, persuade, and convince, or at all events to lay down rules for the performance of the moral laws. But now observe in what a curious predicament the expounders of the ethics of evolution are involved when they begin to frame the preceptive portion of their ethical scheme. If the moral activities of man be the slow result of the continuous working of nature's laws, if morality be a natural science, in what intelligible sense can a man be told that he *must* conform to the laws of nature? For if that precept be enjoined, the assumption is that there is in man a certain spontaneous force which can either assent to or oppose the forces of nature. Why else is he to be told that he *must* conform, except on the supposition that he can resist if he chooses? Epicurus long ago saw the difficulty. If all things proceeded according to the laws of motion and force, how could commands be addressed to atoms which were helpless in the general stream of necessary law? Must not some atoms have a certain wilful spontaneity of their own —an inexplicable *clinamen* from the perpendicular lines of downward motion? The modern scientist will make use of no such puerile fancy, but he pays the penalty in his logic. How can a being, who is simply the result of natural forces, be with any reason told that he must conform to those natural forces? The only logical result of the scientific hypothesis is fatalism.

Observe again, what curious discords are introduced by scientific ethics between what we revere in art and poetry, and what we maintain to be true of the moral self. There is only one thing which is unreservedly admired in art; it is mastery, initiative, force. All our artistic ideals, whether in poetry or painting, rest on this ground—the exhibition of free original power. But how comes it that we can venerate such ideals, when, if we turn to what we know of man, we find him the creature of circumstance and nature, swept along in the current of mighty forces, which he can neither control nor resist? Can it be that man admires what he knows he can never attain to, and that his worship is a sort of despairing reaction from his own impotence? Mr. Herbert Spencer is probably an unwilling witness, and therefore it is not a little consoling to find that he, despite himself, bears testimony to man's free personality. What else can we make of that "active energy as it wells up from the depths of our consciousness," of which he so eloquently speaks in his *Psychology*,[1] or of "the fountain of power within us," of which he makes use in establishing the distinction between subject and object?[2]

But there is a yet simpler consideration, which may possibly throw light on the matter. When we are establishing a great law of evolution, which is to prove not only that morality is the natural development of instinctive self-preserving actions, but that man is the last term in a series, of which the first is the ascidian, it is clear that man, who is the result of natural forces, is himself framing a theory of those forces. Is not this a monstrous supposition, that the potter's clay should be able to form a theory of the formation of the clay, ay, and of

[1] Psychol: Vol. II. p. 479.   [2] Pp. 482, 483.

the potter too? For, in no intelligible sense can a consciousness, whose natural genesis can be traced to molecules, itself stand over and review the process which culminated in its own inquiring activity. What is the conclusion? It can be stated in a sentence. The consciousness which makes us men is independent of time and development. In the last resort we can know of nothing except as it appears to consciousness. With our own active consciousness we begin, and with it we end. It is understanding, as Kant says, which makes nature, or, as Mr. Lewes puts it, in language which should be acceptable, as it is from the pen of a professed scientist, 'The world arises in consciousness.' And if consciousness be thus active in knowledge, if it is owing to its synthetic capacity that there is for us such a thing as Nature to know, it is only reasonable to suppose that it is equally active in morality. It is only on such a supposition that we can explain the moral ends which a reasonable human being sets before himself, the obligation that rests on him to do right; the remorse which poisons his life if he fails. Conscience is then to him a reality, for it is the voice of the universal reason which lives and moves in him and all men, the universal consciousness, which is none other than God. If humanity, in this sense, be held to be the mainspring of morality, we can assent to what M. Renan says of ethical systems:—'Les croyances nécessaires sont au-dessus de toute atteinte. L'humanité ne nous écoutera que dans la mesure où nos systèmes conviendront à ses devoirs et à ses instincts.'[1]

[1] 'Revue des Deux Mondes,' February, 1882.

CHAPTER IV.

On Pessimism, as a Reconstructive System.

PESSIMISTIC philosophy is essentially reconstructive, although the reconstruction is more important from the point of view of Metaphysics than of Ethics. It seeks to deduce knowledge, existence, and such morality as it admits into its scheme, from an ontological principle. It is, therefore, necessary to say something of the systems proposed by Schopenhauer and von Hartmann, although, as we shall see from the ethical point of view, the reconstruction must be pronounced inadequate and futile. We shall not be here concerned with the arguments for or against the possibility of happiness for sentient creatures like ourselves. Our object will be simply the examination of such systems as forming a practicable basis for morality, together with such outlines of their general position as our special inquiry seems to presuppose and require.

§ 1.

According to Herodotus, a division of the ancient Thracians, the Trausi, practised a singular custom.

"When a child is born," he says, "all its kindred sit round about it in a circle, and weep for the woes that it will have to undergo now that it has come into the world, making mention of every ill that falls to the lot of humankind; when, on the other hand, a man has died, they bury him with laughter and rejoicings, and say that now he is free from a host of sufferings and enjoys the completest happiness."[1] Here is an ancient instance of the unconscious Pessimism which underlies the thoughts of many people in different ages of history. The feeling, however, was not common to the Greek world, for reasons which are somewhat significant for us in our present study. In the first place, the strenuous and restless activity of the Greek world left them none of those bitter after-fruits of contemplation which find expression in Pessimistic complaints. In the second place, the clearest and best intellects were occupied in the study of moral philosophy, and made thus early the discovery which the latest critics of Schopenhauer and the German school of Pessimists have constantly insisted on, viz. that morality is only possible on the assumption that happiness in some shape or other is the end of human life, and that, therefore, Pessimism can afford us no basis for ethics. The Greek moralists at all events—Socrates, Plato, Aristotle—assumed as a matter of course that the end of life was happiness, and that the wise and proper methods of attaining it were the actual laws of morality. How then could they possibly acknowledge that for human beings it was unattainable? To do so would be to find their occupation gone, to propound as the end of life that

[1] Herod: v. 4.

which was in itself impossible. David Strauss makes an acute remark which goes to the root of this matter when he says, "Every true philosophy is naturally optimistic, or else she hews down the branch on which she herself is sitting." Once, and once only, so far as I am aware, was Pessimism formulated as a doctrine in Greek Philosophy. There was a certain Cyrenaic philosopher, called Hegesias, who had the sombre title of Death's Advocate (πεισιθάνατος), because he accepted the avoidance of trouble as the highest attainable good, despaired of positive happiness, and considered life to be intrinsically valueless.[1] There is something significant in this sudden appearance of the Pessimist among the ranks of the Cyrenaic School; for the line of thought of which this was the culmination had begun with materialism and the doctrines of the school of Atomists. To men who had thus reduced themselves and the world around them to a fortuitous combination of warring atoms, the next step was scepticism in knowledge and morals, and the pursuit of individual pleasure as the only possible object in life for man. From Scepticism and Hedonism there is but a step to Cynicism—that debasing Cynicism which holds that there is nothing new, and nothing true, and it does not much matter. And then, last scene in this eventful history, the inevitable Hegesias, Death's Advocate, with his querulous complaint that life is not worth living. Thus an examination of Greek philosophy leads us to three conclusions. There are three ways in which we can become Pessimists. In the first place, if we pursue a line of thought which

[1] Diog. L. ii. 86, 93.

leads us further and further from the recognition of man as a spiritual and rational creature, we can then become Pessimists by first becoming Materialists, Sensationalists, and Sceptics. In the second place, we can become Pessimists if we resolutely shut our eyes to the problems of morality. And in the third place, which is, indeed, only the outward and visible form of our second point, we can become Pessimists if we give up a life of strenuous activity, and resign ourselves wholly to the enervating luxury of contemplation.

It is this last point especially which is illustrated by a study of Indian philosophy. Here we are in the ancient home of Pessimism where first it saw the light, and where it was first fashioned into a system to which the modern German Pessimist reverentially returns. The contrast between early Greek philosophy and the Indian is as striking and suggestive as the contrast between the local conditions of the two countries, on which such effects in large measure depend. If any one desires to see how much thought depends on conditions of climate, let him study the difference between Indian and Hellenic philosophy. A sky intense, fervid, and lowering, a vast luxuriance and rich extravagance of natural forms, a society composed of but two elements —a dominant priesthood and a degraded people— what should be the tincture of thought under such conditions? A philosophy, clearly, of quiescence, of mysticism, of absorption into the divine essence, a thought which would hold up before it as its highest ideal the negation of practical activity, the consecration of a spiritless and nerveless repose. Both of the main forms of Indian philosophy—the Brahmanic and the Buddhist—have the same object before them, the liberation of man's soul from the troubles of existence. "The sense that life is a dream or a burden," says Prof. Max Müller, "is a notion which the Buddha shares with every Hindoo philosopher."[1] With the keen sense of human misery to start with, there can be two conclusions. According to the more orthodox philosophy—the Brahmanic—though the created world is a regrettable accident, its effect can be neutralized; for the human soul can, by a long series of sacrificial rites, asceticism, and profound contemplation, be absorbed in the universal spirit of Brahma, the true source of life, thought, and happiness. But Buddha (or his followers) denies the existence, not only of a Creator, but of an absolute being. There is no reality anywhere, neither in the past nor in the future. "True wisdom consists in a perception of the nothingness of all things, and in a desire to become nothing," to be blown out, to enter into Nirvana, that is to say, extinction. The Indian Pessimist, indeed, had to face a problem which was more horrible than that which presents itself to his modern disciple. It is bad enough for the modern Pessimist, who limits suffering to the world we know; but the Indian had a belief in the transmigration of souls, since to the present life was added another and yet another existence in which the dreary drama of torture was to be enacted anew. And thus it was that the Buddhist philosopher thought it absolutely necessary to stop existence at its very source, to deny the will to live by a resolute asceticism, by a resolute

[1] *Chips from a German Workshop*, i. 226.

adherence to a condition of mind free from all desire and feeling. The moral of this Indian thought is easy to draw. Pessimism is the child of inactivity, and a disease of speculation. If it be once assumed as a postulate that life is suffering, there are two possible alternatives. Either you must transplant the happiness which you despair of attaining here to another world,—this was the course of Brahmanic mysticism,—or else you must sit down under the burden as best you may, and seriously envisage annihilation as the only issue for life and hope. And the last was the alternative which the Buddhist accepted.

Of Pessimism there can be as many varieties as of individual character and circumstance. As most of us are said to carry a dead poet within our breasts, so also it may be said that we most of us are, or have been, Pessimists. In the majority of cases the cause is the pressure of some actual misfortune, which, with the rapid habit of generalization from single instances common to all illogical minds, we are in haste to transfer from ourselves to the majority of the human race. Nor are the subjects in which this Pessimistic feeling can be exercised less numerous than the mischances which can call it forth. A study of history may make us despair—the discovery that men do not get wiser as they grow older, that the same criminal errors and frailties characterize the later as well as the earlier phases of human society. The study of politics may make us despair, when we discover that politics is but a game, that the secret of political life is an easy acquiescence in dishonourable compromises, and the character of the distinguished politician a mass of subterfuge and charlatanism. The study of Nature may make us despair, its chief lesson being that right is might, that to him that hath shall also be given, that the law of life is the survival of the strongest and not of the ideally best, and that the rewards of persistence and self-perpetuation are given to those creatures who can most successfully unite brutal force and dastardly ingenuity. Or, lastly, the contemplation of the life of humanity, as apart from that of the race, may make us despair when we see the large preponderance of pain over pleasure in a lifetime, and make the discovery of the Hebrew preacher, that "he who increaseth knowledge increaseth sorrow." But all these varieties belong to what may be called 'unreasoned' Pessimism, as distinguished from that which bases its doctrine on a systematic philosophical scheme. Speaking roughly, Pessimism itself can be divided into these two forms —unreasoned and philosophic. Examples of the latter are to be found especially in Schopenhauer and von Hartmann, the two main representatives of modern German Pessimism. Examples of the former may be found in poets and meditative writers in every age and country. They do not base their gloomy thoughts on a systematic creed, but are either at the mercy of chance moods of depression, of which we have many instances in the Hebrew Psalms, or else carry the individual peculiarities either of their character or circumstances into the views they take of man and existence. In the case of the philosophical Pessimists such explanation of their opinions is not so easily made, for their opinions rest on a reasoned basis; they construct a metaphysical system first, before they draw their conclusions, and their Pessimism is to be judged in reference to a given structure of dogmatic thought. I propose to take examples of both classes, in order to illustrate these two forms which Pessimism can assume.

"Manure the human soul with despair," says a vigorous writer,[1] "and if only it be genuine, you will have a noble harvest." A harvest indeed, but of what kind? Of poetry, first of all; and that is the reason why so many despairing thoughts are to be found in poets of every country. The fierce despair of Byron, the more refined complaints of Shelley, the cultured and cynical indifference of Heine, the wild laughter of Baudelaire, are familiar instances. Pessimism is familiar to the thought of a Hamlet, who expresses in significant form the natural sequel of a life in which contemplation played more part than activity, and which was originally warped and distorted by the sudden and grave calamity of a father's death. By way of illustration of this form, which I have called unreasoned Pessimism, I will take the Italian, Leopardi, who wrote lyrics of singular power, and essays and satirical dialogues somewhat after the manner of Lucian. The characteristic of unreasoned Pessimism is, that it is without difficulty explained by individual circumstance and individual character. Leopardi himself was very anxious that his speculative views should not be construed in reference to the incidents of his life. In a letter written to one of his friends, he enters a protest against such a supposition. "It is the cowardice of men," he says, "who would fain regard existence as something very

[1] Rahel.

valuable, that instigates them to consider my philosophical opinions as the result of my sufferings, and that makes them persist in charging to my material circumstances that which is due to nothing but my understanding. Before I die I wish to make protest against this imputation of weakness and trifling, and I would beg of my readers to burn my writings rather than attribute them to my sufferings" (May 24, 1832). Despite this energetic disavowal, let us cheerfully bear the imputation of that cowardice to which Leopardi refers, for what are the circumstances of his life? Here is a man, with all the subtle susceptibility of a poet's disposition, doomed to bear the weight not only of ill-health and personal disfigurement (he was half-blind and hump-backed), but also surroundings utterly alien and unsympathetic to the cravings of his own nature. Born at Recanati, a small town about fifteen miles from Ancona, in 1793, he was the victim of a paternal control, which in many ways aggravated the sensibilities of his temperament. He was at first dedicated to the Church; breaking from the narrowing bounds of ecclesiastical discipline, because full of a precocious culture which wasted the early years of his life in intense study, he then seeks to find the larger air and the more intellectual society which Rome held before his youthful imagination. Quickly disillusioned by the scholars whom he met with in the imperial city, his subsequent life is a constant migration from town to town in search of that more health-giving atmosphere, which was an impossible blessing to his feeble constitution. He had the luxury of one great passion, of which the fruition was quickly put beyond his reach; and the comfort of one friend, Ranieri, whose only office was to close his dying eyes. His intellectual life runs through those alternations which have become tolerably familiar to a modern age of transition and disappointment. His first attitude is the attempt to find in the doctrines of the Church the refuge against the scepticism produced by a study of the ancients. For him, at first, the philosophy of the ancients was the science of endless discord. Aristotle condemned what Plato taught, Socrates mocked Antisthenes, and Zeno scandalized Epicurus. Pythagoreans, Platonists, Stoics, Cynics, Eclectics, *et hoc genus omne*, scuffled with and ridiculed one another; while the truly wise laughed at them all. To live in the true Church seemed to him the only way to combat superstition. Then he discovers that his antidote for superstition is itself full-charged with the poison he sought to destroy, and his next solace is poetry. When literature itself proved no bulwark against the thoughts which beset him, he turned to philosophy, only to find that that too provided no anodyne for his wounds. "Another thing," he says, in a letter written in 1817, "that makes me unhappy is thought. I believe you know, but I hope you have not experienced, how thought can crucify and martyrize any one who thinks somewhat different to others. I have for a long time suffered such torments simply because thought has always had me entirely in its power, and it will kill me unless I change my condition. Solitude is not made for those who burn and are consumed in themselves." And then his physical incapacity gained over his mind a fatal influence. "My ill-health," he says, "makes me unhappy, because I am not a philosopher who is careless of life, and because I am compelled to stand aloof from my beloved studies." From Recanati he goes to Bologna, thence to Florence, Milan, and Pisa; wintering now at one place, now at another, in search not so much of health as of repose. Here is a touching letter which he sends to his Tuscan friends in 1830, by way of dedication of his poems. "My dear friends, accept the dedication of this book. Herein I have striven, as I have often done in poetry, to hallow my sufferings. Ere I was twenty years of age my physical infirmities deprived me of half my powers, my life was taken, yet death was not bestowed on me. Eight years later I became totally incapacitated. This it seems will be my future state. Even to read these letters you know that I make use of other eyes than mine. Dear friends, my sufferings are incapable of increase: already my misfortune is too great for tears. I have lost everything, and am but a trunk that feels and suffers."

Is it wonderful that his thoughts should take a Pessimistic turn? For him the universe is an enigma totally insoluble. Men's sufferings exceed the good that they can experience. Progress and the increase of civilization, so far from alleviating, only intensify the capacity for pain. They augment indeed to some extent the means of enjoyment, but this benefit bears no proportion to that vast total of sorrow which it makes realizable and possible. What was there that could console such a man? He had found in his father a systematic tyrant, he had extracted from the passion of love more bitterness than joy, and his poem *To Aspasia* is a frank confession of his humiliation. With genuinely pessimistic touch he visits the whole female sex with his condemnation. "Rarely," he says, in the same poem, "is the woman's nature comparable with that of the dream image. No thought like ours can dwell beneath women's narrow brows. Vain is the hope that man forges in the fire of those sparkling eyes. He errs in seeking profound and lofty thoughts in one who is by nature inferior to man in all things. As her members are frailer and softer, so is her mind more feeble and confined." Add to these sombre experiences all the querulousness and irritability produced by constant ill-health, and the Pessimistic result is not only explicable, but even logically necessary. The final state is reached in the pathetic poem *A se stesso*, which might have been uttered by some poetic Buddhist in the Indian peninsula:

> "O weary heart, for ever shalt thou rest
> Henceforth. Perished is the great delusion
> That I thought would ne'er have left me. Perished!
> Nought now is left of all those dear deceits:
> Desire is dead and not a hope remains.
> Rest thee for ever. Thou hast throbbed enough;
> Nothing here is worth such palpitations.
> Our life is valueless; for it consists
> Of nought but ennui, bitterness, and pain.
> This world of clay deserveth not a sigh!
> Now calm thyself; conceive thy last despair,
> And wait for Death, the only gift of Fate." [1]

The secret of such lives is in all cases the same. They have before their eyes a noble and stately ideal, born of their poetic aspirations, and their own sensitive capacity for enjoyment. The actual circumstances of existence form a dreary contrast to such pictures,

[1] Essays and Dialogues of Leopardi, translated by C. Edwardes, p. xxvi.

and in search of a possible reconciliation they turn, it may be, to art or philosophy. Art does not satisfy all the needs of their intellectual nature; philosophy actually affronts their difficulties by a complacent theory of optimism. Here is a Leibnitz, for instance, who tells them that this is the best of possible worlds; that out of all conceivable universes God chose this one as the most perfect; and that evil, consequently, is either a moral discipline or a metaphysical limitation, serving as a shadow to a gorgeous picture. A human being, with all the reality of his daily sufferings giving themselves emphatic witness in each hour that he lives, has a right to turn and rend the shallowness of these quack doctors. He will not acquiesce in the truth that his ideal is too large for human life and circumstance. To him the contrast between ideal and real is an insult to his better feelings and his imaginative intelligence. And, as he will not submit to the antithesis between his hopes and his senses, he embraces the tenets of despair. For those who are not strong enough to hold the balance between what might be and what is, who cannot in such conflict possess their souls in patience, no other issue is possible but Pessimism; the Pessimism at least of those who break their dolls, because they find they are only stuffed with sawdust.

§ 2.

The principal works both of Hegel and of Schopenhauer appeared almost precisely at the same time. Both promulgated essentially monistic systems, but it would be impossible to imagine a greater contrast than that between the respective standpoints of the two philosophers. The contrast is instructive, for it exhibits the two antithetical extremes in which a reconstructive philosophy can exhibit itself. The ultimate ground of all reality in life, the absolute noumenon, or Ding-an-sich, can be envisaged either as rational or irrational, as blind force or logical idea. "When several philosophers synchronously appear, they will represent," says Hegel, "different aspects of a single whole."[1] According to this dictum Schopenhauer's 'Will' represents one side, Hegel's 'Idea' the other side, of some one great ontological principle. But one can imagine nothing poorer and more infertile than the absolutely irrational will, as first principle of things. The Hegelian principle, on the other side, is the rich culmination of that dialectical treatment of self-consciousness which was begun in one form by Fichte, and carried on in another form by Schelling. According to that evolution of thought, the 'Idea' is alone the being of thought and the world. Logic is consequently ontology, and the dialectical movement of the concept is the world-process. Four different systems contain the exposition of the latter principle, while Schopenhauer's principle ends with himself. The first effort of his successor, von Hartmann, is to relieve the Will, as first principle, of its absolute irrationality by conjoining it with the Idea, so that Will *plus* Idea may represent the double aspect of the true thing in itself.

The main currents of philosophical thought which meet in Schopenhauer come from different ages and

Hegel, xv. p. 619.

continents. Of the four books of which his principal work, *Die Welt als Wille und Vorstellung*, is composed, the first is derived from Kant, for part of the second and part of the third he is indebted to Plato, and for the fourth to the Buddhists and mediæval asceticism. The effort of Schopenhauer is to find some conception which shall explain the inner secret and reality of the world at large, and of our own thinking and feeling selves in particular. Ordinarily, indeed, what we mean by the world is but our representation, our idea; the world as it seems to us, not the world as it is in itself. From this point of view, the world, as interpreted in our own knowledge and by our forms of perception, must be wholly and completely relative, and accordingly, in a sense, the existence of the world is dependent on the existence of the first knowing and perceiving being. Yet at the same time it is none the less true that the knowing being is dependent on the life of the world; he is but one link, and a tolerably late one, in the course of the world's evolution. How is such an apparent contradiction to be solved? The logical analysis of knowledge proves that objective reality exists for us only in accordance with the forms of our perception. Scientific study proves that the world existed long before intelligence had birth. There is only one way out of this difficulty. The world as it exists in itself must be one thing; the world as it exists for us, and as we know it, must be another. Our notion of the world, then, needs to be supplemented by the discovery of the inner verity of the world itself. This inner verity is named by Schopenhauer the Will; by which he meant a blind but irresistible effort to exist, a craving of inexpugnable but unconscious strength towards life; an endless, aimless, limitless struggle into the light of existence. It is the will which lies at the basis of all development. It is will which successively presents itself in higher and more evolved forms. It is will, finally, which throws out from its inner capacity that intelligence which is the chief attribute of man. How do we arrive at such a startling generalization? It is this that Schopenhauer sets himself to explain at the beginning of his second book. Not very satisfactory, indeed, is the answer he gives, for we are here at one of the chief difficulties of his system. If knowledge is all phenomenal, if the way in which we set before ourselves the world is wholly relative to our own modes of perception, how is it possible to learn what the world is in itself? We can never learn it, answers Schopenhauer, but we can feel it. Let a man think of the life of his own body. He knows not what it is in itself, he only represents it to himself according to the form of his own perception; but he can feel what it is, it is actualized will. Our body is mediately presented to us by the intelligence, but immediately by the will. So we come to be aware what we are,—force, power, activity, striving and impulse to be—in one word, will. Apply this to the universe, and we thus become aware of its secret essence also. We have transcended the limits of relative human knowledge by the discovery that the world in itself is Will.

Here at once Schopenhauer's critics must feel themselves aggrieved. What right have you to transfer the results of your study of yourself to the universe at large? What right have you to speak of your own personality under the one title of will? These are but two of the numerous questions that might be raised. To the latter Schopenhauer would reply, that the word 'will' is used with a new and extended connotation. Will includes the spheres of emotion and feeling, as well as volition proper. But even so, the question still remains, how far volition and feeling can be thus exempt from all interference on the part of intelligence; how far a man's will can be conceived as working in complete independence of his intellect, so as to be himself, while the intelligence is only part of himself. To the other question, How do we transfer results obtained in a personal sphere to the impersonal objective world? Schopenhauer's doctrine gives also a not very satisfactory answer. A man must start, he would seem to say, with the only knowledge which is practical or possible, *i. e.* the knowledge of himself. Having satisfied himself on this point, the next question as to the existence of other men and creatures and an objective world, can only be solved according to the analogies of his purely personal investigations. To a man, therefore, who believes that he himself is in his essential nature will, the only form which the question as to a real external world can take is this—Are these other objects also manifestations of will? If he says no, he condemns himself to a strict theoretical egoism—the belief that he is the only individual in the world—and his home, says Schopenhauer, is the madhouse. If, on the contrary, he says yes, the deduction which Schopenhauer draws is affirmed.

Will accordingly, being the secret of the world's life, the individual forms of existence are by it successively developed. The lowest stage in the 'objectivation' of the will is that occupied by the general forces of nature—gravity, elasticity, electricity, and the like. The next stages are plants and animals up to men. But all these developments are carried out in accordance with archetypal ideas. These ideas are purely Platonic, they are the originals of which individual things are imperfect copies; they exist as forms, out of all space and time, immutable, eternal, uncreated—the only things that are, while other things become. We do not at once see the object of this revival of Platonism until we come to the third book. The third book is devoted to an elaboration of Schopenhauer's theory of art, a theory over which he seems to have bestowed especial pains as affording one outlet for the victim of Pessimism. When Will has entered upon the higher stages of its development, it throws out from its creative capacity both cognition and intelligence. Originally and properly this cognition thus educed is the servant of the will, the wheel in the hands of the potter. So we see it in animals whose instinct only serves to guide the all-powerful will or impulse; so too we see it in men during the greater part of their lives, of whom it is true to say that their will forms their understanding. But some moments of release from the servitude to will are possible. When a man arrives at the cognition of ideas he is no longer a slave. For a moment he has burst his bonds, he sees things not as an individual, but becomes lost in the contemplation of the universal forms; he considers no longer the where, the when, the why, but sees only (not in abstruse thought, but in contemplation) the what. This, then, is the purpose of the ideas; they are to serve as the object for artistic contemplation; the art-critic and art-worker find in the ideas objects of study which free them from their bondage to the will, as well as from that partial knowledge which views things merely in relations. But these moments of relief which art can give are only single instants of repose in the midst of a life given over to restless toil. There is nothing lasting about them; no such perennial satisfaction as seems adequate to the needs of our conscious nature. By the very constitution of things, life for us must involve a continual effort, and all effort is painful. The inmost reality of life is, as Schopenhauer has declared, Will; and Will is only ceaseless, objectless striving, the result of which is necessarily painful. Want, striving for some end, attainment of that end discovered to be only illusory, fresh striving, fresh effort, and everlasting disillusioning; such is the picture of the life of conscious creatures in our world. Will is only blind irrational impulse; and blind irrational impulse triumphant in the whole universe means universal misery. The phantom that is ever playing before the eyes of human beings, the *ignis fatuus* that is always glimmering over the quagmire of disappointment, is happiness. First, men think that they can attain it in this world; then, conscious of their failure, they transport it to another world; and when this hope too has failed, owing to the want of logical basis for such substantiation of their ideal, they then seek for consolation in the future happiness of the species, even though the individual is doomed to misery.[1] Each delusion in turn is proved to be idle, but the formless

[1] The formal description of these illusions belongs to von Hartmann.

impulse which lies at the basis of their nature is ever impelling mankind to renewed struggles, checked and thwarted at every turn by disaster and despair. It might be different if the struggle were controlled by intelligence—intelligence which works in view of certain ends, in pursuit of which it might mould and fashion for itself its own proper means. But in Schopenhauer the intelligence is the servant of a blind irrational will, and is therefore always feeling the curb of its despotic master. Partially pitiable, partly dreadful, the drama of human life is played out by puppets, moved by the strings of one over-mastering power; for, given a masterful will, working blindly in channels it knows not of, led simply by the dominant impulses of each moment as it comes, with such intelligence as it possesses serving only to throw a dismal light on the waters whose turmoil it makes more hideously patent, the Pessimistic conclusion is at once natural and inevitable. All is vanity and vexation of spirit.

Are there no means of release from such a burden of unhappiness? The ordinary methods of release are, we are told, valueless. The man of the world may declare his intention of gathering the rose without the thorn, but he is doomed to awake from his dreams. The consolations of art serve only to disguise momentarily the wounds they cannot heal. The man of action may seek to assuage his *weltschmerz* in a life of constant energy, but the issue of constant failure will at the last leave him face to face with the problems of his own unsatisfied yearning. There are only two ways of release, of which the first is an inward and spiritual gift of sympathy, and the second an actual and visible denial of the will to live. And this last is the only adequate resource. The denial of the will to live means for Schopenhauer the annihilation of life, not by suicide, which is a selfish expedient, but by continuous and prolonged asceticism. If we refuse to be active, if we cut off and control the various impulses which drive us from time to time to manifest our activity in some fashion or other, either in the pursuit of pleasure, or the pursuit of love, or the pursuit of fame; then we negate the action of the will at its source, and so relieve ourselves from the misery which it brings in its train. Thus in a sense the ideal which Schopenhauer sets before us is an ethical one—the duty, namely, of endless self-denial; but self-denial rather by way of asceticism than active effort for the sake of others—the Nirvana of the Buddhist rather than the self-sacrifice of the Christian.

§ 3.

The interest and importance of the work of von Hartmann (*Philos. des Unbewussten*, Berlin, 1869, and enlarged edition, 1871), largely consists in his critical attitude towards his predecessor. Nothing could better illustrate the strange solitariness of Schopenhauer, as author of a philosophic system, than the fact that his illustrious disciple, who also calls himself a Pessimist, feels it necesssary to differ from him on three points of almost vital importance. That Schopenhauer's Pessimism was the bizarre product of a man of singular gifts of genius and literary style, who was himself an unique phenomenon among the modern philosophers of Germany, is sufficiently obvious from the literary labours of Frauenstädt. But that no sooner had it gained the ears of the public than it was doomed to barrenness and infertility, is brought out in especial clearness by the *Philosophy of the Unconscious*, which in many ways is designed by its author to mediate between Pessimism and Idealism. For von Hartmann, who has gained something from both Leibnitz and Spinoza, a great deal from Schelling, and little or nothing from Kant, professes to reconcile Schopenhauer's system with that of Hegel, as though he were dealing (in the spirit of Aristophanes' tale of the sexes in Plato's Symposium) with the divided halves of one perfect philosophy.

Nothing is more characteristic of Schopenhauer's system than his derivation of all the wealth and variety of the world's life from the single blind principle of Will. It is in this respect that he has done his best to introduce Materialism into Metaphysics, to provide some accommodation for the Scientist within the sanctuary of a transcendental Philosophy. For his monistic system is as dogmatically materialistic as any professor of Science could desire, who wishes to trace back everything to 'the promise and potency' of matter. All that might interfere with this conception—for instance, the phenomenon of Consciousness—is asserted to be actually the creation of the Will, the late and arbitrary product of a wholly unintelligent principle. Now the monistic principle of von Hartmann, to which he gives the name of the Unconscious, is not the brutal and savage Ding-an-sich of his predecessor, but is a combination of Will and Idea. Nor will he leave us in any doubt as to the reasons of this change. He expressly asserts that he desires to bring some illumination into the blind principle of Schopenhauer, to provide it, so to speak, with eyes, and to enable it to become a possible author of the intellectual as well as the material world. "In assuming will we assume idea, as its determining and distinguishing content, and whoever refuses to recognize the ideal content of representation as the What and How determinative of action, must, to be consistent, also refuse to speak of an unconscious will as the inner cause of the phenomenon." That is to say, as we recognize in human action the necessary combination of will and idea, as we can not imagine a will which should not have some illuminating idea to guide it, or direct its activity, so too we must conceive that the Will, which is the ultimate cause of all, has a necessary accompaniment in Idea. Will and Idea are in fact the two poles about which the whole life of the mind, and also of the world, turns. "This simple consideration exposes the singular defectiveness of the system of Schopenhauer, in which the Idea is by no means recognized as the sole and exclusive content of Will, but a false and subordinate position is assigned to it, whilst the maimed and blind Will nevertheless altogether comports itself, as if it had a notional or ideal content."[1] It is true that the ideation for which von Hartmann contends is an unconscious one : but this by no means affects the important and almost revolutionary char-

[1] *Phil. des Unb.*: W. C. Coupland's Trans. i. 120 ; cf. ii. 63, ii. 150.

acter of the addition. The late birth of the Idea in Schopenhauer's system is therefore a great element of weakness, according to his successor. There is needed, he thinks, 'a remarkable restraint' to put up with the poverty of this absolutely irrational first principle: and hence the dilettante colouring which, with all its intellectual wealth, the philosophizing of Schopenhauer possesses, and the 'sigh of relief' when in the third book we approach "the great inconsequence of the system, the Idea."

There is another point of difference between the two Pessimists, and a more vital one, because it affects the very structure of the metaphysical system. Schopenhauer, as is well known, was to a large extent a Kantian, and more than one critic has remarked that Kant's *Practical Reason* minus its rational qualities, becomes a sort of Schopenhauerian Will. In particular, the first book of the *World as Will* is written under Kantian influences, as the author without hesitation ranges himself with the Subjective Idealists, and asserts at the outset that the world, as we know it, is nothing but our subjective representation. This causes, as we have seen, some awkwardness in the sudden change from Subjective Idealism to the Absolute Principle, which is to explain both objective and subjective worlds, for the Will is postulated as an absolute thing-in-itself, albeit that from the point of view of an individual consciousness there is, strictly speaking, no absolute knowable at all. But the point wherein Kantian influences have brought Schopenhauer into flat contradiction with Science, is the doctrine that Time and Space are only forms of our cognition. If Time belongs to our modes of apprehension, there can be no meaning in speaking of a development of the world, an evolution, a world-process. This is the criticism which von Hartmann urges, in order to prepare the way for his own Teleology. For with Hartmann, there is a real world, and a real development of that world: a final cause even can be assigned to the world-process, viz. the emancipation of the Intelligence from the Will. And thus a sort of evolutional optimism can subsist side by side with eudæmonological pessimism: though happiness be impossible, yet hereafter there may be painlessness. But all this is impossible, says von Hartmann, without the presupposition that Time is real: and the fact that Schopenhauer was so untouched by the modern idea of development, deprives his system of much of its usefulness. He broke with Christianity, but could substitute nothing better for it than Buddhist asceticism as an ideal. He is unable to rise to the thought of the possibility of a positive principle for the historical future, and is "without the trace of an understanding and a love for the great endeavours of our time, which are abundantly represented in all other philosophers." [1]

If the character and reality of the world-process gain a different treatment from the later Pessimist, no less difference between the views of Schopenhauer and von Hartmann is observable in their respective attitude towards the final end of individual life. To the earlier philosopher, since all life is misery, the only end is, not indeed suicide, but starvation, asceticism, the denial of the will to live. It is

[1] '*Phil. des Unb.*' (Coupland's Trans.) iii. 94; cf. iii. 163, 185, 323-326.

difficult to see in what sense the individual, who is only phenomenal appearance, can negate the will which is the sole being of the world, his individual volition being only a ray of that one Will. For at most, supposing this to be possible, one of the rays, one of the many objectivations of the Will, goes out, as it were, and is deprived of actuality. But the Will remains as before, with unenfeebled energy, and can bring forth from itself fresh creations of its absorbing activity. Nor is it so easy to understand how suicide can be foolish, because in this there is no denial of the will to live, and yet asceticism be the proper duty. For asceticism is just as much a destruction of the body as suicide, only prolonged over a larger amount of time : and the man who is "obliged to *kill* first his body by *refusal of food*, proves by that very act that he is not able to deny and abolish his unconscious will to live." All individual asceticism, then, is a mistake, not indeed in aim, but in method. "And because the goal which it endeavours to gain is a right one, it has, when rare, by ever whispering in the world's ear a *memento mori*, a high value: it becomes, however, injurious and pernicious when, attacking whole nations, it threatens to bring the world-process to stagnation, and to perpetuate the misery of existence. What would it avail, for instance, if all mankind should die out gradually by sexual continence? The world as such would still continue to exist, and would only find itself in substantially the same position as immediately before the origin of the first man."[1] Asceticism, in its most pronounced form, is seen in

[1] *Phil. des Unb.* Coupland, Vol. iii. p. 129.

pure Buddhism, where it appears as "the union of hopelessness for here and hereafter, with the still uneradicated egoism, which thinks not of the redemption of the whole, but only of its individual redemption." The last sentence strikes the keynote of the change from Schopenhauer to von Hartmann. For the latter, negation of the will must be universal and cosmic, whereas for the former it is individual. Moreover, while to Schopenhauer, negation of the will is the present duty of the individual, the 'cosmic' negation can only be performed at the end of the world-process, forming the ultimate goal of development. Therefore the duty of the individual is not negation at all, but rather affirmation of the will to live. We all, as individuals, must co-operate with the development of the principle of the Universe, must help on that development by every means in our power, and make, as von Hartmann says, the ends of the Unconscious the ends of our own Consciousness.

But what is this principle of the universe which von Hartmann calls "the Unconscious"? A few words are necessary on the constructive portion of this system (which we have hitherto only seen on its negative and critical side) before we are in a position to estimate the nature and value of the reconstruction which it offers. The 'Unconscious' is only one instance of the monistic impulse which appears to dominate philosophic systems in the nineteenth century. Such a return to the older ontological systems always envisages its single ultimate principle with attributes which belong either to thought or to matter. If the Hegelian system represents the former of these two alternatives, the system of Schopenhauer represents the latter. The logical *Idea* with its dialectical movement representing all the vitality and growth both of the world of nature and of the world of spirit, stands over against the brute unintelligent *Will*, ever advancing with devouring and unsatisfied rapacity to new forms of objective existence. The function of von Hartmann in philosophy is, as he interprets it, to find some ultimate principle which shall combine in one the element of intelligence with the element of material force. Further, this ultimate reality must, if it is in any way to represent the germ or embryo of a future development, be expressed in some term which shall represent the indifference-point between the two attributes of intelligence and matter. The life of the spirit must not feel itself estranged from such a primal source, nor yet must the corporeal and physical activity, which makes for us an objective world. It is thus that von Hartmann invents the 'Unconscious,' which is defined as a combination of 'Will and Idea,' from whose perennial vigour the streams shall flow to nourish alike the soul and the body. That which is described as unconscious, might well be interpreted as the author of all physical vitality, while the conscious life of intelligence might also feel that between it and the parent of its being there was a difference not of kind but only of degree. Can it be said, however, that such an ultimate principle is in reality *single* enough in its nature to satisfy the monistic impulse of modern thought? 'Will' and 'Idea' placed thus in external and arbitrary juxtaposition, form an unity only in name, while below there is barely disguised a real and substantial dualism. There is indeed always a preliminary doubt whether this monistic impulse of which we have spoken has or has not a proper legitimacy. The ordinary attitude on the subject is something of this sort. When we are brought face to face with certain metaphysical principles assumed to be final and ultimate, we feel ourselves carried by an irresistible compulsion to the supposition that there is behind them a yet more ultimate and single substance or subsistence *whose* principles they are, and to whom they belong. Can we ignore for all practical purposes this necessity as something merely subjective, or shall we allow it to be a transcendent and objective necessity ? The first position is arguable, but the history of philosophy seems to decide for the second. If that be so, we return to the ' Will *plus* Idea ' principle of von Hartmann, and ask whether this satisfies the conditions of the problem. Von Hartmann would reply that ' Will ' and ' Idea ' are really identical, being only functional differences of one single reality, viz. the Unconscious. The obvious analogy here is the system of Spinoza, with whom von Hartmann has many points in common. Just as thought and extension are declared by Spinoza to be merely the two attributes of one original substance, God; so too ' Will ' and ' Idea ' might be affirmed to be the two functions of the impersonal indivisible and individual thing called Unconscious. Thus, while monism appears to be a necessity for thought, yet Hartmann assures us there must be an immanent duality within it : an absolute dualism is of course untenable ; a relative dualism, however, is, we are told, necessary. Yet the subsequent fortune of Spinoza's speculation does not convey a wholly favourable augury. From Spinoza's Pantheism both the religious world and the ethical consciousness of mankind started away. Religion appeared to demand a sense of dependence on an absolute being which was not satisfied by the relations between the partial and the universal; while ethics in its turn appeared to require the subordination of the individual consciousness to an absolute and independent moral law, which was something other than the one absolute substance of Spinoza. In these cases the assumption of a relative dualism, immanent in a monistic principle, seemed to break down. Perhaps the natural criticism on the similar assumption of von Hartmann is, that unless the Unconscious be understood as a principle independent of and superior to the two principles 'Will' and 'Idea,' the system remains despite all verbiage an emphatic dualism, and the monistic impulse is yet unsatisfied. If this impulse be in itself a mistake, it is better at once to define it as a purely subjective necessity, not to seek to satisfy the ostensible requirements, while in reality the fundamental divergence of the two principles 'Will' and 'Idea' is only partially concealed. It is perhaps some feeling of this kind which leads von Hartmann to describe his philosophy as essentially a *Spiritualistic* Monism—the ultimate principle being an individual *Spirit*, not indeed Self-Conscious, as would be the view of a Theistic philosophy, but Unconscious.[1] But if he thus leans to one of the two fatal alternatives, he affords no longer a reconciliation between Hegelianism and Materialism.

[1] "The one 'super-existent which is all that is,' we may now therefore define as pure, unconscious (impersonal, but indivisible, therefore individual) *Spirit.*" *Phil. des Unb.* (Coupland's Trans.), iii. 194.

The Materialists would naturally feel that they were rapidly becoming Ishmaels in the speculative kingdom.

Let us grant, however, that the one absolute first principle is satisfactorily determined. The next question, which is one of almost primary importance for us as individuals, is as to the birth and origin of Consciousness. Such a problem is of course rendered exceptionally difficult if we have to explain how Consciousness arises from something totally unlike itself. To us who are seeking to interpret the origin and development of the world in which we find ourselves, the whole reality of the world lies *in* Consciousness. If, then, some principle is found which is wholly outside the only reality which we know, if in other words consciousness has to be shown to have arisen from conditions which are not in consciousness, a remarkable feat in mental gymnastics has to be performed. There will always remain something incongruous in such cosmogonies, as though a man were attempting the impossible feat of exhibiting as so much knowledge that which essentially and *ex hypothesi* is antecedent to knowledge. Von Hartmann's attempt to solve this problem is only so far more tolerable than the theories of materialism, in that it has to deal with a first principle, which has a sort of distant relationship with the conscious conditions of which alone we have experience. According to von Hartmann, the 'Unconscious,' at a certain stage of the development of its activities, finds itself confronted by the sudden appearance of opposition. Suddenly the Will finds itself opposed by something not proceeding from itself, and yet sensibly present to itself. Such opposition it naturally cannot understand: and the startling character of the obstacle, the stupefaction of the Will at the existence of an idea, not willed by it, and yet sensibly felt, is the phenomenon called Consciousness. Before there was complete harmony between the two elements or functions of the one 'Unconscious.' The Idea only existed as content for Will, the Will gave force and direction to the subordinate Idea. When, therefore, the Will finds its yokefellow ranged in opposition to itself, there is a jarring sense of stupefaction, contradiction and discord, and from this conflict is born that which we envisage to ourselves as Consciousness. Consciousness is essentially the emancipation of the Idea from the Will, and the opposition of the Will to this emancipation.[1] But how this opposition can in the first instance arise, is by no means easy to see. How, we naturally ask, can the Will oppose something not proceeding from it, if it is the great efficient and dynamical force of the whole? The answer, I suppose, is to be found partly in the different organization of the Will in different parts of the world, so that one part—say external nature, or object—can oppose another part—say internal nature, or subject : partly in the fact that the Unconscious, the 'all-one,' is composed not of Will alone (as was the opinion of Schopenhauer) but of a combination of Will and Idea. Certainly, the essence of Consciousness is the opposition and antithesis between subject and object, and the fact that consciousness appears to rest on this primary dualism is undoubtedly the great difficulty in the way of all monistic schemes. But assuredly this sundering of the intelligence against itself is not more satisfactorily

[1] Cf. von Hartmann (Coupland), ii. 78—118.

explained by the device of von Hartmann than it is by the rigid subjective Idealism of Fichte. Somehow (for that after all is the only explanation vouchsafed) the two functions of the one identical principle turn against each other, as though they were not so much functions as opposing forces. But whether the possibility of this discord does not seriously affect the theoretical value of the one ultimate principle, von Hartmann does not seek to explain. The central difficulty, however, remains. For not only does Consciousness rest on a primary antithesis between subject and object, but by the very conditions of its nature, it for ever excludes any theory of its origin, which is exhibited in terms that are *un*-conscious. Physiologically, the fact of unconscious states, underlying those states which we know and feel, may be a valuable discovery. But it cannot be too often insisted upon that we throw light upon these unconscious states from the illumination afforded by the conscious ones, and not *vice versâ*. Consciousness in point of fact gives whatever meaning there may be to the expression 'unconscious states,' which in themselves form a perfectly negative idea. Take, for instance, the mode in which we interpret animal life. We speak of the instinct of animals as something distinct from the rationality of human beings, but for us the instinctive actions have no meaning, except as interpreted by our rationality. We read ourselves into the animals around us, and it is from this point of view that we suppose a dog to be happy when it wags its tail; or a cat angry when it arches its back. To what these particular actions are relative in the sentient organism of the animal, we can never know.

We interpret their actions by the analogies of our own conscious states. In our dealings with the world below us, and the world above us, we are guilty of equal anthropopathism: we make our animals as well as our gods in the likeness of men. Of all the most curious logical inversions of which the human mind is capable, the most curious is the idea that the instinct of animals can in any way explain the rationality of human beings. For it is we who animate the actions of the brute creation with motives like those of which we are conscious in ourselves. It is from our own point of view that we say that a cat has no instinctive faithfulness, and that a dog can show penitence for some wrong doing. We know much better what we ourselves are than what animals may or may not be. It is the commonest mistake of a sensitive man to fancy other human beings as sensitive as himself, or for a woman of imaginative power to think that other women are equally capable to become artists or authoresses. In much the same way it is the Conscious which gives light to the Unconscious, and it is the Conscious, therefore, which remains as the fundamental fact. If this be so, all schemes of philosophy which seek to demonstrate how from some primal and unconscious germ such life as we know had its rise, are foredoomed to failure; they mistake the nature of the problem, and seek to overpass the limits of possible knowledge. Consciousness can only be understood by us as arising from conditions which are already conscious, from an Idea, a Spirit, a God.

Let us pass to the final end of the world-process as defined by von Hartmann, on which the morality which is possible on this scheme must be based. For if, as its author declares, it furnishes an adequate foundation for ethics, such as was lacking in the pessimistic system of Schopenhauer, we naturally examine it in the light it throws on the scope of all individual effort. What, then, we ask is the final end of that development which flows from the untiring activity of the Unconscious? A first point of importance is to clear away all misconception in this matter. Does the activity of the Unconscious make for justice and morality? No; experience does not bear out this assertion. Is positive happiness, then, the end? Such an answer is obviously impossible in a pessimistic system. Can freedom or evolution, considered as an end in itself, be the divine event to which creation moves? Neither of these solutions appears to answer to the conditions of the problem. On the assumptions of von Hartmann's creed—the relation that is to say which obtains between Will and Idea, the two elements or functions in the one Unconscious—the only end of the world-process must be the development of consciousness. Yet this can hardly be regarded as anything but a proximate end. If the only result of the activity of the absolute first principle was the development of consciousness, the life-torment of conscious creatures would be doubled. To suffer in ignorance, to be the sport or plaything of a cruel and ironical destiny, and to know it not, this is an unhappy fate. But to have light added to the darkness, to know and feel how close and galling are the fetters which enchain us, without deriving any power from such illumination to procure delivery, this is a doom more awful still. It is at this point that von Hartmann is decisively in advance of Schopenhauer, for he provides us with some better chances for hopefulness than the asceticism and the denial of the will to live of his predecessor. The essence of consciousness is, as we have already seen, the emancipation of the intellect from the will. If, then, the unconscious makes the development of consciousness the end of its activity, it must work for the emancipation of the intellect from the will. The essence of will is the ceaseless yearning for satisfaction: if consciousness can relieve the intellect from this tyranny of unsatisfied craving, we reach a certain negative or semi-positive condition, not of actual enjoyment, but of painlessness. The intellect has thrown off the fetters of its tyrant, the fierce desire for satisfaction is over, and the unconscious has at last reached the final term in its evolution, viz. painlessness.

How does such a piece of teleology form the basis for positive ethics? In this way. The final end of development cannot be reached except by a corporate act. At some time when the major part of will is concentrated in the human species, an universal cosmic act of negation is to be performed. No individual can by his unaided powers negate the will to live, but the consentient masses of mankind, when thoroughly enlightened as to their duty in this matter, can by one supreme effort set up some will for rest in opposition to the positive will for activity. Meanwhile the moral duty of the individual is the co-operation with the unconscious: or to speak more explicitly, it is to devote his energies towards the gradual carrying out of the emancipation of the intelligence from the will, not indeed by personal asceticism or self-mortification, but by cultivating to the full his intellectual energy in the knowledge that thus most surely will the final end of the world-process come. Von Hartmann's ethical principle is expressed in the sentence, that we are to make the ends of the unconscious the ends of our own consciousness. Thus while Optimism by easy unconcern, and Pessimism by Nihilistic despair, lead to enervation and morbid quietism, the peculiar system which von Hartmann adopts (described as 'Eudæmonological Pessimism and Evolutionistic Optimism') leads to effective activity, in the help to be rendered to the development of the Unconscious.

It sounds, however, almost like a solemn mockery to call so abstract and fantastic a principle the foundation for an ethic. For work and activity are always proportionate to the end which they are supposed to attain, and no labour will be effective which is designed to secure a colourless state of pure indifference. Our quarrel with Pessimism is that it destroys the reality of all effort; and on effort morality depends. Can it be said that painlessness affords a better scope for effort than the Nirvana of Schopenhauer? To speak of a co-operation in view of a certain ultimate redemption of the world from its suffering is possibly an inspiriting idea, but the question has yet to be asked what the character of this redemption is to be. When we learn that it is not some positive state, some full fruition of all labour, or perfection of all the capabilities of our nature, but only painlessness, we begin to feel ourselves the victims of an elaborate deception. The moral life seems to demand the realization of at least one of two conditions, either the recognition that effort is in itself valuable, or else that it is designed to secure a valuable end. Pessimism secures neither of the two conditions: it deprives labour of any intrinsic value, denying even that effort can be pleasurable; and it adds to this humiliation of a life's activity, the further avowal that the end of life is something far short of the positive blessedness which our nature seems to crave. Nor is it at all certain that such a combination as von Hartmann proposes —between Pessimism in the present and a species of Optimism in the evolutional future—is logically tenable. The doctrine itself of evolution can be equally made to support an Optimistic and a Pessimistic conclusion. Mr. Herbert Spencer, whose speculations revolve round this central tenet, embraces a most sanguine form of Optimism, and Mr. Sully labours to prove that not only does history show an advance in intellectual enlightenment and an improvement in 'social medium,' but also that science points to a future amelioration in the conditions of development. For, he says, that the rough and cruel methods of natural selection are in the higher stages of advance supplanted by methods consciously directed by humane minds—methods dictated by sympathy as well as by higher foresight.[1] But it is an open question whether the exercise of sympathy does more to advance than to retard the world's progress. By preserving the weaker alive it might reasonably be held to interfere with the action of the law of natural selection, and so to enfeeble the advance of the strong. It is obvious too that on more general lines evolution may be considered to point to an end rather of disintegration than of progress. Just as side by side with attraction there exists a force of repulsion, so too by the side of

[1] Sully's *Pessimism*, pp. 375—397.

evolution exist those agencies which lead to degeneration. "To speak of the final triumph of good," says Dr. Maudsley, in his curious book entitled *Body and Will*,[1] "is as if one were to speak of the final triumph of gravitation." Every organism, social, natural, or individual, when it has reached a certain stage of complex evolution, inevitably breeds changes in itself which tend to break up its unity, and finally to destroy it. The law of life appears to run through the following stages. First, there is slow acquisition, then a state of equilibrium, then commences a gentle decline of power, succeeded by a more rapid decay, which finally ends in death. If this be true of the life of an individual, it is quite conceivable that it may be true of the life of humanity at large. "Moreover, the evolutional nisus depends," says Dr. Maudsley, "ultimately on the sun's energy. When the sun has exhausted its powers of combustion, the history of evolution is over." From all of which considerations it is clear that von Hartmann's 'corporate effort of an united humanity to secure the world redemption' seems, to say the least, improbable.

The fact is that evolution, taken by itself, as a scientific dogma, does not necessarily imply amelioration, as so many thinkers seem to suppose, but only advance. And a moral theory which is based on evolution does not derive from it the explanation of a moral ideal, unless there be added to the dogma an ontological principle, which can be construed as conscious intelligence. The scientific theories of current materialism, so far as they adopt the notion of a development of matter, are consequently unable

[1] Maudsley's *Body and Will*, pp. 137—141, 316—332.

to say more in their ethical department than that man's conduct becomes more complex and more heterogeneous as humanity advances. Complexity and heterogeneity do not in themselves mean a necessary improvement. Von Hartmann's theory of a great Unconscious, which slowly evolves throughout the history of the world, until one of its two functions finally reduces the other to impotence, is equally unable to account for either the moral imperative, or the moral ideal. . If an absolute and conscious spirit were in some way or other involved in the development, we might account for these features in the moral problem. For whatever elements a constructive system of ethics may be held reasonably to embrace, it is clear that it must include at least two assumptions. It must include, in the first place, the assumption of the real value of effort and activity, for without a belief in the real value of activity, no moral scheme can exist. It must include, in the second place, a larger assumption than this; one which belongs to a metaphysical system, but which finds almost its best exemplification in the ethical sphere. Morality requires the supposition, not only of an Absolute, in contrast with ourselves, who are relative and individual, but an Absolute and Self-conscious Spirit. Without such a supposition the moral law lacks validity, the moral ideal has nothing whereby to explain its aspiration, and, more than this, the amelioration of the world and of humanity is an impossible conception. To such a conclusion have we been brought, before on purely ethical grounds, now on grounds connected with the development and evolution of nature. The ethics which are based on Pessimism include neither of these assumptions, and therefore bear the stamp of a system which is only partially reconstructive and of purely transitional value. As metaphysical systems have always felt secure against the ugly dream of materialism, so the ethics which are based on God are safe against the pessimistic suggestion that life is nought and moral action absurd.

www.ingramcontent.com/pod-product-compliance
Lightning Source LLC
Chambersburg PA
CBHW030731230426

43667CB00007B/675